GIFTED TO LEARN

GIFTED TO LEARN

Gloria Mehlmann

THE UNIVERSITY
of ALBERTA PRESS

Published by
The University of Alberta Press
Ring House 2
Edmonton, Alberta, Canada   T6G 2E1

Copyright © 2008

Library and Archives Canada Cataloguing in Publication

Mehlmann, Gloria, 1941-
   Gifted to learn / Gloria Mehlmann.

ISBN 978-0-88864-498-5

   1. Mehlmann, Gloria, 1941-. 2. Indians of North America--
Education--Saskatchewan. 3. Educational change--Saskatchewan.
4. Indian educators--Saskatchewan--Biography. 5. Indian
women--Saskatchewan--Biography. I. Title.

LA2325.M44A3 2008   370.92   C2008-900626-7

The University of Alberta Press is committed to protecting our natural environment. As part of
our efforts, this book is printed on Enviro Paper: it contains 100% post-consumer recycled fibres
and is acid- and chlorine-free.

The University of Alberta Press gratefully acknowledges the support received for its publishing
program from The Canada Council for the Arts. The University of Alberta Press also gratefully
acknowledges the financial support of the Government of Canada through the Book Publishing
Industry Development Program (BPIDP) and from the Alberta Foundation for the Arts for its
publishing activities.

  Canada Council   Conseil des Arts
for the Arts   du Canada

I HAVE LEARNED SOMETHING THIS YEAR THAT
NOT MANY PEOPLE WILL BE GIFTED TO LEARN.

—Excerpt from student letter by Paul Shapiro, June 1967

For my deceased parents, Leonard and Delma Stevenson, and brother, Anthony, whose residential school experiences wrested from them as children the gift of learning and the joy of becoming.

CONTENTS

Acknowledgements

MY DEEP THANKS TO CELIA LOTTRIDGE, one time writer-in-residence at the Regina Public Library who helped me select a title for this book; Dianne Warren, writer, who wrote encouraging notes and gave pointers throughout my initial draft; Brian Mlazgar, Canadian Plains Research Center, for carrying out an evaluation of an early draft with his reviewers who agreed: we need to see the author's sense of her own First Nations background play out in the narrative; I thank the Saskatchewan Writers Guild, in particular Susan Hogarth and Amy Nelson-Mile who facilitated an evaluation of the draft with an anonymous writer who, among valuable suggestions, said: "...it (racism) belongs in this memoir, perhaps even more upfront."; Isabel Andrews whose scrupulous research affirms the oral history of my parents and kin; my daughter, Jacqueline, who said, "That professor's words would give your story the edge it needs." I thank the Saskatchewan Archives Board for its unstinting support of my research. I express my deep gratitude to the Mackenzie Art Gallery in Regina for its constant and timely compass; Michael Luski, Linda Cameron, Alan Brownoff, Cathie Crooks, and Jeff Carpenter, University of Alberta Press, for their insights and guidance; Cynthia Chambers, Professor of Education, University of Lethbridge, for her rigorous analysis; Merle Harris, story teller, for her persuasive understanding of the narrative; Peter Midgley and Mary Lou Roy, University of Alberta Press, for keeping the editing process crisp and clear; and, my editor, Meaghan Craven, peerless sentinel for both reader and writer. I also thank the Cowessess First Nation, people of home; the Ahenakew people of Ahtahkakoop for their work in education; and especially Peter Mehlmann, who managed my life through my writing hours. As for all that illumines what I try to reveal about the myth and the reality of teaching and learning, I thank Paul Shapiro, Daniel Shapiro, and my fellow teachers, parents, and children with whom I have had the privilege to work and learn.

PREFACE

THIS PERSONAL ACCOUNT OF AN EDUCATOR, told out of school, illustrates how societal change and reactive policy affects teaching and learning.

As a First Nations woman teaching mainstream children in an urban setting in Saskatchewan during the 1960s and 1970s, I learned that what is invisible to the eye nonetheless touches the life of a school; it affects teachers, administrators, trustees, the individual child and his or her parents. It's been said that a child's success in school is the acid test for how well a society is tending to its future. I believe that is a reasonable statement.

Within the pages of this book live the actual children I taught. Theirs is a story of growing stress at home and at school that took its toll on learning. As their teacher, with pressures of my own, I figure uniquely into the account.

Initially, I tried to spare the reader my life story because, by the simple act of its telling, the tentacles of bigotry long buried in my beloved profession would be exposed. Through the narration of my life story, the reader would also find the mistaken ideas about Aboriginal people that are deeply rooted in Canada's public policy. There was no way around revealing the racism and ethnocentrism I encountered. As early as when I first set my career goal in high school, I worried that I might not gain entry into the teaching profession at all, much less remain in it, were my background to become known to my superiors. Criteria for suitability as teacher candidates acceptable to teachers college, largely unwritten, were nonetheless "readable": family background, academic achievement, social connection, personal commitment, gender, and potential for lasting acceptance by the larger community. I saw my score as two out of six.

Government policy had decreed that I live my life as an Indian on a reserve. In those days, Indian and reserve were words that ignited all kinds of negative images in the minds of people, many of whom might be among my professional associates. Would it even be possible to avoid mentioning the prejudice that tracked my career?

Add to this, as a writer, I was concerned that my life story might detract from the real focus of my work, the important story of children in school in difficult times. But the highly experienced writers I talked to, including family, friends, and colleagues, pointed out emphatically that the reader must know the writer. I take that to mean the truth—so, here I am.

I hope that readers sense what was truly unique about teaching in the 1960s and 1970s, that the times were very much like our own. Except, the beacon of change carried into a new century shone brighter then. It shone so brightly, in fact, that it left a few indelible lessons for us, for now.

The decade of the 1960s began with an optimism that saw the global village unfold in an endless stream of possibilities. People responded. Some took risks in lifestyle. Others sought innovation in specialized fields. Artists and writers pushed creativity to new heights. Psychologists added new dimensions to what was known about the human mind. In Saskatchewan, politicians established universal Medicare and established the right to vote for Indians. This was Saskatchewan flexing mind and muscle.

Across the world and at home on the prairies, untried young people of conscience turned themselves into a high-profile population with social protest as its forum. Some led marches against war, for example. Some pursued "mind-expanding" drugs. Many found unique personal relationships. A number of people involved in these early explorations ended their forays in disillusionment and even death. For the lucky ones, the next decade began a period of reflection. Awareness came to those who kept their eyes, ears and hearts open. Teachers often count themselves among this group.

Change entered our classrooms in the 1960s and 1970s; and, because it was impossible to analyze the trends in their totality, doubts assailed me in my career. Although I was lured by the excitement of change, I was uncertain where it would lead. By the end of the 1960s, I asked myself if it wouldn't be best to abandon teaching after all. Later, I would want to help overhaul the provincial curriculum that defined how Saskatchewan children acquired the skills and knowledge that enabled them to reap the benefits—on an equal footing with their peers, presumably—of a new world and its offerings.

Despite the brambles of dangerous times, a light was cast upon things in a letter from a grade-six boy to me, his teacher. It remains among my prized possessions. In part it reads: "I have learned something this year that not many people will be gifted to learn." That one sentence became my story, in fact, the story of all of us. This story of how a teacher and her pupils make their way into an uncertain future reflects the fact that I was young, new to the city, naïve in my expectations, but curious and willing to learn. I didn't know then what I share now.

Two decades of school life implies success. And most of the children I taught grew up to lead happy and productive lives. They made, and are making, fine contributions to society. However, beyond the stories of achievement by lawyers, doctors, accountants, business people, government workers, and the musicians who once sat in my classroom, a painful story is told. Readers, like most people, learn from mistakes, from conflict, and from pain. Ask the writer, the poet-philosopher, the artist, or the movie director how. And, ask the child.

In my memoir, I do not stay a sequential chronological course. Instead, I invite the reader into the many rooms of psychological time where stories dwell. Each story's essence lives unbounded by time. But to make clear our path of discovery, I set out a few time posts with a few dates nailed on. This way we can look forward and backward as we like. The years I do mention in the following book correspond to the years in which the events described actually happened, except for one or two stories that former students might recognize and grow distressed about. Such stories are put into another school, hence another year. Because the stories belong to actual lives, I have taken great care to protect privacy. Real names are used only with permission.

Is this book aimed at scholars? No, not primarily, though imaginative scholars are rarely disappointed by truthfulness. You won't find this work packed with references to all I have read and studied. I do, however, give credit to those to whom I am indebted, from Plato to Picasso, though we need not be shy in the presence of genius. Let me illustrate. Plato spoke of a cave wall upon which "reality" is but a scene of dimly reflected shadows. This compares to what we "know" of a child from the year of his or her birth to when she or he turns eighteen. Picasso taught us to look for the simple (the essential simple) in the complex. Together, Plato and Picasso illustrate the mind of a child affirming his or her latent gifts.

Memoirs are something like what is seen in Plato's cave, even in the light of reflection. A lot remains unseen despite illumination. So I prepared for this story as best I could. I started with a list of the children whose stories taught me about a side of teaching, a side that says more than university courses are required to elucidate. I narrowed these down to one roomful of pupils. (I end up with fewer.) Then I consulted the annual records of the Canadian Test of Basic Skills to determine the year and school in which I taught each child, and at what grade level. It was not that I really needed to do this—each child's story was crystal clear in my memory. But psychological time is not chronological, and I needed to lay a path.

The next step was to cross-reference the list of names with a timeline of my life. I was glad to find records of my life, mainly correspondence, in an old grey filing cabinet in my basement. Then, I delved into a wooden sewing box packed with dog-eared song sheets and concert programs that I keep beside the piano. Finally, I re-read parts of books that had moulded my thinking over the years, all of them with passages underlined, with notes in the margins showing youthful inspiration, indignation, and counter argument. All of my records confirmed my recollections.

To bring the memoir up to date, I decided to share the names of some of today's thinkers who ring the bells of the past with far more vigour than I am able. But a word of warning: from there, the children's stories take us to whatever place the adult mind and heart are capable of reaching. I invite you to come along and see for yourself.

I hope the reader recognizes that I, too, am struck with the youthful naïveté found in the following stories, namely my own. But I persist in staying true to my observations. Besides, this book tells a story that has no end, if you believe in education and its importance. And if you love the coming generations.

ONE.

IF IT WERE UP TO ME

THERE IS NO EASY WAY. Becoming a teacher of children takes a lifetime of study. Throughout my teaching career, I often wished that when I had first got it into my head to become a classroom teacher someone had taken me aside and set me straight. They might have at least said that teaching is difficult, emotionally draining and that I'd be washed up at the end of each and every day. As it was, people only smiled when I talked about my life's plan. Others said, "Thanks, but no thanks"; the thought of daily combat with spoiled brats was just too much to bear. There were better things to do with one's life than to become a poorly paid pillar of society.

I paid no attention. Something about teaching drew me like a butterfly to candlelight, if not like a moth to a flame. Even my aunt's practical advice to take up a secretarial course so that I'd have something to fall back on struck me as so patronizing that I was hugely insulted. "I'm not about to fall back on anything," I replied in a huff. I knew what I wanted. I had no intention of changing my mind for anyone, including a dear old aunt who purportedly knew the ways of the world and yet fretted her way through life. Perhaps she thought my headstrong ways would draw me into situations I ought to avoid.

In the thick of teaching, though, there were times I wished I had taken my aunt's advice, not to mention the advice of Goldie, my life-long friend, whose notes and letters to me throughout my career had nevertheless helped me steer a course. There would be moments when I'd picture myself fleeing the young idealists who headed down College Avenue bordering Wascana Park, on their way to the red brick building known as "teachers college." In fact, there would be many times I'd scold myself for not having leapt out of the taxicab on my way to the Regina Public School Board office, the day of my first job interview.

Instead, I remained seated stiffly in the back of the cab, feeling skinny and insubstantial as we hurtled downtown. My impatient driver suddenly asked what the address was. I erroneously thought all taxi drivers knew where everything was in this small city of the 1960s. After all, Reginans had planted every single tree across the city by hand. As for me, I was fairly new there, having come into town to seek my fortune, a farmer's daughter in search of her destiny, as it were. I had no idea what the school board address was and said so. The sweating cab driver unexpectedly tossed a telephone book into the back seat beside me and, impatient, ordered me to look the address up. Instead of telling him to look it up himself and then jumping to the pavement in my brand new royal blue suit and shiny black pumps, I panicked. "What do I look under?" I asked.

"You should know," came his reply. "You're the teacher, aren't you? If you're not working with them Catholics look under Public Schools."

I had just failed a test of worldliness. I had exposed my ignorance, and likely, my humble origins. Obviously, the driver didn't take me for a teacher, even though I was smartly dressed—to the nines in fact—and carrying credentials. The incident unnerved me, and I sat wondering now just how much of my real life story I should talk about in the interview. I wondered if my ability to teach would be the main impression

I could leave. I reminded myself that I had come one hundred miles, practically, to reach my goal and should not let doubts interfere at this stage.

But another incident burst into my mind as I sat in the cab. Obviously, I hadn't succeeded in erasing a defining moment with a cold-eyed misguided zealot of his time. I had hoped to be able to put the memory of that life-embittered man aside as I took up responsibility as a teacher. Now, recollected in the "tranquility" of the Regina cab, it was possible to consider that it was indeed that professor's job, in that interview not so long ago, to evaluate my potential as a teacher—that, and only that. His job was to do this openly and fairly; and, on behalf of the institution, to formally welcome me as a teacher candidate to the college. Or advise me to leave. Instead, he'd held himself apart in a tight pose and coldly looked at me when I responded to his question, that yes, I was from the Cowessess Indian Reserve, just north of the town of Broadview, Saskatchewan.

Like all student teachers, that week, I participated in a one-to-one interview with an assigned professor. All of us had to go through this formal screening process and I had awaited my turn with great happiness in my heart. On the appointed day, confident and full of anticipation, I walked, chin up and shoulders back, into the bright light of the empty classroom that served as an interview office. My professor, grey-haired, in a pale grey suit, smiled and asked me to sit down and to tell him about my life: he wanted to know specifically where I grew up, who my parents and grandparents were, what they did for a living, and why I had decided to become a teacher. Well now, the truth was a shining possibility. I was eager to share the facts of my father being a war veteran and a farmer on the reserve; of my mother, an inventive housekeeper; and of my grandparents who boasted life accomplishments due to people in their old age. The professor, however, grew silent, his gaze turning into a cold stare. Then, leaning forward in his chair, he delivered, point blank, a statement that would visit my life as a young teacher time and again. His words were a direct slam to the solar plexus. "If I were head of this institution," he said, "you wouldn't make it through the front door."

I stood up and left the room shaken, judging by my trembling knees. But I was undeterred. I decided to hold my head up. I had no idea what he'd based his reaction on. If his behaviour bespoke what it seemed, and, given his age, it very likely did, then here was a bigot with a row to hoe. I mentally stepped back to remind myself that I could not forget that in residential schools the mouths of children were taped shut, like my mother's; that the reserve had no library on it; and that "our town" had often demonstrated prejudice to be met only with the silence and dignity of grandmothers. For certain, the professor brought home to me my family's struggle to learn, to teach, and to become. Tears pinched my eyes as I walked back to my apartment, my interview over. I talked to myself. In the final analysis, the professor was not an Indian Agent backed by federal authority. No; here was a modestly equipped thinker of another age and, therefore, dying on the vine. In contrast, the future was as it had ever been—a good and greening spring. And that was a source of great courage for me.

So, inside the cab, watching the trees along the streets fly by, I reviewed all aspects of my background as I sat mustering my courage. I had to decide what was tell-able from what was probably not even say-able. There'd be no turning back. It was a matter of light and infinite horizon.

In truth, I was buoyed up with the feeling that I was ready. I knew I had grit and useful life experience—perhaps until that cab driver had spoken to me. And I recognized, too, that had I listened to advice, especially to that of my sophisticated friend, Goldie, I would have been spared this odd moment. Unlike me, she was in Toronto becoming a dentist, "a surefire way to manage gold," as she'd written in one of her worldly notes. It was possible that she'd begun her habit of promoting her preferred profession of dentistry over teaching the exact moment I began the walk up those shallow steps leading into the Regina Public School Board office, that spring day when my whole life changed. Had

I followed her advice, I might have been spared years of struggle to become this thing called Teacher.

But then, I would have missed the opportunity to learn a few things about children, parents, school boards, life itself, and even something about teaching. Success in my profession would mean that I finally understood that teaching is about nurturing the gifts for learning; and this meant more than standing at the front of a room lecturing. Teaching had more to do with the life story of a child. I would come to understand all this in what would sometimes seem an officious and impersonal profession.

It was 1963 and the realization that my pupils would need paper and pencils by nine o'clock in the morning jarred me out of my reverie that first day. Nine o'clock! No time left to sit imagining neat rows of captive angels bending to their work. Nine o'clock! No use pretending that spellers, erasers, and dictionaries would appear magically out of thin air. Nine o'clock! That hour forever alerted me to the fact of living, breathing, jostling children at the door. A cacophony of cherubs and urchins, from far and wide, they came to scatter the myth of unending innocence and the myth of classrooms as protected places.

JAY

I see him today as a red-haired boy of nine in grade four, thin as a reed, one eye askew, buck teeth, and a habit of holding his head to one side. I could never figure out whether he was waiting for me to say something when he tilted his head or whether he was listening to some inner dialogue of his own. His name was Jay, and he was forever doing one of two things; thinking with his head tilted to one side, or reading with his head tilted to one side. And what a reader! Read, in fact, was all he wanted to do, and all he would do for hours on end, despite my protestations.

My problem was this: here before me was a child caught up in the excitement of learning, and already in possession of a key skill. He was a reader. But he couldn't, or maybe wouldn't, write. For one thing, he was physically unco-ordinated. I was concerned that Jay might be jeopardizing a bright future despite his intellectual gifts. He was certainly capable of pursuing a specialized field one day. His curiosity and intellect might lead him to altogether new and emerging fields of learning. In 1961 Yuri Gagarin had become the first human in space. Jay might someday want to contribute to that work, to the excitement of manned space flights. As his teacher, I knew that no matter what lay ahead for him; Jay had to learn to write. It was my job to help him develop his skills, to make him sit at his desk so that regular sheets of paper mirrored his growth. But Jay's mind raced on far ahead of his clumsy scribblings.

He had great difficulty pinning his thoughts to paper and, so, wouldn't even try. His grip on the pencil and his physical approach to the task was clumsy from beginning to end. His wildly formed letters toppled this way and that as they headed out across the top of the page only to become hopelessly tangled before hitting the bottom. More often than not, his letters ended up dancing all around the words he tried to tack down, and he'd look up from his page, his blue eyes sparkling with humour, and say, "Just let me say the answer—my one true talent. It will be faster, like an elixir."

It had been so easy in teachers college to imagine myself at the front of the room effortlessly filling young minds with everything there is to know. In my imagination, children behaved in ways that made their governing a thing of joy. They automatically held up a hand before speaking; they said "pardon me" when they erred; they moved about with purpose; and they would do what I asked. But our professors had warned of trials ahead; social realities influence learning, they said. And, here was the nub of it; a teacher's lack of understanding about the true nature of each learner reduced his or her potential. With the exception of this forewarning, I planned, back in teachers college, to ignore the professors' full catalogue of warnings. I wanted to come to some of my own conclusions about managing children. Had I an inkling of the difficulties that lay ahead, as a student teacher, I might not have pursued that career at all. I might have chosen a less captivating destiny. For certain, I would have missed exchanging those odd little notes with my big-city friend, Goldie, over the years:

I can't make him write, Goldie, and writing constitutes more than half his marks. I'm desperate!

Pillar of Society,
I am but a dentist-in-training. Let him suffer the consequences. At any rate, all you can do is give him time and wait until he comes around.

Despite my concern for him, Jay taught me that learning to teach comes with the children themselves. Talents lie numberless among them, ready and waiting to be developed. Certainly, Jay's gifts were without number. A nod of my head and he'd unleash the most amazing descriptions of what he'd read and digested. He shared these with such lucid insight and curious detail that my own imagination would be carried along by the genius in this little boy. He expounded on any given topic. His verbal accounts, for example, of chemicals in the bloodstream "like an interconnected city," or of kings "ranting and dying in agony of lost power," or of mythical creatures "clashing among the mountains," stuck in the mind. Here was genius too silvery quick for the banal medium of paper and pencil. And here was I, a novice teacher, already at a crossroad.

The professors had missed something crucial, I could tell. They hadn't provided enough instructional time for us to discuss the unique qualities that make up individuality in people such as Jay. They didn't give us the psychological map, the guide book, the recipe for handling unusual children. Instead they gave us only the broadest of principles and a few broad rules. But a boy like Jay defied description; he could make all his future teachers rethink the rules. The real trouble was that this concern held true for every child. I just hadn't gotten to that yet.

I struggled to find the sense of Jay. Was it so important that he write down what I wished him to think? Maybe there was another way. Yet the accepted principle was that I treat all children consistently. What I expected of one, I had to expect of the others. My lecture notes from teachers college seemed vague. What did they really mean? It seemed now, too, that the professors stood outside my classroom door, their codes for success in hand. I told myself that some of the rules just had to be wrong. I had a strong case of inward rebellion to contend with. What does "consistency" have to do with it anyway, I asked myself? What about the child—just as he is?

One day, I forced myself to sit down and analyze what we'd been told about standards. I needed to understand how to apply these to Jay and if indeed they applied in the first place. The professors had made many a reference to standards. My notes said that these were expectations that, once set, ought to be maintained. All right, that was straightforward. For example, a moral standard laid out the expectations for a good life—such as, observe the Ten Commandments. That was direct, too. The professors, though, spoke of standards for teaching and learning. Well now, what were the expectations? What did these mean specifically? With that question, the sense of direction I was after got lost in a sudden fog. My class notes proved scanty: all things being equal, a standard was the level of achievement most children were capable of achieving and were expected to achieve, if they consistently put their best effort forward. So then, I reasoned, this meant that I, in turn, had to establish expectations so that the path was clear for each of my pupils. If teachers saw to this, the professors seemed to be say, standards practically took care of themselves. I had difficulty with this, however: Jay had to know exactly what I expected of him and then he had to get in line. But did standards mean that every pupil must toe the line in exactly the same way? At the same time?

Here was Jay's assignment being verbally handed in again—and could he, please, please, please sit behind the classroom bookshelf, out of sight, to read a bit more? He was at this very moment, you see, pondering a problem in planetary orbits and had to look up the details from a book on loan to his father from the University of Regina for the day. In spite of my college notes, and despite the fact that he hadn't written a single word all day, I'd agree—and I'd grow guilty, once more. "As long as you tell me what it is you've learned."

These moments proved unstoppable. Consistent behaviours lead to expected outcomes. That relationship, I told myself with my pupils sitting there, in front of me in rows, was addressed much too lightly in teachers college. Yet, back then, the professors seeded our heads with their ideas about standards, and they had sprouted into absolutes in my mind. They seemed massive in substance and in structure, like oak trees standing out on a level field. Standards, I fathomed, were big unshakable truths handed down by the world's great thinkers. It remained only for succeeding generations of teachers like me to maintain them. Here in my classroom, with a boy like Jay and with every single child thereafter, the substance of standards died and withered like fall leaves caught and blown away in a September squall. Only later did I begin to understand why.

I soon saw that, far from being absolute, standards wavered, maybe only slightly, but waver they did. They were only as reliable as any fact in its proper context. They vacillate because of children, because of the unique way each child approaches learning. This realization stood in stark contrast to my earlier belief. I thought teaching would be straightforward. I saw a polished portrait, a cameo, with me in front of a roomful of adoring children: I stand at the blackboard, wearing a green velvet dress with an elegant, white lace jabot at my throat. Bright red geraniums sit on the windowsill. In my hand, I hold a piece of snowy white chalk as I lecture on every subject known to the modern world, including spelling. Peace reigns in the heart. The children sit like nodding flowers, all of them smiling in the golden sunlight that streams in through the window.

Needless to say, the real world changed that picture from top to bottom.

My dreams of perfection faded with the realization that teaching means learning how to think about children and to act accordingly, along with a whole lot of other things. My indifference to or excitement about learning about each child revealed the struggle, again and again. Conflict arises as soon as one believes that a clearly articulated connection exists between practice, theory, and learning. I came to realize that professors might refer to "standards" as if they are written down in big permanent letters; but, what remains of standards within an actual classroom setting was a perplexing study in fairness, especially when I tried to interpret and apply them. I was an arbiter of fairness in a world of ambiguity. What was the standard? What did "fair" mean?

I talked to myself. I had to weigh whether or not it was fair to ask Jay to put aside his curiosity until he mastered the skill of putting his thoughts to paper. I also had to determine if it was fair that he be given the privilege of sitting at the back of the room behind the bookshelf, reading while the others tediously wrote out their lessons. But the worst was trying to decide if this writing down of things was indeed the crafting of a child's own thoughts, or if some disguise lay there. Might there be too much too soon, or too little too late? It was no simple matter to simply put my foot down and force Jay to stop thinking about orbits and to get on with his confounded writing assignments.

During these moments of doubt and exasperation, professorial warnings sprang to mind in random order. You will need to make important decisions on the spot...Learning moments and teaching moments rarely coincide and good teachers must come to recognize this swiftly...Wisdom comes with knowing that a child's mind rarely springs to readiness on command...Lesson number one for you, novice teacher, is never, never, never...

This was only my second month of teaching and, already, I was willing to forego the geraniums. I might have realized the need to put aside the lace jabot as well. And I was likely not alone in this. Jay's handwriting challenge remained unresolved; although, at the end of the school year, he amassed a goodly sum of readable pages to his credit, all of them cleared of even a single misspelled word. In May, when the Canadian Test of Basic Skills booklets were scored, he came out at the top of the class in all subjects. If anyone had learned a lesson it was me. I had, at some level, adopted the erroneous attitude, quite without realizing it, that a child's mind learned best under adult direction. Jay's mind learned under his own direction. I had only been smart enough to stay out of his way, by default. His lack of interest in handwriting resulted in raising the bar of my awareness about how far my attitude ought to take precedence over a child's unique act of learning.

Soon it would be me trying to put the same objective distance between parents and their child.

When I began my second year of teaching, I had reason to believe that our professors had not fully explained the vagaries of parents to us. No professor came right out and said that parents, with good intentions, can curb the power of a child's dreams—as in the case of little Herbie Davis. Neither were we told that parents who are overly ambitious for their children can come close to denying imagination altogether. "Parents can be overly grounded in the practical," was how it was put to us. Our professors, however, were unanimous in saying that the aim of public education is to help the learner become a productive member of society. They said that the teacher's role was to develop the student as a "well-rounded" individual, not unlike the Renaissance Man.

Herbie

When I met Herbie, I realized that, as a result of upbringing, even before a child is a six-year-old, his or her blossoming personality can be weighed down by an imaginary briefcase under his or her arm, or with the tools of some trade. This sad circumstance happens because of a narrow view of what schools ought to teach, that once a child is in school he or she should suppress the innate curiosity and focus on getting a job. His or her inherent joy of learning is replaced with ideas on how to hurry the apprenticeship along. Yet, didn't the professors plainly say that schooling is to prepare the child for life as opposed to a job? They ought to have told some of the parents I came to know.

As a beginning teacher, I told myself that I must always make the child's own interests a priority. My parents never got to learn about the things that interested them. Choice wasn't an option. But, with Herbie, I also had to consider the fact that without parents my pupils wouldn't exist, nor would my profession. I therefore paid close attention to what parents said about a number of things. That was the easy part. It took me a while to hear what they might not be saying.

Some parents held such high ambitions for their child it simply exceeded common sense. They disregarded the fact that the intellect develops at a different rate for each and every human being on Earth. Learning doesn't march along in time to the rhythm set by the school, in every subject, in every term, and in every mind. Children rarely excel in everything all at once. Our everyday experience tells us that. Nevertheless, trying to persuade mom and dad to go easier on their little son or daughter was hopeless, once their minds were made up.

I met one such parent in Herbie's mother. She appeared at the classroom door unannounced a week before the teachers and children returned from summer holidays. She got right to the point of her visit. Her son, Herbie, would be in my class this year and she'd be helping him with his assignments. He had a handicap, having lost sight in one eye at the age of three and needed to wear glasses with a strong lens for his seeing eye. I promised I'd watch for him the first day of school and that I'd send homework with him.

Mrs. Davis laid a firm hand on my arm, "I implore you," she said, "send his school work home with him, every day. I must keep a strict watch on his progress."

There was an edge to her voice, and I hurriedly replied that I saw no harm in Herbie taking his work home with him, any time. However, I felt a little uncomfortable about her request. Her tone had an urgent quality to it. The problem was I didn't know the family or Herbie all that well. I couldn't take a firm stand on anything and didn't know if this would be required. Mrs. Davis was a tense person and also very conscientious. She looked older than most mothers of sixth graders and appeared formal and authoritative in her bearing. I thought that it would probably be wise to wait and see what Herbie was like.

When the nine o'clock bell rang that crisp September morning, a familiar excitement, as well as fear and trembling, gripped me. The night before had produced an anxiety nightmare: the children in my charge had gone wild. The principal, down the hall, raced toward me at full gallop...I awoke stunned, still apologetic, and then glad it was only a bad dream.

What did the year hold in store? Would this be the year of having to teach that unmanageable child whom fellow teachers spoke so lightly about? There was a boy in last year's grade five class, apparently, who had spent a great deal of time in the principal's office. Fellow teachers said similar things in the privacy of the staff room. I hoped to be lucky and stay lucky.

I spotted Herbie among the others as the boys and girls filed into the room. You couldn't miss him: he was the smallest one. His seeing eye was magnified behind the lens of his glasses, and that other eye appeared permanently focused on the heavens. He smiled shyly at me and then stumbled over his own feet as he all but fell into the room. We'll get along, I thought. He walked to the back of the room and disappeared behind the boy sitting in front of him. It was now or never; no child with vision problems should sit at the back.

"Hey, you at the back of the room," I called out. "Just because you're good looking doesn't mean you can throw your weight around in my class. Up to the front with you!"

He walked to the front of the row, enjoying the amiable laughter and teasing of the bigger boys, and sat down. Herbie, I knew instantly, would not be the sort to compensate for his lack of commanding stature by acting up. His was a gracious spirit.

I sensed a problem soon enough, though.

Herbie froze at the first sight of an assignment and gripped his pencil as though he intended to carve stone with it. He obviously didn't expect learning to be easy. Nor, it seemed, did he expect it to give him any joy. He pressed down so hard on his pencil that it left imprints two pages deep. He meant business. I worried that his determination might get in the way of his learning. Try as he might, Herbie simply could not make himself hurry, and his anxiety slowed him down to a snail's pace. He demanded such perfection of himself that his thoughts, instead of being free and exploratory, were cemented to the written word. Learning obviously meant getting words down on paper. I worried about him in a way I did not worry about Jay, who put his pencil aside as often as he could. Herbie kept his good eye glued to the assigned page, pencil in hand always. It was as if he was setting down proof for others, proof that learning was taking place. A worried frown haunted his small face, even as he read.

A week later his mother rang the school and invited me to come "for tea and talk." How lovely, I thought to myself, tea after school. Yet on another level, I felt constrained. As a novice teacher, I wanted to be sure that tea after school didn't imply a study of grave matters that ended with a scowling principal back at school. I quelled my nerves by deciding that nothing would distract me from enjoying a cup of tea in good company.

I learned when I arrived at the Davis house that Herbie was away at the conservatory for music lessons, so Mrs. Davis and I had the house to ourselves. And what a lovely home it was; gleaming floors of amber-coloured wood and French provincial furniture set off by pale blue walls. Mrs. Davis was perfectly groomed, almost for a formal tea. She wore a string of pearls. I grew embarrassed in my ordinary khaki skirt, white blouse, and navy sweater. A slight feeling of distress reminded me that, prior to setting out, I renewed a promise to myself that if my hostess were to ask me my nationality, I would change the subject, and if pressed, make light of it with an airy comment, or two. I needn't have worried; Mrs. Davis had other things on her mind and was likely one among those who understand that curiosity and courtesy have their place. I relaxed into her sofa, free to be me.

Sunlight slanted into the room across a green and rose floral-patterned chaise longue. Mrs. Davis's glances quickly pinpointed this and that as she laid bits and pieces aside in her mind. She reached for my sweater and placed it neatly on the sofa beside me. With nervous smiles she poured the tea, all the while ignoring my attempts at genial exchange. This was a meeting that was clearly in her hands. And it was full steam ahead.

"Herbie has a hard life ahead of him. He's not naturally gifted, you know. I spend hours tutoring him, seeing to it that he does his work perfectly. I do so every day and have done so since kindergarten. I intend...that is, I must do this for the rest of my life."

It was clear that Mrs. Davis did not expect me to interrupt. Indeed, the flow of her words made it impossible to do so.

"We are a family that cannot rely on numbers. Herbie is quite alone in the world and there are no children forthcoming. It's natural enough to accept that we, his parents, might well be dead long before Herbie comes of age, certainly before he has children of his own, should that ever become a reality."

Mrs. Davis's face was criss-crossed with pain, and it was apparent, in the afternoon light, that she had troubled her face with too much powder. It made her skin look thin and papery and, yes, older than I expected. I wanted to say something but she raised her hand, "More than likely, Herbie won't have the good fortune to marry, considering his appearance and his handicap. His lost eye and his small stature constitute major strikes against him. Herbie understands that he will be all alone, soon. So, day by day, we go over his work; sometimes late into the night. And, if need be, we work until two in the morning. Herbie must have his grades!"

Mrs. Davis glanced in my direction and proceeded, in a tone of immense authority, "Herbie's father, you see, is a civil servant and knows from experience how troublesome things can be out there, even if one is in full possession of one's faculties—and handsome enough..."

She cleared her throat, catching herself saying more than she intended. "I do go on," she continued, "but you must understand absolutely, that I will be relying on you to send all of Herbie's schoolwork home with him. Every single day. I will not rest otherwise."

This was not the kind of visit that lent itself to mutual understanding, I realized in sudden desperation. I responded as best I could, saying that Herbie was very bright and that every child under the sun had his own way of learning, in good time. I found myself scrambling for words. I hurriedly pointed out that tests and quizzes and chapters read at specified hours in school are only rough estimates of what children actually learn.

"Every child learns in his own time," I heard myself insisting. Mrs. Davis's closed expression held and the lines around her mouth tightened. I began to feel, with a sense of rising panic, that

Herbie was being pushed by forces beyond my control, under my very nose.

"Mrs. Davis, this has to do with what true learning is all about, in the first place. Deep oceans of true recognition...of vast ..."

Mrs. Davis's mouth grew tighter at my floundering words, as did her fingers round her cup of tea. "Tests are but rough indicators of real progress..." I finished lamely.

I tried desperately to recall the words of my professors: Determination is something teachers must recognize in parents and it is something to which the teacher must give way. Sometimes the appearance of surrender is the best retreat, especially when a serious regrouping is required.

"You must understand," Mrs. Davis said abruptly, her blue eyes filling with tears, "Herbie's father speaks of leaving us."

The afternoon sun paled. Or maybe it was me, and maybe it was because I saw in an instant how a mother's eyes can appear like a child's, filled with a deep and sudden darkness.

"Believe me, Mrs. Davis, Herbie is doing fine, and I strongly expect he will continue to do so. I suggest that we work together to let him know that his future is not a desperate thing at all. I will send his work home with him."

I was out of my depth. There was more to the family's worries than I had been trained to deal with. I vaguely recalled a lecture snippet that suggested one ought not to pursue private matters if they did not bear directly on the issue at hand. How to decide?

"Mrs. Davis," I continued, "Herbie has determination. He has a lively intelligence and a charming way with people, not to mention a natural flair for life. I will try to see to it that he balances his work with play..."

It was not the time to enter into a theoretical discussion on the importance of play, and so I reached for my sweater. Mrs. Davis, embarrassed by her tears, was already making motions to hurry tea along. I repeated that I would send Herbie's work home and that, maybe, if Sundays were freed up, the boys in his class were forming a soccer team...

"Yes, yes!" Mrs. Davis said, hurrying me to the door. I turned to wave goodbye at the end of the walk, but she had already spun around and slammed the door behind her.

"Certain things are not within your purview to ponder," the professors said in the back of my mind—the why and wherefore of fathers leaving, for instance. "The focus of your concern will always be the child and the troubles that follow him to school." How was I to know when and how to separate them?

Herbie got along fine, that year. I sent work home with him each day with notes that stressed his accomplishments. On Fridays, I sent another note saying that he should be able to finish his work in about an hour Saturday morning. The few times he failed to make more than his usual 90 to 100 per cent grade, such as on his social studies test, I would look at his 89 per cent and give him extra marks for "paying attention to concepts of importance beyond mere recallable detail."

In fact, Herbie flourished. He began to realize that learning is enhanced by having fun. He couldn't help but do so. His classmates saw to it, and his teacher knew the value of jokes, too. Sometimes though, in the quiet of an afternoon with all heads bent to their work, I'd see Herbie's eyes darken, and I'd think of the lives of children and the things they keep from us. Disrupters of classroom order are nothing compared to disrupters of the heart.

I learned that parents have to "contend" with unique differences in each child and often wide differences among siblings within the family. Abilities and interests can be miles apart even if the siblings happen to be twins. When members of the same family end up in the same classroom at the same time, both teacher and parents notice these traits all the more keenly.

New to the classroom, I was amazed at the range of differences among my pupils. I was trying desperately to teach by the book. That year, I became truly aware of the importance of talking openly with parents about their children, especially in relation to expectations and what these mean and do not mean. Some parents recognize from the start that today's struggle leads to tomorrow's mastery; parents often have to put their hopes for the child's immediate success aside. This was true of Mrs. Morgan, whom it was my pleasure and privilege to know.

MEGAN AND SARAH

The two Morgan girls were in my fourth-grade class of twenty-seven pupils. Winsome as can be, they were the sort of little girls one imagined as once having wandered through primordial times when peace and harmony reigned among all living and non-living things. In other words, they were the stuff of fairy tales. Yet here they were, in modern days, these two sisters with eyes as bright as stars, their glossy brown hair tumbling to their waists, and their light cotton summer dresses skimming the floor. Sunshine followed them into the room when they arrived at the door. Dear little Megan and Sarah!

The girls brought more than sunbeams into the room. They often appeared in the doorway just before the nine o'clock bell with daisies and snapdragons from their mother's garden for my desk. Soon, the freshening fragrance of late summer blossoms would fill the room. And here in the quiet of the day, among the flowers and the children dreaming in their books, were innocence and permanence both. I felt blessed to be a teacher, these times. And though it was unknown to me then, in distant towns and cities, young girls in long dresses, long beads, and with wild flowers in their hair swept headlong toward a time when youthful innocence would begin the search for new expression. For now, in my classroom, I was cocooned against realities to be found in the newspaper headlines that admitted wars, racial strife, drug abuse, and global pressures now brewing in other parts of our globe.

For the time being, in our corner of the world, the children continued to come in from the outdoors after the bell to settle into quiet work at their desks, their faces bronzed and rosy with sun and play. Here were the moments in which I counted my blessings as a teacher. I'd throw the windows wide to the soft morning breeze that fanned the room with scents of new-mown grass and dandelions while, from outside, echoing in the air, would come the high clear timbre of robins.

"Oh, Children," I'd say, "it's God's own morning!" And we would know this to be true. Dreamy, poetic times fell round us then, and our sweet accord seemed forever.

And yet, in our little world, there grew a troubling fact. Sarah and Megan were not progressing in their studies at the expected pace. A year separated them in age but Megan, the younger of the two, had managed to get into kindergarten with her older sister because her birthday fell just before the critical cut-off time. It was the wrong time, as it turned out. The girls were inseparable and had gone on to each new grade together for all their schooling. Mrs. Morgan saw to it. Her candid persuasive manner was easily assented to each year.

"Families who learn together don't become strangers," she explained. The wonder was the girls proved an asset, as a pair, not only to the school but to the room lucky enough to get them. Teachers and pupils alike adored them.

Awful realities caught up, however. Sarah made strides to the top of the class while her contender, Megan, grew weary. She couldn't keep up. When she thought no one was observing her, she'd put her little head down on her desk, fighting to keep her eyes open. Term tests were closing in now, too. Megan slowed to a standstill; it was more than time to call her mother.

Mrs. Morgan sat at the little round table at the back of the room with me, her brown eyes large with sensitivity, her pale mauve suit a lovely contrast against her dark hair. She told me that she'd noticed for some time now that Megan was having difficulty.

"I try to get her to bed early, but she lies there awake, worrying. The work is too hard for her, even with the help of the tutor I hire every year at exam time. I am at loss as to know what to do. Megan doesn't want to be a failure by not keeping up with Sarah. Yet I know she's unhappy."

At times like this, I questioned the fairness of the school's expectations and mine, especially when they force parents' decisions through such rugged emotional territory. How could I promote Megan's success when time just kept marching on to the next lesson, to the next grade, and to the next subject, year after year? Everything was piling up on her. Was there not some huge pretense involved in classifying the levels of learning, putting time limits on them, and then creating tests to measure them? Measure what, I wondered? I felt terrorized by this side of my professional duties. I was to teach according to the child's readiness, but I was to safeguard the overall pace of the system, too. It came as a shock to realize that an unstated issue has to do with what comes first: the child or the system.

Realities gathered round our door. Megan had begun school too early to keep up with Sarah, months older than she. The two bright well-behaved sisters, wishing only to be together in the same class, had to go their separate ways. This would be easier on Sarah, whose ready smile and sunny face saw her through each day. Megan, however, had yet to discover that her progress did not need to be measured against her sister's; progress could be hers alone.

A change in direction was needed. For Megan to work at a pace more suited to her unique learning patterns, she had to remain in the same grade the following year, while Sarah moved on. Mrs. Morgan heaved a sigh of relief at this suggestion and I could see how troubled she must have been. At first, Megan was sad and at a loss, but she blossomed the second year. A few years later, both girls went on to become formidable university students.

During my teaching career, I often thought of Mrs. Morgan and the unwavering support she gave me. Her fairness, integrity, and sense of responsibility made my moments of youthful over-reaction to standards that didn't take into account a child's feelings a lot more manageable. She knew how important it was for parent and teacher to share the same understanding that a child's progress is unique.

I realized at the time how freeing it would be to discuss with Mrs. Morgan my experience of school at home on the reserve. I might have told her about the parents on the reserve whose relationship to schooling was a negative one. The whole of education, for them, meant facing unrelenting machinery that supported decisions made outside the interests of family and community. Reserve moms and dads complied with the educational laws of the 1960s all right, but many stayed away from parent-teacher conferences. At the heart of things, the parents knew the importance of helping the school teach each child the ABCs, but their genuine concern for loss of identity remained unaddressed. Their children were taught a false and damaging picture of who they actually were. Mrs. Morgan would have been dismayed that reserve people did not have the good fortune of living the ideals of modern public schooling.

I periodically re-read the teachers college description of education as "the single greatest endeavour shared by civilization." Mrs. Morgan helped me find the best sense in that quotation: Co-operation between the parent and the school resolves unique dilemmas before a child's chances to grow are thwarted, keeping the child's sense of self intact.

Our professors sent us into the world with a few unshakable truths. But it was hard to see what these were, at times. And there was so much more to know.

TWO.

DISGUISED IN THE OPEN FIELD

AND THERE IT WAS AGAIN: the letter from Goldie. It lay face up on my little round hallway table where I kept an assortment of mementos and reminders until I took action and tidied everything away once more. Goldie's letters always looked the same. The pale blue paper with precise handwriting in navy ink wouldn't lie flat on the table, let alone in the mind. Her words, often ironic, either rankled or inspired but never left me alone. As I studied the envelope with its clear penmanship, it struck me that one of us was bound to end up eccentric, and I tried to feel confident that it wouldn't be me. Words of a friend like Goldie, after all these years, still stung, and still affirmed. Her opening line was provocative, as usual:

> In my books, you chose the toughest profession and I cannot, and will not, commiserate.

Commiserate? That was the farthest thing from my mind! I only asked her to think about my life as a teacher—because she had asked me why I was planning to leave the profession after so many years. I hadn't told her much about the ups and downs of my career, after all. But then, Goldie had a way of reading between the lines and that proved maddening. Some friend, I would think, despite myself. The worst was that when you really stopped to think about it, this was the very quality I wanted in a friend.

We had met in Regina at Balfour Technical High School and did things we thought any sophisticated girl might do. We wore pale cardigans on which we pinned big silk blossoms to set them off and to lend pizzazz to plain A-line skirts whenever we wanted to look ravishing, which was every day. We experimented with lipstick tints in the girl's washroom, cracked gum in public, and flirted with boys half our size. It was after high school that we parted ways. Goldie insisted the good life meant entering the profession of dentistry and "keeping an eye out for gold." I insisted it meant teaching. Now, after all this time, here was a letter that sparked meaning in every direction:

> *Pillar of Hope,*
> *That thing about professional expectations plagues you, I see. I believe it's incurable. I say, come to Toronto for a visit but remember when you get here, I won't tolerate a word about Thinking. Leave it behind—particularly all that pining about children and their connectedness to, what is it, again, society and its battles? Really, Pillar, things do go bump in the night—but if it isn't gold, drop it.*
> *Love to the family and the old tom, Goldie.*
> *P.S. Say the word Curriculum, I scream. Say Values, you're gone!*

So, in Goldie's eyes, my cat was as important as my life's work. We'd see about that. I'd pay her a visit, all right, but on my terms. Goldie would hear more than she'd bargained for, especially about what it takes to become a teacher, even if that meant getting a few main points down on paper for her.

I wanted to put down the stories of my pupils, but in such a way that their significance would be absolutely clear to Goldie. She appreciated frank assessment. But here was my first hard question. Should I write about an incident at school that took place during my first month of teaching? If nothing else, it dredged up a landscape that revealed how I might, or might not, be accepted by my profession, and by my fellow teachers. Beliefs held by any number of teachers in school would be the guide to what I could, or could not, openly discuss. My fellow teachers were expected to teach the history of Canada, and "naturally" the text-book story on Indians. The idea of writing this down even for Goldie depressed me. For one thing, I wasn't at all sure how my background figured into my value as a teacher.

To illustrate, it was September in my first school. On that bright crisp morning three of us stood at the top of the stairs, on hall duty, as we watched the children hurry to their classrooms. The smell of fall leaves and sunshine filled the air. Nervous excitement filled me. Would my children and I have another good day together? The seasoned teacher among the three of us, a woman with a piercing but friendly gaze, remarked to the new teacher, a heavy-boned, square-jawed woman, that the jacket she wore was simply beautiful; to which came the sharp reply, "I saw a dirty Indian woman wearing exactly the same jacket in Fort Qu'Appelle on Saturday. I'm never wearing it again."

Her face softened only when the older teacher remarked, "I don't blame you."

Neither of them looked at me, their eager companion and colleague on duty beside them. Shock and dismay set my heart pounding. Was their hostility a sign that I might be discovered and pushed into a confrontation that could end in me losing my job? I swallowed my fear and anger and focused on the children.

That incident, taken in conjunction with what the professor in teachers college said about his not letting me enter if he were he in charge, crys-tallized the lay of the land in my mind. I asked myself how the parents might feel about me as their child's teacher. This worried me most of all. Should Goldie know about this, not to mention another occurrence? Yet, incidents like these were not the only reason I worried. Time healed, but not everything.

There were permanent life wounds. Four years before I began teaching, I paid a visit to Vital Statistics to obtain a copy of my birth certificate, a document I needed as proof that I was old enough to marry. When I was handed my birth certificate I saw printed on it in large black letters, diagonally, clear across the page, the word "Native." By itself the word said a lot but hand-printed across a copy of my birth certificate was a branding. This oversized grease pencil defacement meant that each and every official who would handle my private information, thereafter, now had a spotlight for reference. Being branded officially meant that any future bureaucrat who might seek to corral my goals, as they had my parents' and my grandparents', had the go-ahead, indeed the invitation.

In the 1960s and prior to that, Canadian society held certain beliefs about the character of Native people. These beliefs had changed little since the days of European settlement. Discriminatory ideas might surface anytime, anywhere; and I worried that I might be considered a source of trouble. I decided to remain vigilant and to protect my right to a career as best I could. I became agile in the art of elusive response whenever I was asked personal questions. Often, I felt like an imposter, although I knew I had no real reason to feel that way. Ignorance about Aboriginal history and Canada's constitutional relations with Aboriginal peoples made many of my fellow teachers imposters to their better selves. If I was a fraud, so was everyone else. Yet, I hesitated, even now, to let Goldie, my old high-school pal and friend, get as much as a tiny glimpse of the underbelly of misinformation and its long management in my profession.

Although the bulk of embarrassment didn't belong to me, its weight was substantial in my professional life. And yet, it was a weight worth carrying, I believed, if I were only allowed to teach and to do it well. Still, Goldie, of all my friends, would be the one most likely to scold me for not having confronted the two teachers in the hallway at school. It was my democratic duty, she'd say, even now. And she'd be right; the two were my colleagues and, in an odd but critical way, my responsibility. But the shock of the unexpected attack and fear of uncontrollable fallout were like hand grenades of historical anxiety easily touched off.

Many times, Goldie's spirited little letters seemed brusque, yet she was a deeply sympathetic and loyal friend. She acted in tune with her beliefs and expected no less of me. Her pattern of communicating was to send an attention-getting note followed by a swift empathetic telephone call. Still, I'd have some explaining to do regarding my silence about certain things over the years.

She would have to be told that prejudice in any teacher rang an alarm bell in my head. Then she would understand why I tried to stay out of its reverberation. Words said with ease of ignorance among fellow teachers, usually in the teachers' lounge at recess, recalled images of my parents' suffering. A flame would inevitably ignite in me. But, fear of embroilment in situations that lowered me and a bigot into the same bath water repelled me. It was a plunge from which neither I nor my assailant might surface cleansed. This meant the stress of hyper vigilance and discretion was to become my life companion.

Added to my fears, if I lost my job my family couldn't help me. My career alone was my way to achieve personal autonomy and vital independence, and it was my escape from soul-searing poverty. My career was worth fighting for in any way available to me. Trouble in the profession could jeopardize all of this.

Still, Goldie knew some things. She once asked me why I chose to become a teacher, given the preference for those of English background. I told her that I refused to be tied to a predetermined existence, a life defined by policy, policy that manipulated the desperate straits of my parents. My source of resolve, I told Goldie, came not only from my willing heart but also from observing my family in the grip of circum-stance. Despite miserable conditions, my parents tried to live each day with a sense of purpose, even as this pursuit of dignity spelled failure.

My father, a decorated soldier, showed pride of accomplishment des-pite his powerlessness to take part in his country as a full citizen after the war. Goldie knew about my mother and often admired a picture I kept of that warm-eyed beauty with dark wavy hair, who had developed homemaker skills with next to nothing. My mother, without picture books or paper and pencil, fed our imaginations with songs and stories from her Saulteaux culture and from my father's Cree background. She impressed upon us the importance of school. I saw the future as one big promise, and I sensed its pressure.

I told Goldie, for instance, about the time two cousins of mine, Ida and Laura Wasacase, came home from residential school and stood at the foot of my bed looking at me. I was too little to be up and about but not too young to feel their indifference to me. I sensed their sophis-tication and saw how crisply their white shirt collars lay against their navy jackets. Young as I was, the feeling of circumstance versus dignity charged the air. I sensed something about myself; I wanted to return their clear and direct gaze on level ground.

Several years later, Ida Wasacase would be working alongside visionary leaders in the First Nations community and in the field of education to establish the Saskatchewan Indian Federated College, where she would become its first president in 1976. A few years later, many more would be working toward the design of a teachers' education program with a syllabus emphasizing Aboriginal history, culture, and language.

Indeed, many people began thinking about the state of Aboriginal education in Saskatchewan in the decades prior to the 1960s. However, it was only in the early 1960s that educational leaders began to take serious note of the shockingly high dropout rate among Aboriginal learners. Although news of such discussions didn't reach the school where I taught, years later I became aware that government had already begun the task of building a foundation for change. Developments had been percolating in the background before I even began my career. However, the purported changes in direction were unknown to me and my fellow teachers, even though we were touted by educational leaders as "the real change agents." Like all my fellow teachers, I was soon very busy concentrating on other matters at hand.

Goldie, studying to become a dentist in Toronto, once asked me what it was like not to be able to go school until I was ten years old. I told her that it had filled my heart with a great and constant wish. For the five years after my father returned home from overseas when I was five years old, I endured the very real pain of wanting to learn, a feeling I never outgrew. There were no schools and few books, if any, on the reserve. My father and mother and other parents were determined not to send their children to residential school. They insisted we not endure what they had in Round Lake, a Saskatchewan residential school that in recent times, it was rumoured, mysteriously burned to the ground.

I was about five years old, in fact, when the Indian agent came to the reserve to speak to my parents. Soon after that, my older brother, Anthony, was taken away. I remember my mother in tears as she washed his face for the umpteenth time that day. I watched how she adjusted his pea cap and tucked his plaid shirt into his trousers as he waited for the truck that would take him away. She refolded his jacket over his arm, again and again. It was wordless crying from her. Anthony stood in the hot sun trying to look tall, his face flushed.

"Next it will be our girls!" My father said. He had only recently returned from the war. His wide, bright, even-toothed smile was gone. He looked pale and grim as he announced to my mother. "The girls are staying put until a school is built, right here!"

As for me, a young hostage and ignorant of the tricks and tools of domination, I wanted only to learn to read and to have a book of my own; and I would have gone with Anthony for this alone.

By the time a school was built on the reserve I was ten, a skinny black-eyed girl in the habit of questioning adults to the point of irritation. That first day of school was when I decided to become a teacher. The woodsy-smelling exercise books, smooth lengths of pencils, short glass ink jars, mystifying brass pen nibs, pure white chalk, and the orange-coloured dust-bane sprinkled over waxed floors at the end of the day—all of it intoxicated me. Without question, I wanted this to be my life.

No, I did not want Goldie to sit and commiserate with me about my career. I wanted her to understand the forces that pulled me into the classroom and what finally took me from it. Yes, it was time to fold up this letter, too, and lay it aside. The thought of Goldie always lightened my spirit. I still saw myself and her as teenagers in school, though we were grown women now. As for Toronto, come summer, Goldie would be the unwilling recipient of one or two pages from my life as a teacher. Make that two hundred.

THREE.

A SURVIVAL KIT OF ONE'S OWN

WE CAME TO THE CITY from across the province for our training. Some of us found room and board in the bigger older houses in and around College Avenue near the red brick building on which we pinned our hopes. Some managed to find rooms at the YWCA on Lorne Street, a few short blocks away. I felt lucky to have found lodging within walking distance of a place that was home to professors and their secrets. Entering the front door would be like gaining admittance to a revered society that took you in and showed you its powers. I harboured all kinds of notions about professors and teaching that needed to be put to the test and would be.

Today I was overjoyed at entering teachers college at last. Having started school late, I was twenty years old, possibly three or four years older than many of my classmates. I was married, furthermore, and a new mother.

My teachers on the reserve had tried to help me catch up to my age group, at least partway; they let me skip grades and combine others to narrow the gap. Today, I was still behind and not just in grades. I was far less sophisticated than my urban peers, especially in this government city I now called home. Still, I was thankful and buoyant with joy.

My husband, Peter, and I scrimped and saved so that I might attend teachers college as soon as possible. A big step because we were alone in the city with an infant and without family support. We kept a roof over our heads and paid a babysitter and, on top of everything, paid for tuition and books. This was at a time when construction jobs for Peter were scarce.

Peter and I were committed to a future together despite that acquaintances reminded us, time and again, that we made an unlikely pair. Peter was a young immigrant from Berlin, Germany, and I was a young Cree/Saulteaux woman from the Cowessess Indian Reserve in Saskatchewan. He was high-summer blond and I was mid-summer bronze. People in town looked at us pointedly as we went about our business. People on the reserve responded in the same tentative way.

Peter and I met while I was in girls' residence in Assiniboia, Saskatchewan, at a church-sponsored teen club held in the basement of the church. I was in grade ten, a sixteen-year-old with plans. Nineteen-year-old Peter was in the midst of his own plan to see the world in the company of two other young men from Germany. All three stayed with a German family in town for a few weeks. For Peter, his tour of exotic countries was cut short by a stopover in Saskatchewan, soon to be his future home. As for his buddies, one fell in love in Vancouver, and the other in Sydney, Australia, so all three ended up settling down someplace quite unexpectedly.

Peter, unable to find construction work in the town of Assiniboia, moved to Regina. He wrote letters to me everyday with the help of an English dictionary. His letters contained impressive but oddly constructed expressions of adoration that worked a certain magic; I told him much later that I was lured by their hintings of Shakespeare.

When he could afford it, Peter would rent a car to come back to Assiniboia to see me at the girls' residence where I lived. When I turned seventeen, he suggested I move to Regina, too, so that we could see each other more often. I agreed and asked my aunt to let me stay with her in her tiny apartment on 14th Avenue until I could find lodging. A week or so later, I was ensconced in the YWCA on Lorne Street.

It was very exciting to be near Peter and the public library where we loved to go and read in the evenings. Peter's command of English, though meagre, grew stronger; thanks to Mickey Spillane and Agatha Christy, two detective story writers whose use of nouns and verbs was concrete, exact, and in the modern vernacular. Peter put his English into practice almost immediately with the confidence of an Englishman, no matter the company. I marvelled at this bold, handsome Berliner whose second language in school had been Russian, not English as he had wished. He read every spare moment, a pile of library books always within reach.

I wasn't happy with my high school arrangements that first year in the city. The public school administration convinced my aunt that because we lived near College Avenue, I should attend Balfour Technical School. I reacted with a panic at the words "technical school." I had no wish to take technical subjects. I preferred to go to Central Collegiate, close by. The academic subjects taught there would allow me to go on to teachers college. I begged my old aunt to intervene on my behalf but she was unsuccessful. So, that fall, I entered the doors of Balfour High with a heavy heart.

I needn't have worried. For the most part, Balfour students could opt for academic classes, though complete escape from the school's technical specializations was impossible. Schools like Balfour Technical Collegiate, which opened its doors in 1931, had been hard won. At that time, instruction was needed to ready pupils for agriculture and the industrial world.

For starters, I balked at sewing. Having grown up on a farm, on the reserve, I worked outdoors and spent much of my time looking after the cows and horses and equipment. This always gave me a sense of freedom; it allowed escape from housework. But soon I was curious and felt challenged by the subject. I ended up making an apron for my aunt and a burgundy-striped jumper that I wore year round over blouses and turtlenecks.

I had wonderful teachers in all my courses. I loved the anonymity of the school's hallways, which teemed with life. The students came from every corner of the world and were not the least captivated by thoughts about one's limited wardrobe. I fit right in and loved my life. There were recreational events enjoyed with classmates. At school assemblies, for instance, we watched football practices of the Balfour Redman supervised by Mr. Gordon Currie, our tall and energetic teacher with bright blue eyes. Mr. Currie was a school football coach of no small fame. Our team won city championships and provincial titles. He was also a beloved classroom teacher who took the time to teach his students the basics of becoming a good human being: to define genuine goals for ourselves and make a genuine effort at all times. This, he said, would root self-respect in each of us, one of the most important powers to cultivate. He said that one way to keep our powers topped up was to make personal time for solitude and daydreaming. "Just lie down on your back in the sun out in a field and watch the clouds in the sky. It can be as simple as that. But do it."

Soon, grade twelve hove into sight and I was very happy. That year, I looked forward to a summer with my YWCA friends and a boyfriend I admired very much.

Peter, a little older than me, was serious about us. One warm summer evening as we walked across Victoria Park downtown toward the YWCA, he asked me to marry him. I reacted in shocked amazement to the suggestion. Marry? I was only seventeen, though soon to be eighteen, and firmly convinced that I would never marry as I had my own plans. My spontaneous burst of laughter hurt Peter's feelings, but he remained constant. I knew I could not marry without my parents' consent until I came of age. My father made it clear to me and my siblings that he didn't like Germans, having faced them in action during the war. He was adamant, and this was a bridge I would have to cross.

Peter and I were each other's confidants in matters such as this. Peter's fellow construction workers told him that if he married me our children would be "half-breeds," apparently a bad thing. As for me, when I told friends that Peter and I planned to get married, someday, I was told that I'd end up with a "DP" (deported person), a bad thing, too. Peter and I found this all very amusing; happy with ourselves as we were.

When that summer came to an end, I signed up for classes at Balfour, again. But, this time, I was told I had to take Home Economics and Home Administration—two separate courses on the same thing, as far as I was concerned. That meant foregoing Biology and Chemistry, at least for that term. No reason was given for the decision. My marks were not an issue. Again, my aunt called the school. She was told "everyone" had to take key technical courses. Lacking any bargaining power, I entered my final year of high school feeling betrayed.

I soon discovered that a number of my former classmates had been permitted to enroll in the very courses I wanted. This seemed a huge injustice. I confronted the vice-principal, a stout man with glasses formally dressed in a dark suit and tie, who proved indifferent to the situation. It was a matter of organization, he said. Hot-headed about the matter, I told him I had no option but to leave this school. He wished me luck, in a grave and kindly manner. I scooped up my belongings from my locker and left. The autumn sun burned my face as an icy river coursed through my veins. Never mind, I would find a way to get my grade twelve classes, I told myself. I needed these for teachers college.

I came upon the miracle of the correspondence school in Regina. It took me a few weeks to gather financial resources, like a government bursary, and to gain admission to the school, as well as to line up courses that included Chemistry and Biology. In the meantime, Peter and I celebrated our good luck at having found a furnished suite in downtown Regina, near the library and close to stores where we planned to move.

We began our campaign to get married. The first obstacle was our parents; Peter's were disappointed in his decision to stay in Canada. My father, particularly, was cold to the idea of my marrying a non-Indian who was German. That was two counts against Peter. Not to be discouraged, we decided that we didn't need anyone's blessing, save the minister of the church who would be the one to marry us in the first place. We met with the minister and agreed to attend afternoon study sessions on the art of marriage at Carmichael United Church. There we learned from a gentle soft-spoken man. The minister, having noted our unmistakable youth, gave us a pamphlet on how to be a couple; we took it home and studied—just to pass that quiz, we joked.

Our situation would take more than passing a quiz. It irked Peter that as a consequence of my marrying him, I stood to lose my identity as an Indian. He took it upon himself to see a federal government official at the immigration government office who handled Indian matters, as well. Peter informed the official of our plan to marry emphasizing that government had an obligation to allow me to retain my treaty status, hence my right to funding for my university education and teachers college. The official, a kindly grey-haired man with glasses, advised Peter that the only option we had was to obtain my parent's consent. The government could not change the legal outcome of my identity. The law was the law. Peter said it felt like he was back in postwar Germany where boxes of approval certificates were required for just about everything. I wanted to say "I told you so" but didn't.

Not to be deterred, we set out to make one last great effort to obtain my parent's approval to marry. We rented a red Volkswagen to take us over the familiar gravel and dirt roads leading to the reserve where a little log house with a lumber porch stood, its stove pipe unfurling bands of smoke. It was an emotional scene with tears all around. We got their approval, finally, and now feeling very free and grown up, we went to the church to set our wedding date for December of that year.

We were happy that we were now able to make future decisions that were best for us. It struck me that our wedding would be a very simple one. We didn't want to present our parents with this concern and so decided to take matters into our own hands. I would wear a simple light beige knit suit and Peter the suit he'd brought with him from Germany. The final question, and this on the eve of our wedding day, was who would cut my hair? I had forgotten all about my appearance, so pleased was I to have something new to wear. Now here it was, already the final hours before the ceremony. Time and cash being limited, and Peter, ever ready to help, said he would cut my hair. I unloosed my pony tail and brushed my almost waist length hair into a smooth curtain around my shoulders and sat in a chair. Peter stood at the ready, huge steel scissors in hand that he'd borrowed from the landlady upstairs. I showed Peter the exact length I wanted, which was just below my earlobes.

"Can you cut straight?" I asked him, feeling suddenly protective.

"Of course," he said. "Wait and see."

There was a grinding shearing sound that made its way around the back of my head from my right earlobe to my left while fronds of whispering hair lengths fell to the floor. I was sorry to see it go but excited to be sophisticated. A final snip and Peter handed me the mirror. The cut was straight as a whistle but, alas, at a grievous tilt! It hung below my right earlobe neat and exact, but it ended way too high above the ear on the left. We didn't know whether to laugh or cry. The only solution was to put my hair up in pin curls and try to sleep on them. The wonder was, the hair looked fine in curls and even softened the look of the suit.

Amidst our joy, the ceremony held a note of sadness. Peter's parents were in Egypt on business where Peter's father was working on the Aswan Dam as an engineer. They sent regrets that they were unable to attend at "such short notice." It was just as well. Peter's construction crew pals, in our part of the world, decided on their own that the wedding couple must be driven to the ceremony in a fully decorated car. Peter and I didn't see the need to fuss, and we told them so. Broad-shouldered Frank, tall Siggy, and brown-eyed Bert appeared to agree but, on the appointed hour, roared up to the house backfiring the car that they had decked out with pink and white toilet paper roses made by their very own workman's hands. My heart sank when I saw the effect. Their old Buick, all shiny and sparkling, was covered in pink and white festoons of what looked like a frothy confection from top to bottom, including fenders and hub caps. The sight made me feel dizzy. The fellows, though, were proud, and their grins were wide as can be. Worse, when we got into the car and set out, Frank honked the horn down College Avenue to Carmichael United Church, a gracious building tucked away in a quiet zone behind the General Hospital. Peter and I sat in the back seat squeezing each other's hands in help-less communication. Thank goodness my parents arrived after us. They might have had cause to wonder all the more about Peter and his friends. As it turned out, we were all very happy together that day.

Firmly settled in our little basement nest, I began my correspon-dence classes, albeit about two months late. Things took longer than we thought. All that winter and spring, I juggled a full slate of grade twelve courses and a university extension English course. I had nowhere in which to do the lab work required in chemistry, so I did without. I studied the periodic tables and deduced other relevant information from the text book and was thus able to calculate the weights of substances that remained when element X was burned with element Y. My answers were always off by a few hundredths but the school didn't find out I wasn't going to lab. My deductive "lab work," however, took hours.

One time, already after midnight, I grew tired as I sat hunched over my books at our little kitchen table. I simply could not keep my eyes open. Desperate, I did what Marie Sklodowska-Curie, discoverer of radium, did when she studied. I filled a pail with cold water, placed it under the table and stuck my feet in. My eyes popped open. My brain perked up. There I read and pondered, among other things, the elegance of chemical equations and the wonders of biological life categories. Whenever I felt I was hard done by, I recalled the brilliant Marie Sklodowska-Curie who, as a young student in Paris, was often so cold at nights in bed that she placed her wooden chair over her blanket for added warmth.

Madame Curie's single-minded struggle against hard circumstances in pursuit of learning inspired me onward in my quest to become a teacher, no matter the odds. Soon enough, teachers college itself rang out the first jarring note, and loud enough to stop me in my tracks if I let it. But my success in correspondence school and my completion of a university extension course, English 101, also by correspondence, proved to me that I could take the next step as soon as possible.

I revelled in the company of my teachers-college-bound companions. It felt like real progress. It told of equality on its way. We were excited that first day in September. We strode tall in our high heels and cotton dresses down College Avenue. A few leaves scurried about our feet and the autumn morning air was sharp and clean. Young men in crew cuts, oxfords, and cardigans affected a smart professional air. It was a manner learned from their men folk likely, and now slightly overdone; in fact they all but swaggered. Their boyishness shone through. But, we are well on our way to becoming professionals, they seemed to say. It was certainly what I was saying. Here was a new life to be explored with new ideas, new associates, and, of course, real insights into the mysteries of teaching and learning. It was exhilarating, to say the least. Soon we found ourselves juggling timetables, signing up for drama, music, and sports and generally luxuriating in the feel of this special place. I wanted it all!

Our professors made a wise move that first day. They stood in line at the top of the vestibule steps waiting to give each of us a formal welcoming handshake. We made our way up the steps to the main floor. There the professors, middle aged and carefully groomed, nodded at us, shook our hands, and addressed us by our surnames. This encounter was the first moment of admittance and obligation. I felt very grown-up, and in a rush I vowed to myself that nothing would detract me from my goal and all its possibilities. I would strive to do my very best, always. Here was the life I wanted coming round at last.

The professors, pleased to see us, didn't waste a moment; they modelled how we would be greeting our own pupils one day. All of our mentors smiled bright professional smiles at us except for one. An elderly professor, standing at the top of the stairs, muttered under his breath as we passed, "Who said anyone can teach?"

I felt a twinge of disappointment and stopped briefly to take a close look at the person who'd made the sinister remark. A man with short white hair, pale grey-blue eyes, and a grey suit—he could pass for anyone's uncle, I thought, though perhaps not mine. I wondered what he considered his job to be. I mentally stepped back and decided that I would prove him wrong. It seemed that with a single step, through the doors of the college, something beyond the magic made its presence felt. I couldn't say what, just then.

That morning, they herded us into the auditorium, a large space complete with rows of seats on an incline with a podium at the front. We sat in random order. I glanced over the heads of about four hundred pupils. In the crowd I saw two First Nations people—a man and a woman—whom I didn't know. The man sat to my right about four rows in front of me wearing a navy suit and tie. The woman, thin in a green jumper and white blouse, sat two rows in front. When the student body was told to shake hands with the person seated on either side, those in front turned to look back at the result and my eyes met those of the woman. The professors stood up on the stage and introduced themselves, each declaring the subject of his or her expertise. Mature and in their business attire, they wore warm smiles; I looked forward to learning from each one of them.

After introductions, the man in the grey suit, whom I had seen earlier, was asked by the principal to say a few words. He stepped forward to the edge of the platform and said, "Look to the person on your left."

I looked and there sat a young woman, smiling broadly.

"Now look at the person on your right."

We did so.

"One of you will be gone before the term is over."

I nodded to the person at my left who nodded back and then turned to my right and said, "It won't be us." A young woman, with a thousand shiny orange waves in her hair pinned back from a freckled face, laughed in such a fresh open way I was immediately drawn to her. "Nope, it won't be us," she repeated.

Her name was Sheila Scott and she and I made friends on the spot. Our association would last through the years. As we stood up to leave the auditorium, I sensed the sombre note that gripped the assembly. I turned to look at the First Nations students and found they were looking at me, too. We recognized one another, although we had never met. What surprised me more was that the moment, brief as it was, seemed fraught with understanding that three is a crowd. It was even more surprising that the three of us did not end up together in any of the classes at any time thereafter.

The professors were helpmates. They divided the students into classes, each alpha group remaining together as a unit for the duration of our training. We would get to know one another, test our strengths and our weaknesses over the next several months, and learn to pool our talents in support of one another. Each professor, with an eye toward growth or failing, tended the flock with care. Their goal was to pass on skills and experience so we could manage our own good progress. In fact, they'd likely spent hours preparing their lessons. Often, however, it would be a rare moment of insight into the events around us that set each of us onto a path of learning. We'd come to consider the importance of key principles of teaching. One came to our attention soon enough: the obvious sheds a dim light. That is to say, the "the obvious" got in the way. Many of us trainees wished to get down to the business of learning how to teach, and that meant now. Groups got together to complain that the masters were not filling our heads with enough practical knowledge. In the same breath, we decried their failure to fill our heads with enough academic learning. We didn't know we were in the midst of an old conflict that is waged between content and process, a conundrum that remains unresolved at the heart of teaching: Was it what you taught, or how you went about teaching that mattered most?

Finding the answers to these questions meant devoting ourselves to a lifetime of study; but, as young teacher candidates, we would have tried to argue against that notion. We didn't realize that our professors spoke from long experience and knew that if you were gifted to learn, you'd be granted enlightenment, and it could still take years.

"Attend to the child," the professors insisted. This rang convincingly in the ear. It sounded like: do the right things and pupils will learn, but there is more to teaching than meets the eye. Apparently, too, we could do everything right and fall short of the mark.

A kindly white-haired professor told us, for example, that life circumstances can make learning difficult for some children. This meant that they could be difficult to teach; but "never say never" was her mantra. She went on to tell us, her eyes locked on a memory as she looked out the window, that a child might lack a sense of personal security, a reality most of us might take for granted. Yet confidence was a key factor of learning. A true teacher built up and protected a child's self-confidence, because a child lacking in this might not be able to learn at all. Hearing this, recalled to me the times I had great difficulty concentrating in school. This was usually associated with tension at home or in the schoolyard with a bully forever baiting his or her little school mates. I grew up with children who failed tests because of this constant fear of violence. Now here was our professor saying that a teacher must remain alert to the role of self-esteem in learning, make no mistake.

Pen and pencil poised, we teachers-to-be waited to write down important facts. None seemed worthy of total pursuit, just yet.

"Should you be lucky," our professors said, "your pupils will have a real thirst for knowledge." By now, we were exchanging glances. Didn't we already know this from our own school experiences?

Sheila Scott, my new found friend and I encouraged one another.

"Surely these dry lectures are meant to illustrate the basics of teaching. But what does it all mean? It's like chasing the wind."

"How do you study for this stuff, anyway?'

One afternoon, Sheila and I headed out across the frost-covered walk that connected the teachers college building to the Mackenzie Art Gallery building, next door. That morning, we learned from our professors that teacher training in Saskatchewan was a relatively new development. In the not so distant past, apparently, trained teachers came from outside the Territories or from the ranks of pupils in higher grades who were pressed into service. In the fall of 1893, the Normal School was set up in a regular classroom to train teachers in an ordinary school in the city. To strengthen pride in our profession's illustrious past, we were shown a 1914 photograph of our old red building with about two hundred graduates in front of it.

Hard snow covered the ground now, and winter was making its presence felt.

"Watch your step," Sheila warned. "It's slippery."

I was paying only half a mind because I was on a rant about those galling weightless study periods in teachers college that weren't doing justice to history. Sheila's blue eyes blazed a warning, her face red in the driving wind. My mind was so occupied I didn't notice the cold. I was in my high heels and nylons, as I reckoned everyone ought to be. Sheila was in sensible flats and overshoes.

"We want fundamental knowledge that explains what lies behind the practices of our profession, once and for all, right?" I was on my high horse while bracing myself against the wind. "Why don't our professors share this critical stuff? Instead, they feed us common sense."

My feet slipped under me. I crouched down into a counteractive ski position and bore down hard to save myself from falling. I straightened up to catch my breath as Sheila burst into whoops of laughter. I turned to ask what was so funny. Doubled over, she pointed to the ground behind me. There, on the sidewalk side by side, lay two little black high heels. I had scraped them right off my shoes. I no longer felt high and mighty. Walking around in my "slippers" all day, I knew I had to learn patience. Nature had given me a quick lesson on dressing sensibly, though humility was a ways off.

As for going to class, I feared the loss of excitement. My mind was on the prowl for facts. These didn't seem to be forthcoming in any degree of speed so I watched for clues. Perhaps the call of the profession meant studying its subtler pathway, I told myself, whatever that might be. I tried not to lose hope of seeing at least one grand monumental tower of knowledge ahead of me. Our professors, oblivious to this concern, stressed yet another common-sense principle. The job of teaching, they said, was to seek and then affirm the special personality of each and every child we met during the course of our work. "If you learn anything of value," intoned the wise, "remember that the learner must believe in himself. Learning takes place then." This, too, was so obvious a truth that even Sheila, the epitome of patience, rolled her eyes.

A feeling took hold that was hard to explain. I had a vague impression that a combination of reward and angst was played out in this hall of learning. I sensed a herding instinct in sway—which, in the midst of everything else we were doing felt like a cold draft from an unknown quarter. Like the rest of my classmates, I tried to absorb the numerous disparate details coming our way, but the big picture was missing. I rarely had time to sit down, much less think about the source of this peculiar weight, let alone decode its meaning. There arrived yet another curiosity; a certain Professor Baxter faced off with a fellow student teacher, Rusty Boulin. Rusty's story is one of control, it seemed, if not self-control.

Like most people, I valued drawing my own conclusions about things. My grandmother who believed strongly in group consensus, often referred to my character flaw as having a mind of my own. And, in a way, that let me know that it wasn't always a good thing. Impatience was something I'd have to manage with care. Still, in teachers college, with so little time to reflect upon what lay at the heart of things, a part of me sided with Rusty Boulin, a student who came under the watchful eyes of Professor Baxter.

Rusty Boulin

There were bound to be personal differences in an institution of higher learning; and when it came to that, I relished the opportunity to argue my points. However, Professor Baxter and Rusty Boulin betrayed something more complex. It seemed Rusty thumbed his nose at professional authority. It also appeared that a mentor cast aside her professional mien to make her point. In my mind, a conflict that reared its head as a consequence of personality alone had no place in the profession.

"What's up with Rusty?" Sheila asked one day, "He's acting like he's got the itch."

"He needs a lesson in respect," I replied.

I thought Rusty really needed to show some appreciation for our institution. In my heart of hearts, I considered teaching the finest of all professions—a remarkable inheritance borne through time by our predecessors. I considered it a legacy worth preserving. My ideal about our becoming keepers of the faith wavered, however, when Professor Baxter let Rusty get the better of her one day.

Professor Baxter taught Health Methods. She became Rusty Boulin's target. Rusty, full of energy and life, had little patience for reflective thought. He often said he wanted the substance of teaching served up, and the quicker the better. I couldn't agree more. Rusty thought such knowledge existed in servable portions that could be digested all at once, and so did I. Since this wasn't forthcoming, he tried to make things difficult for Professor Baxter, who he thought was withholding her best.

Something in the altercation between Rusty and Professor Baxter was being defined that I didn't understand. A couple of classmates pointed out that it was a classic case of man versus woman on a professional plain. Rusty, on his way to becoming a professional man, apparently in the image of his father, felt free to call into question the authority held by women. Added to that, he was a man of means, in a position to call anything he wanted into question. I couldn't believe this.

"Have you noticed how Baxter tries to control Rusty's thinking?" a male student asked.

"And what about Rusty?" Sheila asked. "He's doing the same."

Professor Baxter got my dander up, too, whenever it appeared she was doing my thinking for me. She countered our every conclusion. Her job, she said, was to plant a sense of direction in our heads.

Professor Baxter tried to model correct behaviour. Neat in dress, dry of bone, and generally angry, she was a picture of iron self-possession in the grip of a swirling storm of feelings. It was as if she felt the pressure of time as she tried to impart her subject matter to deaf ears. The thankless reception we gave it finally stoked her temper.

As for Rusty, he lacked true commitment because, unlike us, he didn't need to be in college. He bragged that he could retreat to his father's business and make money hand over fist, anytime he wanted. He said his parents insisted that he get a teaching certificate first, in case hard times returned to the prairies. That teaching certificate was not meant to secure Rusty Boulin a life of independence; he already had that. On the contrary, it was something he would probably never use. Unlike the majority of students, Rusty was financially secure and apparently well established. He'd never have to learn and then live by the codes of professional conduct. Nor would he need to build a reputation that linked him to a network of fellow professionals. He carried that burden well.

Professor Baxter got off to a bad start in General Methods class the day she taught us survival skills of the North. The North— wasn't this extreme? It certainly seemed that way to those of us who wished to be taught the solid and best theories of teaching and learning, once and for all. The dry facts of geography seemed to have little to do with it. Besides, isolated northern outposts of Saskatchewan were for the unlucky. No one in their right mind would dream of going there to teach. Not us; we were urbanites, teachers of the modern age!

Many of us had only recently left rural life and had come here to gain independence along with all the glamour cities might afford. Compared to our city and its promise of ease and novelty, the North was "a desert of ice and isolated communities" as Professor Baxter said. Northern Saskatchewan offered nothing but painful survival, it seemed. It would not be my destination, I knew. I had frozen enough in my time.

Professor Baxter persisted. Knowledge of the North was for our own good. We had to be prepared, male or female, city girl or rural, because some of us would eventually end up teaching where economic interest was growing and where snow and cold had no bearing.

"The odds are against your teaching in our towns and cities," she said. "Fresh water lakes are scarce as hen's teeth in the North compared to its vast stretches of ice, and you have to be prepared."

We were in pursuit of the more alluring aspects of teaching, however. The picture of us chiselling holes through ice for a drink of water was simply horrifying, especially in heels. Never mind suits and ties. Our protests did not deter Professor Baxter who insisted we arm ourselves with the basics of northern survival. Her words fell on deaf ears. Wasting precious class time studying survival skills gave us grief. I felt a stirring of rebellion when she began her lectures but never to the extent Rusty Boulin did. Things came to a head one day.

It began at our first Health Methods class. Rusty arrived and sat down with his long legs poking into the aisle. He waited to see if he could get the professor's goat. Professor Baxter ignored him. Today, she was demonstrating how to wash our hands by using melted ice-water sparingly.

"All you need is a jam can, with a big spike through it at the bottom, hung at a convenient height. You pour in your precious water and push the spike upward from its resting position. This allows the water to dribble down as you lather your hands. The weight of the spike forms a seal against the wasteful downward plunge of water."

Professor Baxter explained the role gravity played. Rusty took another tack, this time turning up the volume. He made a remark about three male classmates who were conscientious and earnest about paying attention in class. "Consider those smart-ass superintendent types up at the front of the room."

Professor Baxter ignored him. She went on with the lesson. Alas, Rusty sensed the common mind was "taking on a rash tone of public good." He declared all the more loudly that we were "becoming increasingly immune to shameless shenanigans that confuse mind with water."

"It brings out the kindergarten in me," he announced.

"It's truly vexing, isn't it," Professor Baxter said, reddening, "that some people are beyond taking professional life seriously. The authorities would do well to pass over such individuals for future positions."

"You mean like superintendents?" Rusty asked, shrinking in mock terror.

"I mean like anyone interested in making it through the doors of this college!" We teachers-to-be exchange glances. There is always the chance. Far be it from us to ruin our futures for want of knowledge about water conservation in the North.

"The president of this institution would be appalled by the lack of professionalism in you so-called student teachers. Imagine the likes of you, being responsible to the public, in perpetuity!"

"Then let us fire the bullies!" roared Rusty, as though mounting the ramparts.

"Class dismissed!" Professor Baxter shrieked.

We quickly filed out of the classroom, young teachers on our way to the North. Out in the hall, we were all a little a dazed with the feeling that we'd just failed survival.

A few weeks later, we heard the news that Professor Baxter was going through a very difficult divorce. The news, discussed in hushed circles during break, settled us down. I began to pay better attention. Now, when a flame of anger crossed our teacher's face, I empathized. Even Rusty shook his head. In those days divorce was a sign of shame, a failing that people whispered about. A good family reputation was the mainstay of a job. Independent thinking and personal independence were not easy companions, then. This meant there were real consequences to being a teacher. Realizing this, I felt a bond with poor Professor Baxter whose life as a professor placed her in a compromising light, especially among her colleagues. Her situation propelled me toward a better understanding of professional life in relation to personal lifestyle. Indeed, when I left teachers college for good, there was a chill in Professor Baxter's parting words.

"The eyes of the community will follow your every step. Never let your profession down. Nor your guard."

So there it was—a first lesson of the profession, a lesson that had to stick to the ribs, no matter what. Success in one's work meant the larger community mattered because teaching calls upon the whole person. None of us really stopped to think this through, even if Rusty's behaviour made it plain that some of our own pupils would be entering our classrooms only because they must. Rusty remained unrepentant to the end.

"You know, a big spike in your back pocket would be murder on the bottom," he'd said. "I won't be heading up North with a little watering can anytime soon. Baxter will have to go it alone." We all laughed. Like Rusty, we had a lot to learn about the real world of teaching.

We were so caught up in the drama of so many microscopic events that it was hard to gather their meaning right away. We thought we only wished to escape teaching in the North. I know I did. Mine had been the confinement of a reserve, and I wanted more out of life. Still, I was astonished at how quickly we had come upon a scene that showed us there was more to learning how to teach than being lectured to in a venerable hall of learning. More facts lay waiting to be discovered behind the scenes in our profession, and many of these implied conflict of all sorts.

FOUR

SINK OR SWIM IN A COMMON FLOOD

VANIA NICOSIAN TAUGHT DOWN the hall from me those first couple of years of teaching. She became a good friend who, as fate would have it, helped me understand the nature of teaching: How a teacher builds meaning even in the absence of the right tools, for instance.

As a student teacher, I thought teaching came with a mental tool kit that I could dip into, as needed. I imagined myself as a craftsman who wished only to accomplish a straightforward task; surely there would be books, films, records, objects, and a recipe box labelled "How To." However, blackboard and chalk would be the only sure things. It would take me a while to see that the senses are as important as the intellect in teaching; maybe more so.

Vania told me of her training as a teacher in Armenia of the Ararat plain where she was raised. Her readiness to teach was tested in her community, a method, which by any measure was composed of fire and brimstone. Her teaching ability was tested and validated on the spot or she would fail in the presence of family and friends.

"It separated the chaff from the wheat in no time," was how Vania put it.

I liked her economy of manner, her compact physique, her clear diction, and her insistence upon using correct regional metaphors. With her bright burnished hair pinned up and her old-fashioned wire spectacles, she had a serious and determined look that, at the slightest provocation, could become the mischievous grin of a child. In addition, Vania had an inquiring mind. Her life experiences had taught her, as mine continued to teach me, that discretion is a high art when differences of opinion, or behaviour, were played out in the Roman amphitheatres of our profession. Our secrets were safe with one another. When she left two years later for another school, I missed her. I lost more than a confidante. Vania's absence meant steering an uncertain course alone.

Our roots and cultural life stories differed. I knew that each of us had relinquished a large part of our personal connection to the past in the interests of conforming. The demands of mainstream life were exacting in our time.

I loved our discussions after school about the power of the written word. Vania understood my concern that so many of the world's children saw comic books depicting Indian people of the plains in negative ways. They were depicted as idle, usually seated on the ground with a blanket wound round their shoulders and a feather stuck in a headband. She said she hadn't seen these as a child and hoped that she would have recognized the not-so-subtle lie before it bent her mind out of shape. At the time we were just a couple of young professional women marking books together, at the end of the day, sharing our stories.

"So, tell me more about yourself," she said.

"You first."

"There's nothing to tell, really," she replied.

But when we got talking, there was more than we knew.

When Vania was a young girl, she left Armenia with her parents for America—first to the States, then to Canada. Her father had to find work. There was nothing to hold him in Armenia after his mother and father were killed during one of a dozen, or more, deportations. It meant she now had no grandparents.

"My people were Christians, so my father wanted us to settle in a Christian country," she explained.

Christianity was another thing Vania and I had in common, I thought as I watched her pile of marked math books grow on the right side of the table beside her.

"We really struggled to learn the English language, the language of retreat. It was taught in our little village. Did you know—I can't imagine you do because it isn't well known outside Armenia—that in our recent past, children's hands were cut off by the enemy?"

"What?" I couldn't believe the terrible image that popped into my mind.

Vania nodded, and her eyes blinked rapidly. She swallowed and continued her story, after a moment. She didn't wish to discuss this further, I could see.

"Armenia is a gateway to the West and the East. It's a small country that hugs Mount Ararat, as in centuries past. It's where Noah's Ark may be resting."

A shiver travelled the length of my spine. I looked at her to see if she was joking. She wasn't. I recalled having heard how scientists thought that a well-constructed ark might still exist and be found, someday. How close and at the same time how far away things are that matter, I thought.

"Poor as we were, the people were cosmopolitan in their awareness," Vania said. "Consider their exposure to the several nationalities trading and passing through our homeland for centuries. Did you know there's an ancient city in ruins high up in the mountains? Our village elders talked about it, but they'd never let us kids climb the hills to see for ourselves. That old city and its secrets still remain out of sight in my mind."

"But why?" I asked.

"They never said. But I have my theory. That protected place could be the site of Noah's first settlement after the flood."

A thrill raced up my spine to join goose bumps on my arms. Was this possible? I wanted to find out more, but Vania said it was my turn now.

"My home is hardly exotic," I began. I saw only my reserve. "However, my people had to learn the language of retreat, too, if you consider that my parents were taken away to residential school to be taught English."

"What do you mean taken away?"

"I mean literally. Some of the kids were rounded up by church authorities. The parents tried to hide them but they were found. The children were to be kept separate from their homes and their family. That was government policy."

"Was it policy enforced by the army?" Vania asked.

"No. We didn't declare war on the settlers. Armies weren't involved. The people made treaty, instead. Our lands and resources were exchanged for rights to health and education."

"But why live on reserves? Why not keep the kids and move elsewhere to hunt and fish?" Vania saw Canada as a huge and bountiful country.

"The land was already surveyed. The people were forced onto reserves."

"You mean by police with guns?" Vania stared at me, horrified.

I wondered if she were thinking about European war tactics that one read of and saw in films.

"No guns. Not directly, anyway. The main weapon was starvation. People died. The winters were as fierce then as they are now and with the buffalo gone, the source of warmth and food disappeared. My grandmothers used to tell us of their fears for the unborn. I suppose that would be me and my siblings, too. You can see how gifts like choice and choosing were out of the question."

Vania was shocked to learn that five-year-olds (my parents among them) were taken to schools that professed the teaching of Christian values and a state-authorized curriculum, both of which were subverted. Inside those walls, such values found no roots: generosity no gifts, respect no grounding truths.

I shared with Vania the horrifying picture of families camped outside the school grounds trying to catch glimpses of little sons and daughters who were not allowed home for months on end. I told Vania that my mom once called out to her mother in the Saulteaux language and was punished, like other children who forgot themselves, by having a half bar of soap taped inside her mouth. Residential schools had begun stilling the voices of a thousand years.

"Your mom! Just a baby!"

I told Vania that we were poor but lucky, too. My father was a veteran who began a farm when he returned from the war. The old people told many stories that Mom translated for us to fill our lives. There were stories of trade in the distant past for example, about people from ancient cities to the far south and huge farming communities to the east and old fishing villages in the west. People around home out on the prairies still traded in items like brown sugar, purple and red corn seeds, silver jewelry, spices, cotton cloth, and natural dyes and herbs. "Our stories speak of a major flood, too," I said. "The story goes that the earth and all the life forms, along with laws to govern their order of interdependence, had been created. Humans, made last, were the most dependent on other living and non-living forms. But they had the gift of dreams. They had the gift of dreams but also the propensity toward negative emotion, like jealousy and envy. After the people destroyed one another, disaster fell. Huge clouds formed and poured down so that even the mountains tops were under water. Every living thing died except for a spirit woman and the fishes and the birds. The world remained flooded for a long time. Apparently, water creatures decided to help the lonely spirit woman and so persuaded one another to dive down into the sea and bring up mud to rebuild the land. The humble and homely muskrat was the one who finally succeeded in grasping the soil and bringing it to the top to form Turtle Island for a new generation of people. "

"Maybe it was the same flood—and animals from Noah's Ark," Vania said.

"For all we know!" We laughed together.

I saw that Vania's spelling books were marked now. Soon we would start on the nature science note books. Marking these meant more than mechanical checking, though. Comments were needed, but we had so much to say that we decided to take the note books home to finish later that evening.

I went on to say that, unlike the experience of most immigrants, the removal of my great-grandparents from the plains to reserves had brought an end to any true horizon for them.

Vania told the story of her professional journey in Armenia. According to her, studying to become a teacher there was a difficult and solitary struggle in a city away from her community, but the end result, her final exam, was the business of everyone back home. By tradition, everybody in her village came to witness a final exam that tested the worthiness of a teacher. Vania recalled for me the terror of that event.

There, up at the front of the room inside the village hall, packed with parents, aunts, uncles, old people, and friends, stood the teacher candidates—five nerve-wracked souls, including Vania. Even the clergy was there, as were veteran teachers and, as luck would have it, a hard-minded professor from the city.

"This was no paper exam," Vania said, "no mere recitation of technique and philosophy. The object was to demonstrate your skills as a teacher—at the drop of a hat."

Each candidate, Vania reported, had to reach into a bowl that was set out on the middle of a small table at the front of the room. The candidate then removed a slip of paper from it. Next, he or she had to read aloud what was written there. The slip of paper described the lesson to be taught, on the spot, stone cold, before the eyes of family and, as Vania recalled, the whole world.

"The worst was each assignment had some special little twist to it," she said.

It was a terrifying experience, she recounted, to know that within seconds you'd be exposing your raw talents and personal limitations to friend and foe alike, many of whom knew more about teaching than a single body could hope to know.

"It was all the more terrifying to be told that your fellow pupils were the ones you were to teach, as part of the audience." Vania's eyes grew big when she told me this.

I assured her I would not have been able to do it and that I would have tried to get out of it, somehow. There was no getting out of it, she claimed, and it didn't help matters to know that five other candidates would be undergoing the ordeal with her.

"I watched the others through a fog as they began to demonstrate their skills, skills that involved things like teaching the national anthem—in a fragmented Armenia, mind you. My trial began when I was called to stand at the front of the room that was now as still as a morgue. I grew numb from head to foot. But I willed my body to keep moving toward the table upon which stood the fateful bowl. I reached in with blind fingers and withdrew a slip of paper. In a voice I didn't recognize, I read the lesson I was to teach: Objective: To teach grade ones the letter O using English words of choice.

"At first I thought there must be some mistake. This was a nightmare. To teach the letter O? What could be more impossible? O was so much like zero, so much of nothing."

I agreed it must have been horrible. A room without teaching aids would pierce to the marrow, all right. Especially without a blackboard and chalk. The lack of those was formidable. A teacher without the tools of the trade would be lost, never mind trying to pass a final exam.

"Why didn't you ask for a different slip of paper, a different lesson?"

"It was against the rules. My moment of truth had arrived. Everything I ever learned fled my mind. I scanned the room for something to help me get started—a child's name that began with O? No such person. The poet, Ovid? No, I'd have to quote him! An oracle?—too close to my own needs just then! Just as I began to feel my courage sink, there it was. In the front row, my mother sat holding an orange in her lap. A beautiful orange! From where I stood I could smell and almost taste it. I reached out for it and my mother handed the orange to me. Bless her soul and God's grace rain down upon her." Vania's eyes shone bright with that remembered deliverance.

She said that she struggled to see the audience as a roomful of five-year-olds. It was a tremendous stretch, but at least now she held a precious teaching aid for her "little grade ones."

"And so, I began the lesson, Do you want to hear it? Do we have time?"

I assured her that I wanted to hear it. The question had crossed my mind a few times as she talked: just how do you teach the letter O to little ones?

Vania folded her hands and rested them on our little round table; her eyes reflecting another time in Armenia. "Well, I held the orange aloft and asked, 'What is this?' My charges responded in unison, my mother leading the chorus, 'Orange.'

"God bless mothers who sway the masses!

"'Say orange again and look at the person beside you. See how the lips shape themselves into a circle? Now say O, and notice how your mouth goes round.'

"My little ones laughed but they began to relax into their role. I sprang into action, 'Let's peel the orange and take a tiny taste.' I said, 'When you taste a drop of orange juice, I know what you'll say.'

"I peeled the orange quickly and handed out the sections, here and there, among my so-called pupils, 'You will say, Oh,' I told them. 'And your mouth will water.'

"I saw the master teacher at the back of the room nodding his approval. I had my pupils' attention. I knew I must be off to a pretty good start—at least I was on the right track. But I now had to apply the principle of movement so I could demonstrate that children learn by doing. I knew it wasn't enough that an orange is worth a thousand words. I asked them to follow my lead. I needed to engage them in the learning process. I had to prepare them for the concept O, as a symbol, at this point. I had to show that I could handle the transition from the concrete to the abstract without losing my pupils' interest. I struggled to keep my charges focused without the small mercy of a blackboard. This is how I did it.

"I said, 'Touch the tips of your pointing fingers and thumbs together to make a circle. Do you think an orange can go through?'

"This method of comparing size, at this juncture, pleased the master teacher. My pupils now related the object to an abstract quality in an understandable way. He actually beamed when I took the time to correlate the concept of O with numerical thinking in this concrete way.

"'Now,' I said, 'Put your arms above your head and touch your hands together at the top, like this. See how your arms make a really big O?'

"I spotted a problem in the back row. Some younger men of the village refused to participate. This could be taken to mean that my approach wasn't inclusive enough: the cardinal sin among true teachers. They sat there scowling, their arms folded across their chests. Yet I had only a limited time in which to make the transition from the concrete to the abstract, to the actual symbol, O. Well, it sure put me in a bind. I had to carry momentum forward or I would risk losing the concentration of most of them. I decided to use my judgement and opted to continue the lesson. I heard myself say, 'When you write the word orange, you start with the letter O.' When my pupils began to draw circles in the air, I understood I had made the grade. Everyone stood up and cheered and applauded—family, peers, and community members, including the young men in the audience. I passed! I was on my way to becoming a teacher."

Vania's story had staying power in my life. It revealed a lot about teaching and learning that held true throughout my career as a teacher. Obviously, she had learned how and when to apply sound methodology. She had taken her pupils through a thinking process that led from the concrete to the abstract. She proceeded from the known to the unknown.

Vania, the well-trained teacher that she was, recognized that if she had simply drawn a circle in the air and declared, "This circle represents an O, as in orange, which starts with the letter O," she would have failed. Further, she would have failed absolutely, had she done this on a blackboard.

"That single orange was my kingdom for a horse," Vania laughed. "And thank goodness my mother was there to get the ball rolling."

There was so much to remember in a key principle: some learn by listening, some learn by looking, all learn by doing. Vania said that during the exam, she'd heard her professor's voice ring in her head: "Learning starts when the senses are awake."

Vania and I agreed that the power of the senses in the act of learning is a self-evident truth, so obvious a truth, in fact, that professors fairly sang its praises: "Learning begins when a student wakes up," we laughed, on that day, satirizing our beloved teachers. I guessed that it would take real children to show just what else our professors had tried to impart.

"If your professors knew you'd become a successful teacher in North America one day they'd feel blessed, I am certain," I told Vania as I packed up my things to go home.

"I live with hope," she replied.

Making my way along the sidewalk, I reflected on the fact that sometimes the obvious got in the way of seeing the basic principle, just like our old professors had said. I'd have to dig deeper, starting now.

The professors had told us many things. And, here I was, as another day drew to a close, another day of trying to feel like a teacher, whatever that elusive feeling was. I saw that confidence might rarely exceed anxiety. Upon first entering a classroom, a teacher has no one but herself to rely on. There is no "How To" recipe. The floorboards beneath her feet can fall away in an instant. I came to experience that sensation, time and again, in my trials as a novice. Inadequacy strikes at the heart. I even began to think I could forestall the worry by planning for every eventuality every day. I soon had to admit that this would be like trying to define and predict all occurrences between life and death and then deciding on a course of action. Planning, I found, was an aid, not an antidote. Predictability was out of the question.

Walking home, I thought how Vania and I hadn't said outright that even our text books today lacked important facts of history. But how do you write about the loss of a child's hands or the loss of a child's mother tongue? How do you expose the secrets?

FIVE.

LOOK AT ME

Our psychology professor once said, "Teaching is more of an art than a science." His words echoed Goldie's, the day she and I argued good-naturedly about the difference between art and science in terms of our future jobs. Goldie liked dentistry, she said, because it was a science, primarily. It was not like teaching, which was more of an art, and hence, clouded by feeling and emotion.

"Clarity in the precise, such as to be found in dentistry, is rare." she said. The spark in her eye said it was anyone's argument now.

"Are you saying the art of teaching is distorted by emotion, hence lacking in the science of teaching altogether?" I asked her, showing my own bias.

She said I was splitting hairs and trying to be difficult. "It is how you go about doing a thing," she said.

That was then. Now here was the psychology professor lecturing about the art and the science of methodology. He said that method involved a world of ideas, concepts, and theories awaiting discovery and analysis. "Classroom walls offer no help in connecting young minds to understanding," he said. "Enter, the teacher."

He smiled prophetically yet added nothing about teaching being "more of an art than a science," as Goldie had argued. Nor did he say anything about the role of emotion in teaching and learning.

I put up my hand. "A teacher's job, I hear you say, is to keep the mind free to focus on meaning, rather than on emotion."

I had no idea where the comment might take us or, indeed, what I truly intended by it, but our professor had definitely skirted around something and I wanted to know what it was. The professor asked me to "explain, please."

My classmates, awake to the moment, were ready to pounce. I casually referred to the times I found myself unable to concentrate, times when I could be so wrought up that the page before my eyes blurred, times when meaning swam away, even after pointedly re-reading.

"Emotion has to be a factor in learning," I said, stalling for time.

"So?" he asked, patronizingly.

I glanced at my classmates. Their smiles confirmed the lure had worked. Substance lay hidden in the professor's remark. We set ourselves to cornering him.

"So, what does it mean, exactly," one of my classmates asked, "to say that teaching is an art and not a science? How does emotion fit in?"

Another asked, "Is it true that teaching is grounded in science, say, like the science of psychology that considers the very nature of emotion, and with apparent exactness?"

"Didn't you just claim that teaching is an art?" I added.

Our professor smiled and replied simply that emotion and intuition, indeed, play roles in teaching and in learning. But both of these things remained tools, period.

Rusty sat up tall in his seat. "If the whole business of being a good teacher lacks a firm intellectual foundation, unlike our professor's own field of psychology, we're sunk, right? And what about revelation, I ask you? Do we deny the role of revelation? Sure-il-y, this is an outrage!"

The class burst out laughing. And, once again, our supposed counter-argument was reduced to nothing more than having fun at our professor's expense.

"Time will tell," was the professor's rudimentary reply.

He reddened considerably toward the end of the period, no doubt feeling protective toward his specialization. Yet, none of us was any further ahead in our thinking. There was so much about teaching that was still inaccessible. And we had not even begun to know what to ask.

As a teacher in the making, I studied the tried and true instructional methods for each subject area, such as social studies, mathematics, and art. I worked hard to make sense of these. I besieged my professors. I wanted to know why knowledge was separated into categories, such as the now familiar subjects of science, psychology, and math, in the first place. There was something vague and unnatural about this, I contended. Yet, had it occurred to me that if learning depended on "doing," that is on a child's interactions with real objects and natural processes being the best teachers, I might have thrown up my hands in despair. Then the whole world ought to be replicated in the classroom! For now, cocooned in my thoughts about mastery, I hankered for a chance to wrestle old ideas to the ground while trying to get a sense of structure and boundary in the profession.

Like many of my classmates I felt a growing impatience. Yet, term had just begun. We were told that certain questions were best left for a contemplative age, an age that would grip the coattails of us sooner than we might think. We wanted answers now, even before we had begun to formulate the right questions.

Our beginner's questions told of our struggle. Wasn't there a theory that linked the way one learns to a construct of knowledge, other than what was separated into particular subjects like science, psychology, spelling, and math? What exactly made these subjects separate and distinct in the first place? We tried every means to get our professors off the beaten track and into the lane of proof, fanciful or not. Your concern, they replied, is to find ways to engage the hearts and minds of the student. No matter how knowledge is bundled, they said, each subject has its appeal and its limitations; each subject remains a discipline unto itself. Only remember, they droned, each and every subject area has the potential to engage the interest of the child.

It took a while to see what they were getting at. Though I still thought there were simple answers, then.

Lisa

When I met Lisa, I had been teaching for almost three years and was due for another lesson. I was convinced that every child looked forward to art period. Everyone, so far, had. I thought a child might have the odd concern with dance, drama, and music, or some aspects of them, but she would automatically be drawn to the visual arts, no matter the challenge. Children took to colouring pictures as soon as they could grip a crayon. Fellow teachers, whom I'd asked, insisted that, along with sports, art period was a saving grace. I was never more surprised to find that not all children like art; some said they disliked it, and, apparently, others feared it. For example, some children acted as though the teacher and the school conspired to expose his or her failing: that they couldn't draw. Whatever the reason, I met in Lisa a little girl whose manner said loud and clear, "I can't draw. And I don't like colouring and painting either."

My challenge was to reverse this feeling, once and for all; after all, the creative drive remains an important avenue to learning for everyone in the classroom and outside the classroom, the world over. In talking to my colleague from Armenia, Vania, I learned that "creativity and the arts centred the universe, just so." Soon, the importance of this would be confirmed.

I learned from experience that the visual arts, and the creativity they presuppose, indeed do something inexplicable, something extra for the human mind and the positive liveliness of the human spirit. One young lady helped show that to me.

Lisa was in my fifth-grade classroom. Like her classmates, she collected records of The Beatles and posters of all the pop stars she could. She was a tomboy who played hockey and basketball whenever boys let her join the game. Despite her sunny nature, on Friday afternoons during art period, Lisa's personal confidence broke down. Since art period remains a favourite with most children, I had to ease her out of this. All her future teachers would most likely insist that art remain a key part of their instructional programs year round. They had full appreciation of the important role art played in learning. In addition, what is loved universally by children is what teachers capitalize on. And, when one stopped to think about it, in the creation of art, the brain is made to work in consort with the soul in ways that strengthen the mind. There was no getting away from it. Lisa would just have to change her mind about art period so that she could get in touch with her latent talents.

It was Friday again. In preparation for picture-making I had taken the children through a series of mini-lessons in the preceding weeks. These were designed to demonstrate basic elements of the visual arts, such as variety in line. The children came to appreciate certain ideas about line through their explorations of sweeping lines, swooping lines, twisting and turning lines, fat and thin lines, and all the different manifestations of line: lines in leaves, in shoe-laces, in the curve of the chin and brow, and in the swift invisible paths of birds in flight. Many an art period, pencil and crayon in hand, the record player full blast, the children happily pursued lines made in imaginary runs across a basketball field, lines made by skates skimming over a frozen pond, and lines that music drew in the mind.

Lisa made lines, too, but without enthusiasm. She drew her lines in tight narrow runs as though she thought line-making was the law and she a potential breaker of such laws. Lisa approached our exercises in colour, form, and shape in the same way. I hoped these little studies of the basic elements of the visual arts would prepare all the children, including Lisa, for picture-making. This was the day. Real fun and excitement would be ours at last; it was time to put the doubting self aside.

On this day, children would bring to life a picture of their own design through the use of colour, line, shape, and form. The day before we had determined that since autumn is such a colourful season, and since every living and non-living thing seemed alive with colour, our first picture of the year would be an autumn picture. To get the juices flowing children shared some ideas for autumn scenes like the many-coloured trees along the valley, fall leaves blowing across lawns on the way to school, or of vines and vegetation in decline in one's backyard.

As a standard feature of our art periods, the children were free to sit anywhere in the room and with anyone they chose. But then, there was Lisa. She sat alone in the corner of the room, her face a misery. Today, again, Lisa chose to sit alone in art period. She sat staring bleakly at her paper. I had to do something.

"Lisa," I said, pulling up a desk beside her, "may I sit with you? The others won't let me help them. It isn't fair. I get so excited about making a picture but I can't always join the fun."

She shrugged her shoulders as she looked at me.

I continue, "What would the principal say if she were to come and find me sitting in a corner colouring by myself instead of minding you children? Besides, if I ask Janet or Bobby to let me colour with them, they'll just tell me to get lost."

A smile tugged at the corner of her mouth. It was her decision.

Lisa smiled a big smile, "Not me. You can sit with me. And you can do it all."

I made a deal with her, "Let's work on our picture together. That way, if anybody makes fun of our work, we'll stick up for each other."

"Okay," she said.

Lisa confided that she imagined her uncle's farm. A farm scene meant I could be a good guide for Lisa because I'd grown up on a farm, too, and farm families in Saskatchewan, on reserves, or anywhere on the prairies, share many of the same life experiences and certainly the love of land and animals. Together, Lisa and I would be able to get at the details of any farm picture she wished.

We talked about farmyard life from quarrelsome chickens to fragrant cornstalks in the garden. We decided to begin our picture by sketching an outline of the barn against an open field. By word, and gesture and minimal demonstration, I showed her how to sketch a thing, how to capture it softly by leaving out details, attending to the larger shapes for now. Quicker than you can blink an eye we had the big elements of our picture positioned to our satisfaction.

Lisa and I made another deal; if we didn't like where we'd placed certain objects once we began to colour, we'd change them. Colour, I told her, often demanded its own way. Lisa giggled at the idea as we worked.

I was mindful that the other children might need my help and attention, too. As is often the case, however, in the close company of their friends, particularly in an atmosphere that says "mistakes" are learning opportunities, children become absorbed in what they are doing. This is especially true in the act of creating some-thing new, when the serendipitous calls into being subtle hints of something even more beautiful. I sensed, however, that I should stay connected to all the children in a way that they could feel the connection. Yet I knew that I had to keep my interchanges with Lisa going. There is always a way, and I reverted to my usual method.

"You others hush, now," I called out. "I speak only to the angels and half-angels in this great palace of learning and gracious living"

The giggles began.

"I just want you to know that Lisa O'Donahue and I are creating a wondrous picture." More giggles. "So mind your own business and leave us alone." Laughter and sounds of mock outrage—"Genius must be left alone."

There was then huge laughter, including some boos.

"Then it is you who should leave us alone."

The class bursts into laughter, once again. It was Tom as usual, ready to take the least opportunity to riddle even the most serious talk with some witty remark, alas, often cheeky. The children happily settled into their work. They knew I was thinking of them, too.

In the meantime, Lisa didn't let a moment go to waste. She coloured with a gleam in her eye. The moments passed.

"The sky..." she burst out suddenly. "It doesn't look like a sky. It looks like a kindergarten sky!"

Everyone stopped to listen. They knew that Lisa grew discouraged in art period. It was plain that they'd been exposed to her predisposition before. They sat and stared at us, dear little classmates with their tag-along histories, already.

"You have an artist's eye, Lisa," I said this loudly enough for the others to overhear. "And you're absolutely right."

Now the children were really listening. They exchanged glances.

"Our sky is as dead as a doorknob," I said. "It needs life and you spotted that right off. It has to do with colour. The thing about colour is that it's always alive, just the way light is. In fact, colour is light, Lisa. And light has all the colours of the world in it."

She stared, listening.

I pretended that I was slipping in and out of my own thoughts. I pretended I didn't know all ears were listening.

"Colour is motion at play, just as people in this great world go about in their work, in joy or in sorrow. That's the secret, Lisa. As soon as we put colour to rest on the paper, it can die. There is no motion anymore and the light can't show the colour that's in everything."

The room was quiet with listening, as though something precious hung in the balance.

"Let's try something. Great artists do it. Let's mix different colours in the sky. Let's gather all the blues and purples and pinks and, good grief, oranges and yellows."

Some of the children got out of their seats and edged toward our desk, leaving their work momentarily behind. Never mind. This would be a lesson for all.

"Which reminds me," I said, "of the story of Vincent van Gogh and the way he used colour. And the way everyone laughed at him. And that appalling thing he did to himself."

Lisa, listening with every fibre in her little frame, added bits of colour to the sky. More children slipped out of their desks to see. We had an audience. But I pretended to be so absorbed in the story of van Gogh that I wouldn't notice children out of their desks in a million years. I told them of his pain and his pride, his tragedy and his triumph. I told of his courage in breaking through the boundaries of photographic realism into a bigger universe of colour and motion. I told of his isolation, his suffering, and his rejection by the people of his day.

"And then, there was the love for his lady," I said. "There was that terrible cutting off of his ear and sending it to her in an envelope. And, yes, how he was seen running later that day, running down the street around the corner, out of sight, holding his hand over a most dreadful wound, the wound of his heart and soul."

The story took up a good part of the period and all the while the children, including Lisa, were intent on their own masterpieces, some taking great liberties with brilliant colour combinations.

Gone the fear and loathing from our Lisa's eyes! Her picture was a thing of joy: barnyard chickens armed in red and orange feathers and mad blue eyes scampered over and under burning bushes. Trees of magenta and purple branched out over bluish-green grasses that sizzled in a dazzling sun; several plum horses crowned the hills. And that barn, and that brilliant sky sprung to life with embroidery of swooping birds.

Alas, it was time to put our artists' tools away and tidy up for the weekend. The children demanded to see Lisa's picture. Here was the moment of truth. "Oh, Lisa," I thought.

"I wish I could say I painted it," I said, stalling for time. "But I got carried away with a story. Lisa's done most of it. Mind you, I did put some red on the barn, not to mention most of the handle on a dear little watering pail..." I tried to gauge Lisa's courage.

"Hold it up, Lisa," they called to her. "Go to the front and hold it up."

Lisa at first hesitated, but standing tall, she walked up to the front of the room. She held her picture up high. It was downright astonishing! Lisa's picture was alight with shimmering colour. It was something fierce. We simply stared, unaware that Lisa was growing uncomfortable. She was fairly squirming by the time I noticed.

Suddenly, Tom called out, "Lisa, cut off your ear!"

All of us, including Lisa, burst out laughing.

It became our little joke. In subsequent art periods, the children called upon Lisa to help them with their colours, and she took great joy in sharing her liberated sense of colour, and her courage. Thank you, Lisa. Thank you, Vincent van Gogh.

Thank you Father in Heaven. Because teaching is like that: filled with reward. Lisa, and other children like her, encouraged me to go on with teaching, or put another way, to help the young free themselves from blinders and, as I was to discover, from all kinds of untruth.

Lisa helped me see that creativity centres the self. I noted the professors' words: "When in doubt, give something for the emotions, something for the physical being, and something for the mind." In short, appeal to the senses but attend to the child. Because under real conditions, my professors had warned, a teacher's challenges are of infinite hue and, as often, alarm. The teacher, the blackboard, and the chalk in a sea of classroom walls are all there ever is, as starting points.

Even in my youthful days dreaming about the glamour of teaching, I never let go the chalk. Glamour has little to do with teaching and less to do with children. In fact, a beating heart, not glamour, lies at the centre of this endeavour.

The discovery of latent gifts can happen anytime, the professors said. Lisa's artistic rendering of a rural scene might now help her to see the possibilities in art period and, I dared to think, to see her world more fully. Beauty, after all, is a constant teacher and artistic works, like the natural world, would help her learn to trust her ability to find and give expression to her innate gifts.

It seemed that when Inga, another little girl, came to my class, she was already on the verge of giving up on herself. She had fight in her still, but this was turning into anger and self-destructive behaviour. I learned that her father believed in order, order imposed by authority. He demanded "correct" feelings and "correct" behaviour of Inga, no matter the circumstances. I thought more about the meaning of my profession when I met Inga, a little girl who did not know her own worth.

INGA

Whenever I recall the pain of being a teacher, I think of Inga Konig. When a child is at home with herself she stops worrying about how to fit in, how to be noticed, or worst of all, how to be invisible. Learning means putting aside the doubting self for the curious self. It means abandoning self-consciousness for the anchor of self-awareness that allows one to pursue knowledge fully and joyously.

I learned from my grandmothers that human beings—including me, they were careful to point out—are uniquely gifted. As I studied Inga I was reminded that there had to be countless ways in which a child gets disconnected from a healthy self-awareness. No one, least of all a little girl, should have to carry the weight of self-doubt. How this burden is shifted onto a child is rarely obvious. Inga, however, showed me one way.

My training told me that Inga had difficulty with what is known in the field as a good self-concept. To help her overcome this, in the few short months she was my student, I had to watch for certain cues about her abilities and personality as quickly as possible. The teacher in me knew that somehow I had to meet her unique needs. Yet, when all was said and done, it was still possible for me to fail.

Inga Konig was square in shape from top to bottom. Her face was flat in profile and her lips tight and wire thin. Her eyes were her most compelling feature: pools of grey ice rimmed in steel. They were filled with deadly warning and were welded to a manner that commanded others to back away and stay away. Inga flouted my attempts at affection. She looked coldly at my hand if I happened to touch her. She lurched aside in an obvious manner if I stood close to her. She shrugged off pats on the shoulder. In short, she made it impossible for me to establish a comfortable footing with her.

Yet, here was the contradiction. This nine-year-old wanted to be included in every conversation and in every activity, though on her terms. Her attitude said, "Teacher and classmates, try to get me involved and I will remove your innards. Ignore me and I will stare at you in terrible silence. You cannot and will not win."

She was a challenge all right. As a young, optimistic teacher, however, I was convinced that all she and I needed was time. A teacher can be persistent but only for so long since attention must be given to at least twenty-three others, and all at the same time. "Every child comes round eventually," I told myself, particularly if left to her own devices. Especially if something catches her interest. I'd have to be patient.

As a neophyte teacher, I acted on what I'd been trained to do. I tried to make my teaching methods as interesting and inviting as possible. A resolute singer, a tottering poet, and a storyteller rolled into one, neither the sting of bee nor the sap of honeysuckles escaped my strivings to make knowledge come alive for children. I knew, too, that every child settles in only when she is comfortable and has a sense of belonging. So, for the time being, I left our little square-chinned Inga to herself and watched for signs of response.

One day, I announced that we would be studying the country of Holland. I told the children that I wished I knew someone who had lived there, because it would be great to have him or her come to the school to tell us about that fascinating land. It was hard to believe, but Inga held up her hand.

"Yes, Inga?" I said, my heart in my throat.

"My parents are from Holland. They came when I was small. My dad would be able to come and tell us about it." Her cheeks reddened.

"Inga, that's wonderful!" I said. "Would you ask him? Shall I call him?"

"I'll ask him," she said as she glared horribly at her astonished classmates.

Inga did ask her father. And things should have taken a turn for the better from then on. Other parents had come to tell of their experiences in the bigger world, and our studies had benefitted from those visits. I had reason to hope that the real Inga, who remained hidden away, now had a fine opportunity to burst out into the sunshine. It was not to be.

I hadn't met Inga's father before his visit, but I once spoke briefly with her mother. This was at the beginning of the school year, at the time of the annual open house when parents and teachers are invited to come to the school to meet the teacher and one another. I was surprised at Mrs. Konig's physical appearance. I had based my imagination of how she might look on Inga's build and manner. I presumed she had a matronly no-nonsense style, wore heavy flat shoes, and had tightly knotted hair. What appeared in the doorway, however, was a young willowy woman of radiant charm who was bursting with cheer. She wore a bright yellow sweater, a red leather mini-skirt, and long purple boots. Golden hair fell in waves about her shoulders. She was a woman of the 1960s, very "mod." In a quick light voice she laughed and called out to other parents in the room. An air of excitement hung round her.

Mrs. Konig told me that she worked as a waitress in a local club and that she was in a bit of a hurry. Up close, I could see her nicotine-stained fingers and yellowish teeth. And yet her vibrant nature outshone the minor flaws. She hardly seemed a mother beset by burdens. Mrs. Konig explained that she didn't have time to talk about Inga, at this moment. She was on a quick coffee break from the club and meant only to poke her head in. We promised to call each other the minute we sensed "a big looming," as she put it. That gave me even more time to put my thoughts in order. Had Mrs. Konig asked me how Inga was doing in school, I would have had difficulty expressing my concerns accurately. I knew that when it came to sharing views with parents regarding their child, it was wise to know exactly what you meant to say. I reminded myself that presenting issues without clearing my assumptions first was plain folly, and it occurred to me that I was beginning to sound like a professor I once knew.

The day of Mr. Konig's visit arrived. From the time he entered the room until he left, he was the centre of our undivided attention. He arrived promptly on the day of his talk about Holland. He was much older than I expected. He was the most formal of gentlemen and impeccably dressed. His manner was part commander, part old-world nobility. No nonsense tolerated here, only order and correctness.

The children and I sat at attention. Mr. Konig had prepared his lesson as masterfully as a military strategist. He drew a precise map on the board that showed the distances from one place to another "...with the sea ever at your doorstep," he stated.

The children settled into a receptive attitude, and I breathed a sigh of relief. They were as attentive as I had asked them to be. Courtesy demanded it, I told them. Our attempts at dialogue with Mr. Konig were cut down to brittle snippets. Mr. Konig liked his audience to attend, not speak. No questions or comments, please. In some ways, he reminded me of my father. I had learned as a child that a soldier who comes home from the war is tall, uniformed, and called Dad. (Mine had not been home in five years.) He tossed you high in the air, asked your name, then set you down and told you to be quiet. His arrival home marked the beginning of military-like discipline and manners in my life.

As Mr. Konig lectured on, I found myself recalling how my brother, my younger sister, and I sat on our mother's bed as she excitedly opened a parcel of Christmas gifts sent to us by our father who was overseas in the middle of World War II. Mom's hands had trembled as she loosened the wrapping paper to reveal a rubber ball, a teddy bear, a doll, and a little truck. There were three pairs of wooden shoes from Holland, bleached, and hand-painted. None of them fit. They were too narrow, too short, or too long. There was a green dress for our mother, with a letter tucked inside its folds wrapped around a small bottle of a sweet smelling perfume. She read our father's words aloud to us and hugged and kissed us, as if he were asking her to do so in the letter. She handed us the bright red candy he sent, too. That letter made our mother rush about the house the next day, cleaning and tidying up with joy in her eyes. Our father was coming home someday soon. I was curious to see him. I knew he was called Leonard and that he was a soldier far across a deep dark sea somewhere in Holland.

Suddenly, in the midst of dreams about wooden shoes and sparkling skies, windmills and canals, and row upon row of aromatic bulbs, Mr. Konig barked out, "Inga, pay attention!"

Inga had been looking out the window, thinking her own thoughts as she often did. She whirled about, her face bright red. My heart quaked. She sat bolt upright and stared straight ahead, her hands clenched in her lap. Tears brimmed in her eyes. Poor Inga! And in front of everyone, too! What now? Had her father only seen how importantly she'd flounced into the classroom that morning, her stiffness gone and her squareness all but disappeared from her small frame. What now? It was impossible for me to concentrate on the rest of Mr. Konig's lesson. The children exchanged looks with each other and stole glances at Inga. All this was lost on Mr. Konig. He was fixed on his aim, proud even, that he was the disciplinarian, the lecturer, the commander.

Our feelings limped along to the end. There was a sense of relief when the briefcase on the desk snapped shut and the last of measured footsteps down the long hall could no longer be heard.

Mr. Konig had given us brilliant insights into the heart of Holland and its history, but he was not the father of mindful regard when he needed to be.

In our follow-up activities on Holland over the next few days, Inga exhibited anger and, at times, sadness. She performed her tasks in a perfunctory way and looked out the window. There was no help for it. Nothing I could say or do was going to make her reconnect with us, just yet. It was back to the waiting game. Somehow, something had to spark her enthusiasm. When all was said and done, though,

I wanted her to know that problems in her life were not because of her. That she was fine human being just the way she was.

Near the end of school that year, I realized that the best I could hope for was the odd smile from her, followed by angry withdrawal. Inga had eluded me. She had gotten through the year without being reached, without feeling free to be herself.

The last time I saw Inga was at the end of June 1966. This was the last day of school and it was time to reflect on what might have been, had circumstances allowed. Inga was a case in point. I looked out my window at the glorious morning and studied the scene before me. Someone caught my eye. It was Inga pushing her baby brother in his stroller down the street, past the classroom window. I longed to run outside and give her a big hug, once and for all, but why make her angry? She appeared to be in possession of her day, of herself. She held her head high and savoured the breeze while she pushed the stroller along. The toddler waved his arms and crowed at the top of his lungs. This was a picture for all time—a little girl, a happy baby, and a clear blue sky arched over a fresh green lawn.

Suddenly, Inga began to pick up the pace. She ran now, faster and faster—and without warning, she gave the stroller one almighty push. It careened down the sidewalk and hit a bump. It flipped over and the toddler tumbled out, head first, onto the sidewalk. Inga stood frozen to the spot, her hands clamped to her mouth. Soon her father came running down the street toward her. There was a huge scooping up of the crying boy and a swarm of slaps and pushes and shouts for Inga, who was running, running home.

The weight of the year entered the heart of me. I never told Inga she was a good little person. When could I have told her? A year is not long enough. A lifetime might be too short—but this was surely an excuse. I vowed, then and there, that come September I'd seek her out. By summer's end, all memory of these bad occurrences would have faded and we'd make a new start. Even if she wasn't going to be in my class the next year, I'd seek her out in her new room. I'd hug her, too.

Hopes of seeing Inga Konig that September fled with the sad news that her family had left Canada over the summer to live in Belgium. Once there, Mrs. Konig abandoned the family for a life of her own. Inga's father took what was left of his life and returned to Holland. I would never see Inga again, never be able to reach out to her and do something about the sadness of her young life.

As a teacher, I could never forget the student I didn't reach. The pain of that stays. Consider the very last day of school, that June. Consider the fond farewells and the artwork the children left as parting gifts. Consider the touching little messages they placed shyly on my desk: "I will miss you. You are the best teacher of my whole life."

Imagine toward the end of the day when final reports are done and put away, that, while looking in a pile of drawings and messages, you find a picture made just for you by, of all people, Inga Konig. It is a black crayon-drawing of a little girl, all by herself in the middle of a blank page. Indeed, the little girl is a mere triangle of a wee dress with head and limbs affixed. But what is this across her chest? A tiny message cut out of a magazine. Bending close, you are barely able to make out the words: Look at Me. And that is all it says.

That little girl, alone, with a single wee message glued over her heart struck my own. I put my head down on my desk on top of my mound of gifts and cried for Inga and for me and for all the years we wouldn't have together. In time, I came to see that the science of teaching can be thought of as established methods of instruction, methods guided by theories on how we learn. These methods can be applied as an aid to learning. The art of teaching, on the other hand, might adopt the scientific method but it also takes into consideration the life circumstances, personality, and temperament of the learner. The logic of method is thus raised to higher levels of engagement by the illogic of the unique child as learner. I felt I'd failed Inga by placing greater emphasis on method than on heart.

As teacher candidates, we thought we understood everything. Sheila Scott and I were reminded almost daily that good teaching means being vigilant about meeting a broad range of student needs. I felt lucky that Sheila and I took our internships at the same school and in the same classroom in the city. Many of our fellow classmates had chosen rural internships. Sheila and I knew each other well enough in our direct but constructive criticism of each other to say what was working, or not working, for a child.

"Your introduction to the lesson was too long. Robby got bored and started colouring in his scribbler."

"The illustration you drew held everyone's attention, but you spelled 'receive' wrong."

One day we were in the midst of conducting an evaluation of a poster on dairy food products made by a student under our host supervising teacher. Sheila, ever quick to spot the essentials of good instruction, said, "Hmm. Good correlation." The teacher had asked her pupils to measure the dimensions of each hand-drawn product. "Math, health, and art all in one lesson," Sheila said. I was reminded of the practicality of our professors' lessons almost everyday, now.

Our professors had stated, categorically, that as young teachers we might allow ourselves to be swept along by an enthusiasm for the mechanics of teaching, which would be like casting seed upon stony ground. Any one of us might pin our hopes for instant success on an instructional technique. They'd said, this dangerous tendency might take hold long before our budding knowledge could be tempered by children. Had I paid better attention, I might have been prepared for Inga.

In his own way, one of our professors demonstrated that a scientific attitude might hold the mind, yet leave matters of the heart in disarray.

His gaunt facial features often held a tired expression during lectures. I saw that same look on my father's face when he came home from the war, when he acted as if he were boxed in and trying to come to terms with life. However, I had no real way to judge how a professor, who seemed to have everything, might share a sense of confinement that could encourage him to drink.

Professor Colter

The rumour went around that Professor Colter, our science methods teacher, was a drunkard. He was seen on College Avenue staggering home many a night. Like other classmates, I wanted proof of the rumour first hand. We could scarcely believe it. Professors alcoholics? Unthinkable! Some of the pupils said that if you chanced to meet Professor Colter heading home from one of his soirees, he'd look right through you, giving no hint that he'd ever met you. Others said if you greeted him he'd tell you to go to hell.

I found this hard to believe. Professor Colter appeared to be such a fine old gentleman sitting, day after day, in his navy blue suit, at the front of the room. I doubted he was, as Rusty Boulin dubbed him, "the intemperate ruffian of College Avenue."

I saw Professor Colter in an altered state once. The day started out as an ordinary busy morning in science methods class. We pupils assembled in the cold glare of the classroom with our assignments dutifully in hand. Professor Colter was late again, not by minutes this time, but by almost half an hour. This was the morning he'd planned to show us how to evaluate the effectiveness of the teaching tool we spent the weekend devising.

"Do what you have to do, but get a basic science concept across in a visual way. And be prepared to defend its usefulness to the death," he said with a wink.

That was Friday, now it was Monday with no sign of Professor Colter. It was important that he come because the marks he assigned our projects counted toward our overall final average for the year. The impatient Rusty Boulin, seizing the opportunity for theatrics, announced to the class that he and his superintendent pal, Eric, would get to the bottom of things. Today, he and Eric Jones would tend to the business of our "tottering intemperate ruffian of College Avenue who must be made accountable for his unbecoming behaviour."

Out of the room and into the hall marched Rusty Boulin, pushing a reluctant Eric Jones ahead of him.

"Off to the principal we go, my son," were Rusty's departing words. "Now move along and look sharp. Remember who you are."

We needn't have worried. Rusty didn't go tattling to the principal with his underling in tow. It simply wasn't his style. He and his appointed superintendent took matters into their own hands, though. They went straight to Professor Colter's house to make a deal. Professor Colter, apparently recovering from a disagreeable flu, agreed that we could mark each other's work in committee and then, individually, take our work to his house the next day for verification. Rusty Boulin and Eric Jones had saved the day. Maybe.

It was late Saturday afternoon and my turn to go. I fretted about how Professor Colter would view my work and the committee's assigned mark. I rang the bell and the door flew open. I was dismayed to see Professor Colter, so very red-eyed, swaying in the doorway. He reached for my project, stumbling as he did so.

"That will do, young lady," he said, almost as if I had been the one to trip and even intended to do so again. "They have marked you fairly?" His tone was halfway between a question and a statement.

"Yes," I replied, "I believe so, though the mark is a bit high, perhaps..."

"Nonsense!" he snorted. "In this world see to it that you don't cast doubt on your work, especially if you have worked hard on something. There'll be enough people willing do that for you."

He gave my drawing a cursory look and held it in the wedge of sunlight that streamed through the door. He gave the drawing a shake, as if by doing so some greater meaning might tumble out. It was, after all, only a hand-drawn cross-section of a volcano, brightly coloured and carefully labelled.

"And what might these veins demonstrate, young lady?" he asked, as a long nicotine-stained finger traced the length of a rivulet of molten lava.

"The basic concept deals with erosion, sir..." I began, "As one of the forces of nature..."

"Yes. Yes. It's perfectly clear. Excellent concept! Bound to time, you understand. Erosion, one of man's afflictions. You have gone to the heart of the matter, my dear. You have captured the pulse, exactly. Excellent and truly drawn—full marks. Yes, indeed, now then, good day. And watch your step."

"Good day, Professor Colter. Thank you."

On the way home, it occurred to me that, when you really stopped to think about it, Professor Colter might actually have confused my volcano with a human heart! And I had got marks for nothing. This was humiliation itself. I was livid to think that Rusty Boulin likely knew in advance what the outcome of such an arrangement for marking assignments might be. When I confronted him in the hallway, on Monday morning, to tell him Professor Colter very possibly confused my volcano with a heart, he burst into peals of laughter, "You want to be a teacher? Then swallow your pride. Or take drawing lessons. Mind you, there's always the nunnery or heart surgery, though I see your temper forbids it. Too volcanic!"

Feeling stung, I told Rusty he'd better watch his step. I hear his laughter to this day.

The notion began take hold in my mind that our professors might, after all, be human in the fullest sense. They, too, suffered pain; being a professor didn't protect you from the human condition nor from life's failings. I began to appreciate that this might be so. I tried to imagine what the professor's life must be like with his condition and his having to focus his mind and heart on the challenges of teaching.

On one hand, teaching seemed to require a kind of detachment, a degree of objectivity that relied on the power of the intellect alone. Pure logic, the science behind things, must be a first principle. Yet, on the other hand, there was an emotional connection necessary to empathy, a matter of the heart that breathes life into reason. I sensed the seduction of the intellect while trying to estimate the limits of the heart. Professor Colter was a worry, all right.

Such were my thoughts as I strove to hurry my learning along. A covenant with the self, and self-awareness, was bound up with it, somehow. I certainly didn't want Professor Colter to be a person disconnected from the core of himself while trying to function as my model teacher.

I wrote to Goldie and could scarcely believe she agreed with my assumptions, at least as far as she allowed herself:

Pillar of Strength,
Someone nonetheless has to stay in charge. And there should be science
and art in it both, pal. Feelings and logic keep a sense of direction in
all of us. So, let there be you (teeth aside).
Goldie.

SIX

ONE DAY SOON THE LION AND LAMB

"REMAINING TRUE TO THE CENTRE of one's being is the touchstone of integrity," droned the professor. He was lecturing us on the concept of free will. "Everyone has the capacity to carry a decision forward. There is, indeed, such a thing as free will."

This was Dr. Heinrich's opening statement for today's lecture. Tall, robust, he looked like a farmer with lashes and eyebrows bleached by the sun. Yet his manner of speaking said that he had lived the life of a gentleman scholar for a good long while.

"Just who is our doubting Thomas this time?" Rusty moaned.

I could see why Rusty was impatient. Professor Heinrich, who came closest to our idea of a true philosopher, forever advanced some yet unravelled principle of thought under the guise of the obvious. Today, the topic was choice versus fate in personal affairs. As always, Rusty took refuge in the literal meaning of things even while some of us tried to guess where the challenge lay. Professor Heinrich explained that when one's life decisions are consistent with one's values, human conflict is eradicated. He repeated this. The question, he said, was whether or not this assertion was true.

I shrugged my shoulders at Rusty's indignant glance. When Professor Heinrich uttered the words "true to the centre of being" once again, Rusty buckled over, as though shot. We all laughed. Years later, it would seem wise to have filed away something of this in the back of our minds.

I accepted that teachers work hard to make children feel they belong. It stood to reason, we said, that all children wish to be like their classmates, in ways that are important to them. Rusty made the observation that anyone who stood between a child and his or her sense of belonging ought to be dealt a severe blow with an eel, though he wished it were otherwise.

"Hindrances to learning by design, as opposed to, say, natural obstacles like one's own nature, pose even greater challenges," Professor Heinrich said.

We asked for examples.

"You tell me," he said. "Is it by nature or by design that poverty, as a hindrance, exists?"

Teaching would be so much easier if life and the beliefs of people didn't get in the way. I wrote to Goldie that I feared the "still life" of me in elegant pose with chalk in hand, had worn thin. It was now 1968, and I had almost six years of teaching to my credit. This was the year I taught part-time, from May to June, before finishing my final year at university. Goldie wrote back:

Pillar of Perfection,
I want you to know that I wouldn't waste a diamond drill on something as unreliable as human nature. Give me the gleaming tool, the fail-proof technique, the singular ivories. That is all. Save yourself. Forego the crumbling chalk, Pillar, dear. Else be a poet.
Goldie.

Rosie

I learned more of human nature and people's beliefs when I met Rosie. She looked like a porcelain period doll you might want to dress up in a ruffled gown of rich green brocade and place upon a mantelpiece in full view. Though, knowing Rosie, you'd never get away with it. Rosie spat dragon-fire in seconds when provoked, even if her faded cotton dresses and quiet demeanour suggested otherwise.

Take the day we were discussing American Indians. Rosie didn't like the tone of a passage in the history book I was reading to the children about how Indians lived when the settlers came. She had something to say about it and stood up, hands on her hips.

"If I were the Indians," she said in a voice loud and clear, "I would say to these people, look, I dug this land and I didn't dig it for you!"

She stamped her foot and sat down. Everyone turned to stare as her outburst hung in the air. That such a small passage, read aloud from a social studies textbook could create such an outburst from a little girl astonished me. I'd read and re-read similar passages about "the Indians" as a student, their key messages being three-fold: Indians are caught in a time warp. Their curious culture stands in the way of their progress. Their culture has to catch up with modern times. As a teacher, I had grown immune to everything but the dry "facts" I was trying to impart about life in an all but buried past.

Still, "immune" was hardly the right word. Instead, I tried to hold to a discipline of detachment that allowed me to keep reactive emotions in check. It was difficult to put this detachment into practice, however. For example, I once tried to teach a new perspective about "the Indians." The unexpected response of a parent registered a shock in my sensory system for days. This took place at a time when there were no Aboriginal teachers or mentors in the public education system that I might learn from. There were no Aboriginal teacher education programs that might have helped me build up a personal knowledge base, a base that would then support a sense of confidence. There were no professional groups to help me deal with the loads of Aboriginal stereotyping and unclear thinking that cheapened our textbooks.

Nonetheless, instead of talking things over with my principal, I took it upon myself to deal directly with a student's remark that Indians were "dirty and lazy."

I thought to address this fallacy with a lesson that focused on the many accomplishments of the people. I went so far as to discuss their pharmacology that now helped everyone in our time. I yearned to illustrate this by telling them about my own life. For example, that my maternal grandmother, tiny and very wise, was a respected traditional medicine healer. I might tell them about her skills as a hunter, a doctor, and a vision seeker; I might tell how she kept us alive in the centre of her small sustaining universe. I wished to tell how she went about her daily chores, wearing a pair of old runners, full of holes, a long black dress, and a black kerchief knotted over her long black braids. I knew my pupils would be interested to learn that she spoke Saulteaux, her jet-black eyes shining as I struggled to understand her. They might also want to know that her chores fascinated me and that almost every other morning she'd sort through her gunny sacks of dried roots and leaves and boil the herbs down in old jam cans on the woodstove to make medicinal drinks for people who came to be cured.

I didn't tell the children any of these things. Instead, at the conclusion of my lesson, I said that it was plain that Indian people were not lazy, nor were they drunkards.

A couple of days later, I received a personal visit from one of the moms, a board member whose child I was teaching. Apparently the boy had gone home and told his parents that I had told the class that Indians were lazy drunkards. The boy's mother and I sorted out together that her son must have "drifted off" in the middle of my lesson and woke up to my concluding remark. She was glad, she said, that I had not repeated negative information about Indian people.

And, now, here was Rosie.

I began to pay close attention to Rosie and to her sense of justice. There were times when she stamped her foot and thrust her jaw out like an indignant pugilist. Rosie had a strong sense of what was fair. Every now and again, however, we were reminded of a barrier that made her draw inward. Her family belonged to a religious faith that forbade praying with classmates, singing the national anthem, and creating graven images. At that time, schools did all these things, apparently on a daily basis.

Every morning after nine o'clock bell I would say, as teachers everywhere said in the 1960s, "Bow your heads and repeat the Lord's Prayer."

Rosie would slip into the hall and close the door quietly behind her.

"Stand at attention and sing 'O Canada.'" I would think of Rosie waiting alone in the hall.

Rosie would return, her face drained of colour. Within minutes, however, colour would ignite her cheeks and all would be well again.

We got along fine until Christmas. Without giving Rosie a second thought, the class and I plunged into the annual making of a huge wall-length mural of the Nativity. We were well into the pots of paint, pails of water, and flying sponges with rows of artists on the floor working the skies of Bethlehem. There arose a boisterous good-natured planning of which groups would do which kings and in what colours: who would paint the shepherds, the oxen and the ass, who Joseph, who Mary and the Baby Jesus. Rosie's spirit had dwindled to almost zero by the time I noticed my error. A graven image! There could be no turning back now, not from these golden sands and that bright intended star. Oh, Rosie!

I worked out a plan whereby one of the groups and Rosie painted winter scenes of snowmen with which to decorate the lockers. But Rosie was disconsolate, ever eyeing the growing assemblage of nativity figures against the backdrop of glowing hills and tall embracing palms. She wanted to be part of this creation, part of the groups of children putting the finishing touches to their artistry. I hit upon an idea.

"It is lambs we need," I announced. "Lambs will make it all come to life. Look how the shepherds stand forlornly to the side. Everyone loves a lamb but, alas, all of you are doing something else, I see."

"I will do the lambs!" Rosie called, her face brightening with hope. "I can paint animals," she laughed.

And she did. Rosie had a feeling for lambs. And, as it turned out, each solemn shepherd got a fluffy white cloud of a lamb with strong black hoofs and dark piercing eyes for his very own.

The week flew by. The moment of truth was upon us. The children and I hurried to make the room ship-shape for parents' night. As order and tidiness in the classroom came into being, the magic of the children's artwork shone like a beacon. Colour and form drew attention to Baby Jesus in the manger with the star overhead. The snow scenes and the Christmas letters to family and friends, now decorated with fine detail, drew attention to sparkling borders. Like the others, Rosie's parents were on their way.

At seven o'clock sharp, Rosie's mother and father arrived for the viewing of the room with its bright bordered poems stapled to the bulletin board. They moved quietly, making their way toward the inevitable image. I went to stand beside them, wanting to explain but not knowing quite what to say. Rosie's mother, in a soft beige sweater, surveyed the landscape, her hand in her husband's, and they both looked down at Rosie who stood there in her little pale green dress. Both Rosie and I knew what this might mean. I stepped forward.

"I did the lambs," Rosie said simply.

I was about to explain that it was my fault, that I had insisted Rosie do the lambs. Her parents reached out and put their arms around Rosie.

"I knew it right away," her father smiled. "They're just so beautiful."

Rosie's face was as bright with happiness. I marshalled my feelings, as best I could.

Years later I would still get a twinge of uneasiness whenever I'd think about Rosie and how I had almost put her in the position of having to defend the lambs. She could have easily put her hands on her hips, stamped her foot, and, in so doing, turned us all upside down. Or was it right side up? I began to see that children can manage conflict when grown-ups make an effort to accommodate their unique circumstances of life.

I also began to understand that theories of learning, without real children in mind, can get in the way of seeing the child as a whole person. It was going to take a lot more maturing on my part to finally lay the books aside and contemplate, instead, the perfect sense of each child and every child as they were.

No wonder our professors said we were to take note of the interests of every child as soon as possible. "Do this upon their arrival in the classroom and start from there," they said. That proved harder than I expected. Indeed back in teachers college, I had only wished to get on with the subject matter, and quickly. Tell us once and be done with it, was my attitude. I recalled, for instance, sharing my impatience with fellow classmates one morning in general methods class. I wondered if we would ever get past the obvious. It seemed entire mornings were consigned to self-evident bon mots. My classmates and I shook our heads and I remember feeling high and mighty. No wonder. I didn't know Rosie, then, nor Jay, nor Lisa, nor Inga, nor all the others.

Nolan

A boy named Nolan Cubbin taught me more about matters of the heart. But, he worried me. He was forever gunning for a fight. He was tall and skinny, like a stick bent in the wind clutching an oversized windbreaker around him. Blue-eyed, with dirty blond hair and teeth that protruded, he was not going to win friends on appearance alone. I worried that he might never learn to manage his feelings. He had yet to find the centre of his being, it seemed. For him to attain emotional stability would be a starting point. To say the least, he was wily and cranky by temperament. Worse, he actively hunted for trouble and, if conflict began to wane or fall apart for lack of interest, he did his best to fuel things up again. He raised cane, far and wide. In short, Nolan was a scrapper and liked to make others upset. He taunted kids on the way to and from school and then hid in back alleys around the neighborhood afterwards so avengers couldn't get back at him.

His last year's teacher warned me that he had the shortest fuse of anyone she'd ever known in all her teaching days. Nolan's temper meant that he ended up in a huge fit of crying if he was prevented from hurling curses at his nearest foe. I observed this behaviour in him more than once. Just to start a row, for instance, he'd say, "Ryan's mama dresses like a real old bag." It was his favourite approach. "She should be ashamed of herself," he'd say, knowing full well the intended recipient and friends were within earshot. One day, his impudence made things a little too hot for him.

Apparently, on the way to school, Nolan gave a severe tongue lashing to a much older boy who had dropped out of school a few years back and who had taken to standing outside the school fence calling out to the girls and boys that they were a just bunch of jail-birds. I'd seen the lad before: bored, taunting, but harmless. I told the children that he was just trying to act free and to ignore him. Heaven knows what Nolan said to him! Whatever he said, he was in hiding again.

I wasn't aware yet that this was an established pattern of behaviour in Nolan. Knowledge of that was still to come. I noticed he liked to sometimes stay indoors after school. He'd set up entertaining conversations for my benefit, once or twice until way past five o'clock. It seemed odd.

"Why don't you go home after school, Nolan? You'd think you'd be dying to be let out," I asked.

"Nah, I don't want to go home. There's nothin' to go home for anyway, least not with my grandparents there all the time."

I thought about his family circumstances. His mother was a single parent whose husband left years ago.

"He liked my red hair for a while, I guess you could say. All of a sudden he didn't," Mrs. Cubbin declared as mirth played in her eyes.

She and I were having a heart to heart, that day.

"He ran around chasing wine, women, and song. Mostly wine, though, 'way I see it. I had to bring up Nolan alone. First, we lived on my parent's farm until he was old enough to go to school. Then, I got this job at the printers. It beats running a boarding house, which I tried for a while. The men weren't bad. Some even proposed. Not for real, though, if you get my drift. I guess, in the end, the red hair scared them off, too."

I could see that she and Nolan shared the same wry sense of humour. Mrs. Cubbin was a big woman. Her size made me think Nolan, thin as a rake, must take after his father.

"Nolan will be the death of me but he has to understand that I can't give him all my free time." Mrs. Cubbin's life choices were narrow, as were Nolan's.

Nolan was sitting on the window sill, near my desk, where I sat marking books. "It must be nice to have your grandparents live with you," I said.

I wondered if this would be our topic of conversation, "At least you don't have to go home to an empty house."

"Nah, they fight all the time. My mom and grandma yell at Grandpa the whole day long. Geez, it gets my goat."

"Is your grandpa hard to get along with, then?"

"Nah. It's just they're tryin' to get him to take a bath for the wedding. He baths once a year. He keeps tellin' them it isn't the date yet, and they keep yellin' they don't want to be shamed by his smell. I wish they'd quit buggin' him. It just makes him mad. He doesn't stink that bad. They won't listen though. And tonight they're gonna fill the tub and wrastle his clothes off and dump him in. No use me going home till it's done."

"When's the wedding?" I asked, knowing it would be hurtful to show that I was amused by this predicament.

"Saturday."

"He might do it on his own before then," I said. "And what about you?" I wanted to change the subject, "Are you going to the wedding, too?"

"Yeah, I got a whole twenty dollar bill from my grandpa. Want to see it? I hid it. Bet you can't guess where."

The guessing game. Why did it enchant children so? Nolan's lips were skinned back over his teeth in a wild grin.

"I haven't a clue, Nolan."

"It's in my running shoe! Here, let me get it out," he jumped back up on the window sill, flipped his runner off and handed me a thin coiled paper reef. "Go ahead," he laughed. "It's a real twenty dollar bill."

I unrolled the bill slowly. It was damp from the sweat of his foot; a part of me recoiled but I didn't want to spoil his fun.

"See?" He was practically doubled over with glee.

Then he swept the bill away and cast a worried look outside the window. "I guess I should go now."

He looked worried. Too worried. "Nolan, do you want to wait here till after your grandfather's bath, or what?"

"I guess so. It'll be over soon—once they get his clothes off. The rest will be fast, Mom says."

He glanced out the window, again.

"What is it Nolan? Is somebody after you? Want me to go check outside?" I was beginning to suspect it was more than an incensed schoolmate waiting down the block that he had to dodge. He was too jumpy.

"Okay," he agreed. "Look for a big guy, about nineteen, twenty maybe. Skinny and ugly as a guy can get. He says he's going to kill me if he catches me."

"Who is it, Nolan?"

"I don't know. Just some geezer hangin' round the store. I seen him before, outside the fence at school acting like a big know-it-all."

"What did you do? What did you say to him?"

"Nothin.' I just told him that if he ever came around my yard, or my school, there'd be blood all the way down Thirteenth—his blood. That's if he shows his mug around. I told him I'll be the one to make him bleed like a bloody mess!"

"Oh, Nolan, whatever for? To strangers yet! And twice your size! One day you are going to get what you're asking for. Here, I'll check for you, and then you get right on home. I'd watch my tongue if I were you. Lord Nolan, my son. I mean it! I hope your twenty is hidden away."

It was now after five o'clock. I shielded Nolan behind me in the downstairs entrance and peered outside. The coast was clear.

"You run now, Nolan." I said.

He ran like the wind, glancing back over his shoulder with a wicked grin that fled the instant he turned to pick up speed. I waited until he was out of sight, sure to be home safe. No sound of the enemy. No pumping gravel. No cracking bones.

Perhaps the bath of the grandfather would be over, too. Walking up the stairs and back to my classroom, I reckoned that wry humour might be catching, thanks to Nolan.

A line of verse popped into my mind: "I ups with his heels, and smothers his squeals..."

Few had Nolan's saving grace, which was his way of getting anger out of his system. Mocking others cured many a temporary grief for him, that and knowing all the alleys and quick getaways. He was a survivor. The trouble was that little things, as well as big, got his dander up whether or not it was any business of his.

For instance, he grew upset that spring when the school organized a building bee to enhance the playground. The principal and vice-principal set up a meeting with parents to plan the construction of monkey bars, a climbing apparatus, and swings. The plan was to imbed large tractor tires in the ground and haul in extra soil to build up a hill for the children to play on.

According to the vice-principal, the parents needed no convincing of the importance of proper outdoor equipment. He had gone to a meeting just the night before, armed with a list of child psychology books, just in case. He might have saved himself the trouble as his promotional clout was not needed. After all, we lived in a time of growing public interest in the country's level of fitness. Apparently, sixty-year-old Swedes had something on Canadians. It was worth the school's time and effort to assemble basic exercise equipment for the children. If we co-operated, the chairman of the school board said, our schools would outperform Swedes hands down.

Parents came to help. Volunteer parents always came. For this project, the women held raffles and bake sales. All through May and June they provided coffee and cake and helped the men empty truckloads of dirt. However, the energy and laughter of parents and friends was lost on Nolan. He made it plain to anyone who listened that "this pitiful little scene" was nothing compared to the NHL and even more pathetic when compared to the Grey Cup. Besides, he said, there were so many old geezers hanging around, a guy didn't know what to do. "Why do we put up with this puny stuff? Real football players and hockey players wouldn't." he sneered.

Nolan Lee Cubbin. When it came right down to it, he was, in his own way, a likable student. He had good days. Trying to settle him down to task, however, was like putting a bee back in its hive. As for learning, he worked with fury on the days his world went well. By the end of the school year, he hadn't carried out his threats of hell and damnation on Thirteenth Avenue. And he wasn't likely to—skinny and temperamental, his own shadow sometimes gave him a start.

I now had to admit that some children, like Nolan, came to visit the teacher after school for reasons other than companionship. Some want quiet. Some want a sense of safety. I found it difficult to imagine that even one child in our great province and country didn't have "a clean well-lighted place" at home, the virtue of which was described in a Hemingway short story I'd read. Nolan stayed after school for his own reasons, sometimes out of fear of a coming showdown. When he raged and cried and threw himself on the ground or hurled his thin body hard against the walls of the school outside, I'd let him cry it out. Something would have touched off his anger that day. I sensed the source of his pain might be his father who had abandoned him, but I didn't know his mother well enough to ask her about it. She had no time to come to the school, just yet, she'd say.

Nolan's life had some of the same features as children living on my reserve. In both cases, the children suffered from family breakdown— on the reserve, mainly as a consequence of historical pressures such as residential schools; and, in the case of Nolan, the unexplainable loss of his father. The effects on home life were all the more complex. The parents under such duress faced obstacles to calm attentive homes where children flourished. On the reserve, for instance, the nuclear family had also now to function as a substitute for the traditional kinship system wherein relatives, such as aunts, uncles, and grandparents, helped bring up the next generation. Children suffered while adults grappled with impoverishment and psychological anxiety. In circumstances such as these, children tend to have fewer outlets for their creative energy, a circumstance that plays havoc with their emotional lives and self-esteem.

I grew certain of one thing. No matter what children endure, they can not tolerate injustice very well. The outward appearance of acceptance or submission by them sometimes amounts to suppression of their true thoughts and feelings. This can lead to psychological problems, the manifestation of which can often be traced to societal ills. The professors made it clear that self-control at all times is the anchor to a well-ordered society; so we student teachers had to appreciate the importance of keeping emotional flare-ups to a minimum. Psychic pain, an invisible phenomenon, was easy to overlook in children.

On the reserve, the Indian agent and the teacher lived in homes that had electricity and running water, and even the smallest of their children had rooms of their own. In contrast, our mudded log dwellings crowded everyone into two rooms. There was no running water or electricity. Poverty had a grip on our sense of the future, too, when we saw how poor the old people were. Yet, despite these daily reminders, outbreaks of anger among the children were few. Silence reigned in those seemingly incapable of feeling.

I read that in the 1850s, and prior to that time, the reserve was not a place where people could just be, let alone become. Mere existence exacted its toll. Adults around me lived in a state of unrelenting anxiety. Their parents and grandparents, under threat of starvation, had worked for meagre rations consisting of wormy flour and salted bacon on a reserve that was stripped of any other means of survival. Their once flourishing hay fields had been expropriated without compensation under petition of their neighbours, the Broadview townspeople, with Ottawa's consent. A change in conditions was impossible to achieve. My parents referred to this as "the time people were starved to death."

During the mid-1800s, death from starvation mounted and hunger and fear set in among the weakening men. The men finally took matters into their own hands and went to see the Indian agent. The agent refused to allow anyone near the storehouse of rations that was situated on the reserve. The men broke into the storehouse anyway. They then armed themselves and waited for the law in a house in the valley. Bloodshed and legal redress were barely circumvented when the police and government officials arrived. A deal was struck whereby jail was avoided and "justice served" in the name of "mercy" when four of the Indian men agreed to plead guilty of "theft" and were let go. Times of hunger continued into the next generation, our generation.

I noticed how, in our time, indignation turned to deep sadness in those once touched by youthful optimism. As the months and years went by after World War II a deepening sadness seemed to grip everyone, young and old. Sadness turned into depression. Optimism had no tenure. Many people committed suicide. Bonds between adults and children were all the more deeply rent. The people struggled to find work, just as they had in the 1800s with the help of a sympathetic farm instructor answerable to Ottawa's policy of stringency. In the end, circumstances precluded true industry. The selling of wood and gravel from the reserve was forbidden under the Indian Act. I saw how people with only time on their hands ended up having no time at all for anything. Now as a teacher, I tried not to think about this, but the suffering of any children, such as my pupils, called to mind stories not written in history books.

As a teacher in a city that teemed with resources, I never expected I would have to pay close attention to the private crises in student's lives, at least not so soon in my career, nor so often. Teachers college had told us nothing of this.

I saw that children are capable of learning self-control when circumstances in their worlds remain stable and where fairness prevails. Even in homes where sufficient resources and support create stability, a child's needs might not be met. Nolan, for example, tried to work a towering rage out of his system, and until he did so, he'd be robbed of his own strengths. Crying out to a darkened sky can't be so very wicked, I'd say to myself as I stood, or sat, beside him. Even the Biblical Job had lashed out, in sackcloth and ashes. And, in my work as a teacher, I would come to wish that other children I knew could be more like Nolan. That surprised me to no end.

JOHNNY

Take Johnny. His circumstances were similar to Nolan's. He, too, had lost the ability to hold himself together in the eye of the storm. Somehow, in his short life, this self-centring ability went missing, and it wouldn't be long before I found out why. His case was a difficult one to deal with. Like Nolan, Johnny was being brought up by his mother, even though his father was at home. Johnny Willard's mother told me all kinds of things; but probably not as much as she should have when we met.

Johnny was a well-mannered likable boy but something about him bothered me. Within the first two weeks of getting to know him, my mind searched for words to describe his way of being.

All I could think of was that he seemed to be afraid of life. He was good-hearted and well-behaved, as his previous teacher had said, but something worried me, nonetheless.

Johnny Willard was good to a fault. He apologized for everything that happened around him in the classroom, even when he was out on the playground with the others. My sixth sense told me that if nothing was done about it, he just might go on apologizing for being himself. In one way it was obvious that he needed to see how he fit in. But more than that, he had to know that he was an important part of our world, that his needs and demands were as significant as anyone else's. Johnny shouldn't feel the need to compensate for his existence, I told myself, certainly not as a ten-year-old. There had to be a way to show him.

To begin with, during class, I made up little stories containing seeds of bravery and aimed these at Johnny. "Once, there once was a boy who felt anxious from morning till night..."

There was no telling what might trigger his self-awareness, that he had a right to challenge his limited view of himself. If I were to help and be effective at it, I'd have to learn more about him. But, he gave nothing away. He simply smiled and deferred or smiled and assented.

In teachers college, our professors taught that parents and guardians can come in ones, in twos, or in extended family groupings and that this either helped or hindered a child's development, depending on circumstances. Just another uninspiring fact about character development was my response, back then. The professors went so far as to say that getting to know the guardians or the parents broadened the teacher's view of the child. I decided it wouldn't hurt to ask Johnny's parents to come in for a visit as soon as possible.

I had to do this in a manner that wouldn't upset Johnny. The opportunity came at report card time when parents normally came for parent-teacher conferences. I took pains to schedule the meetings after school when interruptions were minimal and when time available to talk might easily be extended.

It turned out to be a hectic day and I hadn't yet formulated how I would broach the subject of Johnny's lack of confidence. I found it impossible to prepare for Johnny; he gave so little of himself to situations where I could observe him. His participation in class discussions was confined to answering safe questions. When pressed to give an opinion, he'd make the barest reply and then duck his head, or worse, retract his words. I tried to make things easier for him. "What is your favourite day of the week, Johnny?"

"Saturday...Sorry, Monday. Well, any day, I guess. Sorry..." would be his tortured response. He'd turn as red as a beet at these times.

That day was a day like so many, a day when teachers endure nonstop demands and interruptions running neck and neck from bell time at the beginning of the day to bell time at the end. The intercom blasted its way into almost every lesson: insurance forms are to be picked up before noon; book order money should be turned in now; the school nurse is about to begin checking eyes; lost and found articles must be checked over by all classrooms before recess; radio broadcast schedules are being drawn up now—first come, first served; if you think your dog followed you to school...

The day drew to a close and Johnny's mother would be on her way. Not knowing Mrs. Willard made any structured discussion tentative at best. It seemed that, for once, I might choose to ignore the professors' words with a good conscience: It is important to be thoroughly prepared; botched discussions solve nothing and leave everyone dissatisfied.

Well, here it was four o'clock with the children filing out. Mrs. Willard was nowhere in sight. Had she forgotten? Perhaps she got held up. At least, now, there was blessed silence in the room. I decided to wait for Mrs. Willard and to simply go on instinct and sincerity. I began to mark the children's books and was well into a pile of them when a short plump flustered woman appeared in the doorway. Mrs. Willard!

Her coat was buttoned up tight and she struggled to undo the neck button.

"I'm late," she said, breathlessly. "My husband won't be coming, as I said. I have come alone about Johnny. I'm late."

"Here, Mrs. Willard, let me help you off with your coat. I'm glad you've come."

She stepped aside indicating that she preferred to keep her coat on.

"I was just marking books and was on the point of looking out the window for you. So you're Johnny's mom—meet Johnny's teacher."

We laughed as we settled down at the little round table at the back of the room. We talked about the neighborhood, about the prices of things these days, and about the fact that everything was going up. Mrs. Willard, I discovered, was not at loss for things to talk about and needed no encouragement. But she seemed unwilling to settle in for a good talk about Johnny. That made two of us searching for a way to begin or, in her case, not to begin.

Mrs. Willard delved into her past life on the farm explaining how, as a little girl, she was "a most joyous creature" and how she now felt cut off from life and the world.

"There was no more joy, after the farm," she declared, studying her fingernails, "except for a brief time spent in Yorkton where life included boys with all us girls dressing up for dances. Oh, I was something, then! Frilly dresses—real satin ones. Later there was marriage, just when life approached a dangerous peak. I didn't think too deep about life," she confided, "but I wanted diversion and I got none, what with all the heartaches and pains of womanhood."

On and on she talked, her words racing over territory unfamiliar to me. She gave glimpses into the private moments and feelings that unsophisticated young women were not accustomed to having any real thoughts about. I sensed that I had lost all vestige of control over the interview. Prepare, indeed.

"Do you know," she asked, "that Johnny's father is at home right now, drunk as a skunk? And smelling like one?"

I stared at her.

"Well, it's true. Drunk all the time. Won't work. Johnny and I live on next to nothing. But don't you worry, I'll get back at him! I have a Buddha and I plan to use it."

I had no idea what she was talking about.

"You don't know what it's like trying to shield Johnny from the sight of a drunk. The worst is Johnny is reminded of it every time he goes outside. Beer bottles piled at the door, everywhere. Johnny has to step over them just to go off to school. It makes him sick, I know. My poor Johnny! I tell him, 'Don't worry, Johnny. Mamma has her Buddha now.' I have never let Johnny know about my secret, but that Buddha works."

I nodded vaguely, unable to keep pace.

"I got him a several months ago at Woolworth's, and I tell you," she continued as she drew her chair closer to mine. She lowered her voice, "all I have to do is take him to my room at night. I sleep alone while Guess Who is passed out on the only good bed. And I rub his belly—the Buddha's."

Mrs. Willard, thank heavens, didn't notice hysterical laughter threatening to burst its dam.

"I just repeat the name of a person I hate," she said, "like my husband's sister, the one I practised on—Hilda. It kind of scared me. She fell down the stairs at home on the same day I rubbed the Buddha, and her ankle broke. She swears to God she didn't trip. She just fell down as though the step buckled out from under her foot—her very words. She's not that old either, you know. Like me, middle-aged."

Mrs. Willard looked at me and nodded her head as if we shared the burden of shock that must have registered in my face. I couldn't believe she was serious. I tilted my head vaguely, not knowing how to respond.

What Mrs. Willard read there, however, seemed to satisfy her and she continued, "As for my husband, I'm ashamed to call him that—well! We haven't slept in the same bed since Johnny. Just let him get near me and I'll use my Buddha on him."

I was afraid that she'd ask my opinion about those private matters but, to my relief, her train of thought finally turned to her son. "Johnny is a good boy. I tell him to work hard in school. 'Do what your teacher says,' I tell him, 'so you won't turn out like your dad.' He adores you, my Johnny."

Finally, it was my turn to speak. "And I like him, Mrs. Willard. I only hope he stops being so hard on himself, because he is a good boy. I don't wish him to think he could ever be anything but. Even if he were mischievous he'd be a good boy because Johnny's good from the heart."

I sensed the need to martial my thoughts, quickly. "I hope he starts to feel sure of himself. I don't think he's aware of all his talents. This may come with time, but..."

Mrs. Willard, beaming, stood up and re-buttoned her coat. Obviously, she thought we'd covered all the ground we needed.

"This is the best talk with a teacher I have ever had," she said. "You know, I never go out anymore. No money. But I have my Buddha and my Johnny."

With a wave of her hand she was gone. Seeing her disappear so quickly, I now fully understood that, had I taken time to design the discussion, we might have talked about Johnny. But now I had a bit more to go on, perhaps more than I thought.

I had only to reflect on life on the reserve when it came to alcohol abuse. According to the women in our family, drinking became a habit of the men who came home from the war, full of hope. They had energy but no work, and nothing to make work with. The men's bodies turned alcohol into a poison that robbed their physical and mental integrity. Alcohol made home life increasingly miserable. In our home, my father's army pals came to visit with stories of the war where buildings overseas were burned to the ground, where farm fields were blown up with people's arms and legs flying through the air. The men cried, often more so after a bottle of wine. They'd curse Ottawa for not helping them find work and the government policies that denied them alternative opportunities.

The men, newly discharged, often wore their old uniforms when they came to visit. They took great care to keep these clean and pressed. Soldiers made a bed so taut a coin bounced off, they claimed. Like other aspects of soldierly life, they were proud of their skills. The younger men brought along their new girlfriends to the house from the valley, or from other reserves. They'd all sit in our big room, one or two pretending he had more money than the others, or that his life was quite comradely with the English people in town. Later, Dad drank, too, and told stories about the war. Soon these stopped, and then he was just mad at everyone.

When I closed the door of the school and headed for home it was already dark. The wind whistled across the yard. On the way home, I thought of Mrs. Willard. Her coat was much too tight for her true size and she wore it like a little girl. She had made grownup comments, though, and it seemed she was trying to pull the fragments of herself together. Perhaps she was too absorbed in her troubles to see that her life and her confinement, real or imagined, were close to being one and the same. The interview had failed its purpose, and I was too tired and much too inexperienced to round up my thoughts about Mrs. Willard.

The next morning, Johnny came to school practically bursting with song. He seemed relieved of a burden. It was plain he brought more of himself to school that day. He even offered to clean the chalk brushes on his own outdoors. He was swept along in a kind of heady enthusiasm. His mother must have shared with him my view of his potential, however fleeting a reference I had made to it. Now here he was reaching beyond himself.

With Johnny, I began to understand that children measure their worth by expressions of care in adults' eyes. It is as though children look there for a clear view of themselves. In the literary works and biographies I'd read, poets and politicians feared the withering glance. Children have even less defense against the cold gaze from those they admire. They gain confidence in themselves through "smiling eyes," as my own little daughter once said, describing her teacher. Johnny's father might not care that his son existed, and Johnny would have seen that more than once.

It saddened me to think that a small gift of confidence, easily given, can just as easily be withheld. How immense the trust is that society places on its teachers! This fact was humbling. It also disturbed me. As a teacher, there were so many factors to consider, many beyond my control. But I vowed I'd never turn a vacant eye on any child. Nor any adult. Nor living beast. Such were my thoughts when I thought about Johnny Willard.

One day in the middle of math period, the intercom crackled to life. For someone not expecting it, it can sound like a cannon blast. The principal made an announcement. "Swimming for grade fours will commence Tuesday mornings at the YMCA. This marks the beginning of the swimming program for October and November. Everyone is expected to participate. Bus schedules will be forwarded to teachers, today. Have fun learning to swim, grade fours."

Johnny Willard paled and slumped over on his desk. I hurried to his side. Placing a hand on his shoulder I asked him what was wrong. He had turned ashen so suddenly. His small face peered upward and he whispered, "I'm afraid of water. I can't swim."

It was one of those dreaded moments, a moment in which reaction rises like a flood among the children. In an instant, the strong feeling of a single child can become a banner for the others. This is when a teacher has to act quickly; it is called managing the moment: Classroom Management 101. Our situation was that everyone had to participate, without exception. One look at Johnny and my heart sank. Some of the children stirred with excitement while others appeared beset with uncertainties of their own. They looked at me for direction and confirmation. It was plain to me that not everyone liked to swim. The children waited to see how I responded to Johnny. So, this is what experienced teachers mean when they talk about tough love.

"Johnny, even some grown-ups have been terrified. Some people are afraid of water itself. There's this postman in New York who couldn't even stand in a pan of water..." Johnny covered his head with his arms.

"Tell you what," I said, "I'll talk to the instructor, Mr. Jackson. I know him well. He has to deal with a lot of people who are afraid of water, at first. Lifeguards like Mr. Jackson are trained to do this. Don't worry, Johnny, we'll all be together, and you can take your time."

A voice piped up from the third row, "I used to be afraid, too, but now I'm not."

It was Dale Jenkins wishing to encourage Johnny; bless him and all his sprinkly freckles, I thought.

"You want to tell us about that, Dale?" I asked.

"Well, I almost cried at camp," he said. "But the counsellor said just to follow instructions. And I did. I did everything he said and I learned to swim in one day. My dad said it was a miracle."

Everyone looked at Johnny. Some of the children chimed in, telling their own stories of overcoming fear. Johnny was a little less pale now. He said that he was feeling a bit better, sorry, and that he would try.

One of the questions I wrestled with all my life as a teacher was when to push and when to leave a child alone. You can never be sure how deeply rooted their fears are. Nor can you be certain that what you are faced with is but a fleeting momentary lack of confidence that needs only a little help, the one little push that a teacher can provide. All through my teaching life, I found myself wavering between that one encouraging push and the single important need to wait a little longer.

We arrived at the YMCA Pool on the appointed day. I asked Dale if he would be Johnny's partner and both boys seemed pleased as they hurried away to change and shower. At poolside, I told the instructor about Johnny's fear of water. He flashed a brilliant all-knowing smile and winked at Johnny standing near the edge of the pool, shivering in his sagging trunks.

"This morning," the instructor began, his voice full of the cheerful notes of enthusiasm, "we'll start by getting ourselves wet. So, let's get into the water..."

And without so much as a how-do-you-do, Johnny Willard jumped as hard and far as he could right into the middle of the pool and sank like a stone.

Everyone was stunned, including Mr. Jackson who stared incredulously as a huge splash of water shut over Johnny's head. Johnny surfaced, sputtering and choking and flailing his arms, his face white with terror. Mr. Jackson took a short swift running leap and dove into the water. In seconds, he swam up alongside Johnny just as he was about to go under again. In the brief moments that had passed, Johnny lost his mind. He clung to Mr. Jackson in a most maniacal fashion and, despite stern shouts, refused to let go his crippling hold. There erupted a wild thrashing of water in the middle of the pool. By degrees, Mr. Jackson was able to skin the struggling Johnny off his back and then heave him up and onto the side of the pool.

Everything happened so fast, I wasn't sure who was who out there. Somehow things were sorted out. Mr. Jackson stopped to catch his breath, to settle down, and to begin the swimming lesson. Johnny got back into the water with the others. He said that he would just stand in the shallow end for now, sorry.

I still see him there, waist deep in a corner of the pool, a faint blue skeleton of a boy. He insisted on spending all of October and November in his corner like a little sea urchin in disguise. It was only during the final lesson that he ventured a little farther into deeper water.

I never found out whether Johnny Willard ever learned to swim. At the end of that particular summer, he and his mother moved to another part of town, likely taking her distorted ideas of the Buddha with them. I often wondered if Johnny's jumping into the pool with both feet like that would mean, someday, that his courage would rise from a centred self, not from thoughts about miracles, uncaring fathers, or a mother's childish distorted ideas about imagined powers residing in religious figurines.

Over the years, I began to see that a hard part of grounding one's self as a teacher meant coming to terms with the fact that that it is impossible to influence every child's life story to a good end. Nor can you be certain about the fate of the parents, especially mothers, who bring up children alone.

I often grew wistful thinking about all the mothers whose lives brushed mine ever so fleetingly, but who, nonetheless, lent a sense of courage that sustained me whenever difficult days were mine to endure. Those women scarcely recognized their importance to a young teacher whose mental map of what to do next was only about as practical as her own life experiences. The mothers' attempts to support me, as a teacher, helped me gain the feeling of a stable foundation in my calling. The absence of fathers and husbands added to the heavy burden of bringing up children in a changing world. How these women consolidated their strength as they maintained a home and nurtured their children was beyond me. They scarcely had enough time in their busy days to reflect on their lives. Yet the majority came to all school functions, as best they could, and this helped me understand that their home situation continued to impact on the lives of their children and their children's futures.

There was another edge to the worries that surrounded us. How could I, as a teacher, remain true to the centre of my own being? My classroom experiences kept telling me that new and even more compelling societal forces would soon affect the ability of mothers to nurture the learning of a new generation. The requirements of change stretched to the limit the resources and the time available for family interaction. As pressures mounted, the paradigm of the nuclear family with mom-at-home as its centrepiece, changed as the storybook description morphed into a reality of latchkey children fending for themselves at lunch and after school. Later, people began to wonder about the role of television as an appropriate "guardian" of children in defining needs and wants. In the not too distant future, technology was destined to make even greater inroads into the time available for family discussions, a mainstay of home as source and centre of values. As a young woman, I began to wonder if it was only the beginning. I told myself that the thing to do was to get centred and stay centred. To me, that also meant finding money to go to university. I had seen what happened, back home on the reserve, when family life failed. This didn't mean I understood what I saw but it was obvious that children were growing up with, or without, their original parents and in difficult circumstances. I saw the children's fear, anger, and loneliness because I had experienced the same feelings that come with isolation and frustration.

If change continued its course, I wanted to know how that could affect me as a teacher and, ultimately, my little girl and her life. I also had a healthy sense of my own ignorance and wished to study. Yet, my going to university would put a strain on our family's limited resources. We had little cash at the end of each month. Still, I had been teaching almost five years and, in 1967, time kept marching on as before. I decided to confront my anxiety and take on the world, as did the mothers at school who struggled to safeguard their children's future.

My having married a non-Indian man meant that my Treaty Indian status was removed. With that went financial support for my education. I had to take out student loans. Acquaintances impatiently asked why I hadn't opted to go to university before I got married. For those who had learned to work bad policy to advantage, it was clear that I had given away a birthright that should have worked on my behalf. It was discriminatory of government, they pointed out, to deny my right to education. Why had I gone and done a dumb thing?

I had good reason. The fact that I was only able to start school at age ten made me at least five years behind my contemporaries in education; but not in marrying age. Peter and I could have lived common law to maintain my rights. But, in terms of both our parents' values, common law implied impropriety. Common law was out of the question. Besides, Peter and I wanted our children to share our name from birth.

Peter's earlier discussion with a government official about retaining my treaty rights in relation to marriage, as was possible for men and their non-Indian wives, had no effect on a policy that was unfair. I warned Peter that his appeal might come to naught. However, to him, what was reasonable was achievable in this country. I worried that our decision to marry had implications for my daughter and her future education. Anxiety about this felt like a coming winter.

Money or not, in the late 1960s I asked for professional leave to get a bachelor of arts degree. Peter, too, now wanted to study. All his reading paid off, and he spoke and wrote English well. However, our resources couldn't cover the costs of even one of us going to study. He was too proud to ask his parents. This meant Peter would have to take his degree a class at a time while he worked full time, right up until he graduated. He chose to major in English. I chose to major in German.

Like Peter, I wanted to study a language that was connected to a body of literature that in turn reflected a long preserved canon of knowledge. English offered that possibility in spades. In fact, it might have been my first choice. However, among pupils and staff at the university, word had it that the University of Regina had waived English 101 for an Englishman who planned to study and then work in Canada. No other group had this option. Hearing this, the old spectre of unfairness reared up and left me with a bitter taste in my mouth. After all, Peter had to take German 101 for his bachelor of arts and had to cover the course work as thoroughly as any beginning speaker. I asked myself why I should study a language and literature wherein a key grounding class, English 101, might be waived for one person—of the preferred cultural background, of course—who could merely speak the language. I did not come up with a satisfactory answer to that so I decided, instead, to pursue my interest in acquiring a second language.

Having informally read French history books, biographies, and novels in translation (mainly on courtly life and political figures), the study of French literature drew me. But I let my high-school experiences compromise my receptivity to it. A number of English-speaking teachers of French, whom I knew as teachers, ought to have at least tried to learn to pronounce the language with a semblance of true cadence and enunciation; but they did not, or would not, or perhaps, could not. The teaching of French was in a sorry state in my experience, particularly in anglophone high schools. I thought it might be the same at university.

I had an ear for languages and wished direct access to French classical thought as embedded in the language itself. The reading of French novels and biographies in English helped me to get at the history and culture, albeit superficially; but, as literature, I sensed the lack of that spiritedness that permeates French culture. Unfortunately for me, I interpreted a teacher's inability to speak the language a hindrance to expressing clearly the text's original meaning.

Peter, who read German, American, and Canadian literature, loved to engage me in discussions about the relationship of context and story to style and meaning in fiction. He had grown to love the American voice in fiction and remained faithful to his other loves, the poets Blake and Coleridge, along with a few contemporary German writers. I was saddened that no such works awaited my study in the original languages of my homeland, my continent, my country, my province and personal history. Also, First Nations' knowledge could not be accessed through stacks of reading material, concordances, dictionaries, and textbooks in my parents' languages. I might have studied Cree or Saulteaux, but the teaching of these languages at the Saskatchewan Indian Federated College was in its infancy at the time. Judging from the lack of texts and space in the college, First Nations languages were badly under resourced.

I saw how lucky Peter was in his pursuit of great literature that was grounded in fundamental culture and thought. So I struggled with the basics of the German language in my summer and evening classes before going back to university full-time. Because Peter had his own night classes to contend with, I thumbed many a good German dictionary to shreds. I had embarked on the study of a body of literature in its primary language and I was very excited about this. Soon I began to feel very lucky in my choice of major.

At the end of my final year in 1969, I was informed by the German department at the University of Regina that I had won a scholarship to study for one year at Kiel University on the Baltic in Germany. I was thrilled at the idea and began plans to leave immediately, dictionary and suitcase in hand. Peter's cool-headed review of our personal circumstances prevailed. Many things said no: consideration of our little daughter, Gabrielle, now in school; a permanent job waiting for Peter at the University of Regina Library; the hidden and not so hidden costs of living in Europe; the expense of a move; and my loss of right to First Nations education funding.

Circumstance had again foiled my goals, and I cried bitter tears. I wanted to study in Germany and to be able to retrace the physical steps, at least, of Goethe and Schiller and even that surly sixteenth-century writer Martin Opitz, whose gloomy vision had filled many of my study hours with a sense of foreboding. I told my German professors about my decision not to accept the scholarship and why. Dr. Isabel Jones, an elderly professor with a stalwart manner and clarion voice, said, "A closed doorway leads to another open; years from now, you will see what I mean." I clung to her wisdom as I grieved.

But, a door had opened. My former principal, Mr. Hervey Sykes, known as one of the system's finest administrators and teachers, came to my home before the end of spring semester to tell me that the school I had been teaching at wanted me back. Although I had the obligation to return to the Regina Public School System, there was no promise that I ever could return to my old school. Mr. Sykes asked if I might come on as a substitute teacher to complete the year. I gladly agreed because I would be back with the teachers and students I knew and loved and then afterwards remain there in the fall. Looking at Mr. Sykes as he sat in the living room, a smile lighting his face, I felt blessed. I felt hope in the midst of sadness at the loss of a golden opportunity to walk on the same cobblestone streets as the wonderful German writers whom I had grown to love; to go to the German archives and museums to see their papers and objects; and to sit in a German library and read what the old masters had written, in their language. My grief was deep, but the thought of children and my old school cheered me immeasurably. I told Mr. Sykes I was ready to start immediately.

Back in the classroom, I realized that I had not lost touch with my skills as a teacher, but in no way was the work becoming easier. On the contrary, it seemed to increase in its complexity. More times than I cared to admit, the prophetic line "The centre cannot hold" whisked through my mind.

SEVEN.

THERE'S GOT TO BE A PONY IN THERE SOMEWHERE

LEARNING TO TEACH IS DIFFICULT. Little by little, I began to realize that teaching meant deepening my knowledge about the teaching process and its structured content. When I was teaching, the age of personal computers and Internet resources was a long way off. The self-help guides that line bookstore shelves today were unavailable. Still, my needs went beyond the wish for more content. Depth meant learning from the great thinkers of the past. It meant seeking out the help of specialists and the master teachers at school. Such learning would be my life's struggle, I would often think in desperation.

It was about five years into my job, at a time when abstract ideas excited the mind and life had yet to test them. A B.A. had given me the basic concepts of thought in a few areas, including a small foray into the sciences, which was a big help in determining what to read next. In preparation for teaching, I read. I also listened carefully to the wisdom of those around me. Yet, it was only a beginning.

"Why is fire hot?"

Why, indeed? There were theological answers. There were philosophical arguments. I had only basic biological reasons to go by.

The advice fellow teachers gave me, as we congregated in hallways with the children streaming past, lifted my spirits somewhat. I asked questions about how soon I could hope to master instructional techniques. I asked when I would have a knowledge base broad enough to enable me to teach each subject well. It takes time and patience, they replied. I thought answers might be found in the One True Book that teachers consulted. It was time to write to Goldie:

Goldie,
I can't say whether I know enough about what methods to employ. I think I'm failing health, thank goodness only as a subject at this time.

Pillar of Pallor,
I think you might be concentrating too hard on the classroom-contained aspects of the job. Your classroom is a microcosm, a little model of a bigger world. There are people out there to ask. I learned this when I went on an extended rant about something or other. A root canal, I believe.

I sat down and thought about my profession as an organization. I had questions. For instance, I saw no connection between a school division's funding and its numbers of specialized staff. But I saw a pattern. When there was money in the organization, classroom teachers got the help of subject area specialists, like music consultants who could read music, sing, and play instruments. Physical education consultants who knew the name of every piece of gym equipment, and how to put these to use, were also available. I needed their help but they were not always there.

I became interested in another aspect of the organization at this time. I overheard the principal's remark to a young male teacher one day, "The only thing they respect is money these days. When I tell them how much I make, it holds them, all right." I wondered what it was about a teacher's salary that would hold anyone. It took time for me to learn that principals made more money than teachers. It took longer still to discover that men in the profession earned more than women. In teachers college our professors hinted at these trade secrets, as did the specialized consultants I came to know.

PROFESSOR WINFIELD

Our drama professor, Dr. Millicent Winfield, whose teaching skills were nothing short of amazing, warned us about underfunding. Petite, white-haired, and willful, she was not above jumping on top of a table to add fire to the points she made. I loved her even as she scolded us into raising our sights for a larger view of the world.

"There is no room for egocentrism or self-indulgence," she roared. "You're entering a world wherein you must teach. Not with books, even if the school board ever has the ones you really need. Not with pictures, even if the board ever gets these for you. You may never have such luxuries. But you have yourself! So wake up to your voice, your body, and your imagination. Sing! Dance! Get off those fat behinds and teach."

It was instructive to watch her. She was not a shy woman and when she demonstrated the art of storytelling one day, I swear I could taste the soup. It was such a direct and simple story that, when read line by line by a novice such as myself, it threatened to flatten out, curl up, and die right on the page. An old woman wants to make turnip soup. She finds a turnip in her garden. It is much too large to remove by its roots. Hunger drives her to enlist the help of neighbours, whom she instructs to pull on the turnip. Their co-operation is rewarded with a tasty pot of soup for all.

Professor Winfield primed us to watch her transformation as a storyteller, saying she would come round the corner and through the door at nine sharp. "And I won't be me!" she roared.

The next morning, on cue, Professor Winfield charged into the classroom, an old woman hurrying to her garden. When she circled that turnip in the middle of the room, you felt its size. When she seized its top and leaned backward in one almighty pull, you felt the weight of it. When she pushed with her shoulder against it, you sensed its counterweight. Finally, when she called the neighbours in, characters of every shape and size filled her kitchen. You read all this in her facial expressions, by the way she eyed them and by the way she moved in relation to them. When the old woman finally lifted the lid off the pot of simmering soup, a sharp aroma of turnip, onions, and carrots seemed to fill the air. And when she finally lifted the spoonful of soup to taste—what sudden flavour!

It was somewhere between the brief taste of flavour and the picture of an old woman transforming herself back into our Professor Winfield again, that I recognized the power of story-telling. Professor Winfield made us forget that she wore high heels and a pale blue dress with a string of pearls. She made us forget that the sun was not hot on our backs in her garden. I promised myself that, for my students' sake, I would learn the art of story-telling. Stories are like maps that keep meaning alive. I had reason to reflect on this many times as a teacher.

In her quieter moments, Professor Winfield told of her younger days as a beginning teacher in country schools across the prairies. She fought for her children's rights to know. She scoured the countryside for teaching aids and materials borrowed from drama, art, and music.

"Never teach in a vacuum," she commanded. "Correlate, correlate, correlate; math is not shorn of music. Music is not dead to the spoken word. Ask the poet. Ask the scientist. Dig down, deep down."

Professor Winfield pulled no punches when it came to getting the idea through our heads: You have to be resourceful. "And for Heaven's sake, don't confuse reality with cynicism," she said during those last days of teachers college. It was important advice. It told me to avoid setting out on a path of disabling doubts, advice that I savoured especially because I would soon be exposed to the twists and turns of funding policies in school divisions all around.

The issue of sufficiency of resources often seemed to be couched in pure economics: do we fund the basics or some frills, this year? A school board might find itself having to defend, or promote, misconceptions about knowledge and even about learning. Teachers know that art isn't a frill but an important subject area in itself; what's more, all the art forms provide critical avenues to learning. Yet, art consultants came and went while the resources for drama, music, and dance remained spottily represented in the system's classrooms. The passage of time revealed bias in other funding decisions. For example, one other bias that rankled was the unstated notion that women in the profession could make do with less. It appeared that investment in their professional development and in their supports, such as a free half-hour once or twice a week to plan and catch up, was negligible. It was difficult to put a finger on the real problem because bias manifested itself in so many subtle ways. Often it was as plain as the frustration on a teacher's face. Still, I tried not to become cynical but, instead, sought to learn what I could about the limits of fair and informed decision, as did my colleagues.

For the most part, we teachers learned from each other through co-operation at school; and, if the board got it right that year, from actual specialists.

My beginner's enthusiasm carried me far. Like all neophytes in need of expert help, I found myself hurrying off to the school board office building after school, happy and excited to take extra training from subject-area specialists. They represented a survival kit. They fired up a desire to teach their subject. I could hardly wait to get back to my classroom after these sessions.

Miss Della Fillmore

Miss Della Fillmore, the art consultant, welcomed us that first art session. She perched herself on a stool at the head of her class of novices. As she puffed on a cigarette, she said, "The language of art is as important as any of its techniques. It is, if I know anything about it, an important language to learn."

According to her, art was as deserving of a teacher's careful preparation as any other subject. Art period was not to be considered a "free for all," even if the teacher is not especially interested or even talented. Some teachers, apparently, systematically replaced art period with other instruction.

"Art is an amazing teaching tool," she said. "And I suggest you never skip it. Instead, do significant reading in the area and make art a vital force in your lives. For, as sure as I'm not a genius, art is universally enjoyed, loved for its own sake by children young and old. Think back to your childhood days of scribbling and colouring. Don't tell me you didn't enjoy art."

She sat on a stool adjusting her long limbs and rolling her eyes across the ceiling. Taking long puffs on her cigarette, she patted her fly-away hair in place. A she studied us, I began to like the tone of her. There was something of the maverick in her that made me think that there was something about the profession of teaching that not only attracted wishful idealists but, also, strong-minded people with solid senses of personal value. She had decided something about us, too, and having assessed us, said, "So you hate art and are scared to death of it. Forget that! Let's make fall colours, shall we?".

And so began her first lesson. We followed her lead. We grabbed brushes, containers of water, art paper, and water-colour boxes and set these down beside us on long tables. We were to begin with trying our hand at painting. Without a moment's notice, we had a job to do and that was that.

It was a rare sight to see a pro in action. Miss Fillmore moved effortlessly from subject to object, from technique to the life force at hand, and from the imagined object to its counterpart in reality. She both led and followed. She deliberately lost her way—"Let me see, I started with what colour combination?"—so that we could help her find it. In short, she captured us.

"When you teach," she began, "there is nothing more satisfying than passing a painting technique on to a child. It's not enough to say 'Here is a bowl of flowers for you to paint. Be finished at four o'clock, and don't disturb me until it's done.' Don't laugh, it happens."

Miss Fillmore was fascinating to watch. Her drawl and fluid movements combined with puffs on her cigarette. Holding a paint brush in one hand, while steadying the canvas with the other, she ushered in a sense of anticipation. And while demonstrating her techniques, she'd usually say outrageous things.

"Damn the board that doesn't give you materials for your children. Damn parents and taxpayers who think art is a frill. A pox on them! In so-called tough times, it is the very brush you hold in your tight little fist, not to mention the paper in front of you, that disappear the minute money becomes scarce. But don't be misled! Make no mistake; money never gets scarce. Art lovers do. And peace and happiness. Put that in your pipe. And now to the poppies, shall we?"

She chose the subject of poppies, she said, hardly because they were her favourite—indeed, up close, they activated her allergies—but because most parks in the city grew these and children would have seen them. Children, said Miss Fillmore, are like artists; they are captivated by the observable yet remain mindful of the unseen. Apparently, for a child, it was the presence of a pony about to appear where there seems to be only a pile of straw. For the adult, it was that perceived mercurial quality that one senses in, say, a second language text that eludes easy translation. In both instances, the unseen enlivens the mind with possibilities and summons up latent curiosity, the twin companions to learning.

Teacher that she was, Miss Fillmore beckoned us onward, instructing us to follow her demonstrations as she told us about the ways of the world, and of children. Now, here was a model teacher!

"When you paint a poppy, twirl the tip of the moistened brush—notice I did not say dripping wet—in the yellow paint-block first. Why? Because it's smarter to paint in the lighter colours first. Observe the brush sweeping im-pres-sion-ist-ical-ly right across the great divide like so, and soo..."

Here and there across the paper, her brush lightly touched down, delicately as a butterfly to a rose. At first it was hard to copy her technique. A touching down does not a poppy make, but she ignored our faulty efforts and moved ahead.

"Then take a swirl of orange, so...and lightly loosen the petals here, and here, soft as the breezes of the morn, and maybe here, for balance. Now see the red come through where the orange blends with the sunny yellow, here, like so..."

Watching her, you forgot the paper as object and saw, instead, the emergence of big juicy poppies. By the time she deftly patted in light purple trails of shadow, you really wanted to paint one yourself. What's more you had. There on the paper in front of you, fair genius set to bloom!

Now if that didn't send me hurrying back to my classroom, nothing did.

Miss Fillmore made the impossible easy. She set our minds at ease and focused our attention on the possibilities, on what lay just beyond our reach, and, in so doing, she took us through the steps of creative development. I felt I might become an artist, too, one day and maybe a good teacher of art.

Miss Della Fillmore didn't stay long in the employ of the board. She moved away amid whispers, which happens when ground troops aren't told why a change has been made. She had cancer of the larynx, some thought they'd heard. She had a falling out with the board, reported others. Still, others insisted that she fell in love with an artist, a man with a beret and goatee, and that she'd gone to live with him by the sea.

I wanted to think that she'd left on her own accord in pursuit of her art. Miss Fillmore, like many artists before her, was compelled to make a living while, hour after hour, holding the life force of her gifts at bay. I read that great artists starved to death, or lived in abject poverty and in isolation, just to come to terms with the driving authority of their gifts. Maybe Miss Fillmore had such gifts, I knew, but with us students (and the board's funding) she might never get past the poppies. I could only guess the seaside offered her hope and reprieve.

We waited, but the board office shared no facts about Miss Fillmore's leaving, at least not to my satisfaction. They sent a notice to the schools saying she'd left the system voluntarily This was yet another aspect of the profession that hinted at deeper organizational issues. Whereas open communication characterized good teaching, apparently, it made lesser claims on good administration. Good teaching depended on solid support, like Miss Fillmore, presuming one knew her whereabouts; but novices are always kept in the dark, clucking among themselves.

As a sign of changing times, art lessons came to be regarded as an opportunity to have children turn the world's junk—plastic, tinfoil, and assortment of expendable trinkets—into the mock-beautiful. Environmental pollution, as a concept, was gaining attention in the Western world. In the late 1960s and early 1970s, the misuse of technology produced pockets of disaster in sea, land, and air. Wrappers, tin cans, papers, plastic tubes, and bottles added to rubbish heaps. The things we were doing as a society were at odds with the planet. Funding seemed to be tied now to the idea of recycling; gone the various papers, paints, and brushes from our hands. Instead, walls boasted artful contrivances of Styrofoam meat trays, bottle caps, gum wrappers, and sundry. Classrooms spray-painted glued-down macaroni designs on paper plates. It was obvious some teachers misjudged what the movement was really about. Wise inventive children, I would think, poor beleaguered teachers.

I was grateful for consultants like Miss Fillmore. She was one of the many who had gone out of their way to make new teachers, like me, feel comfortable during their visits to my classroom. Fellow teachers advised me not to worry. Consultants were patient with fledgling teachers. Still, it was unnerving to think how easy it would be for others to misjudge my progress. Anxiety increased with the realization that teaching was a complex matter because of practical details and, of course, children.

In the following years, school board consultants would be replaced by teaching teams and co-ordinators. By the mid 1990s support for teachers in Saskatchewan would include training in the philosophy (why and how do I teach this); the content (what do I teach); and the approach to instruction (what methods do I use to teach this objective) of a revised curriculum. In subsequent years teachers could dialogue with experts and access information on just about any subject through the Internet and through the institution of teacher inservice as delivered by trained teams with subject-specific manuals for teachers. Thankfully, down through the years, physical education, another specialization, was not considered a frill. Quite the contrary. Where the arts, visual, dramatic, dance, and music, assisted teaching and learning in unexpected ways, phys. ed. excelled as a truly vital force. However, this was another subject area in which I knew I needed the support of a specialist.

Back in the mid-1960s, when consultants came out to the schools to assist teachers, it seemed to me that physical education consultants had a particular flair for life. They came bouncing into the gym with skipping ropes furling out ahead of them and basketballs whapping the floor. Before I knew better, I envied them. It seemed that they were destined to be forever playing and leaping about in the sun and wind. Lacking fields, any space might do to please the hankering for motion and targets. In contrast, the rest of us were the dullest of drones marking student exercise books in musty rooms after school. Physical education consultants enjoyed their life's work utterly. In their lessons, every single pupil ran and leapt alongside.

But these specialists, too, had their work cut out for them. Life in phys. ed. class is more than a joyful noise. Maintaining a balance between body and mind affects learning. I saw with my own eyes that children were calmer and more studious after a solid workout. The experts were right; physical education is learning's Rock of Gibraltar. I saw a direct link between sessions in the gym and a rise in the perfect willingness of even the most mischievous of children to sit down to work with grace and dignity.

EDDIE

Such was the case with little Eddie Brown, of all people. Eddie often came to school out of sorts with the world and himself. He lived in an overcrowded house filled with odds and ends of brothers and sisters and cousins. His mother worked nights, slept days, and took in sewing on weekends. Eddie's father had walked out on the family and never returned. Mrs. Brown gave her waking hours to the youngest and let Eddie and his older siblings fend for themselves. Eddie, unfortunately, took this to mean splashing water on his face once a week. He let the dust and grime percolate throughout his scrawny frame. His hygiene and often unwashed hand-me-downs didn't win him friends. So, he sought attention any way he could on the playground. He taunted and chased others while holding up his ill-fitting pants with one hand.

At some point in his life, Eddie decided that he was not as smart as the others but that he, nonetheless, had certain powers. He dashed into the classroom at bell threatening to tag groups of horrified girls with his "germs." His brand of warfare increased his personal troubles. It also reinforced his negative view of himself. I spoke sharply, on occasion, telling him that germs are personal and that each had better mind his own, or there would be a terrible reckoning. Eddie responded to the power of vague threats and would take to his seat, content that he, too, figured in the lives of others, no matter how.

Eddie also had a hard time concentrating. He disliked reading but was not immune to praise for his effort. For instance, I told him that he had a steady hand and would probably, on that advantage alone, be able to excel in penmanship. During writing practice he tried his best but then would forget to apply the same effort to class assignments.

One sunny morning, after running across the field in pursuit of a soccer ball and, true to form, slyly tripping a classmate or two, he took up the challenge of penmanship. The task for the children was to write out a definition for the word "bullion" by consulting a dictionary and rewording the entry in their own words in their notebook. "Bullion" had come up earlier, in reading period, and no one could state its meaning. I was never more surprised to see Eddie settle right down to work. A familiarly warm quiet peacefulness transformed the room. Only the sound of pencils writing, the turning of the odd page, and the sniffing of noses could be heard.

From my desk, I surveyed the class. And there they were: a roomful of cherubs intent on their labour, their diligence tugging at the heartstrings. And there was Eddie, a mildly rinsed, chimney sweep of a boy, the very picture of balance and contentment. I couldn't help but think that despite his father's abandoning him to life's circumstances, he would one day come to know himself as a good and able-minded person. I had only to build up his love of reading so that one day he could read of great men and, through that, become master of his own good progress.

It was time to glance over the children's work. I began at the back of the row and worked my way up to the front where Eddie sat. He sat up straight so that I could get a good view of his work. And a wonderful job it was. His writing was impeccable, every single letter straight and true. He beamed with pride as I exclaimed, "A full excellent master-writer, Sir Edward Brown!"

I studied his definition and immediately knew something was wrong. I was not about to say so, however. Hopeful hearts need stout protection, especially when expectant eyes look up from a little sweat-streaked face. A second reading and a glance at the dictionary, open on his desk, explained everything. He confused two words of similar appearance and composed a definition based on both.

By alphabetical rule, the word "bullock" follows fast on the heels of "bullion." So, with scrupulous penmanship, Eddie marshalled a definition, thus:

Bullion-(n.): castrated lumps of gold.

I struggled to keep from laughing. I managed to say with earnest gravity to Eddie that his work deserved the widest praise. I continued to pinch the inside of my arm to counteract a mounting sense of hysterical laughter. Meanwhile, Eddie sat grinning from ear to ear.

"Well done," I managed to say, and the class applauded Eddie's effort.

The important thing was that through this small act of kindness, Eddie's pride in his ability was saved. I didn't ruin his success by reacting to the unintended humour in what was the product of great effort. When the class grew fidgety and audibly restless while awaiting recess bell, Eddie stood tall and called out to his class-mates in a bright proud way, "Quiet, you guys, she's teaching us education!"

Over the course of the year, Eddie grew into a likable boy and even tried to make and keep friends. He helped tidy up the classroom, going so far as to offer to tie the shoelaces for the grade ones down the hall. I worried about him and his slowness to learn. I hoped his next year's teacher would be able to see through the distracting dust clouds that followed in his wake. I thought he would have a lot to offer the world, some day. And it seemed that he might even grow up to be a good and gentle father. Having lost his father while very young, his empathy for children needing a male role model might grow. His pride in having little ones look up to him might also provide an impetus for him to grow into the responsi-bilities of manhood. It was worth bearing in mind as I observed his behaviour each day. For now, I was glad that recess provided time for him to expend his excess energy as well as the opportunity for him to learn to get along with others. I was gladder still that the curriculum helped me bring formal structure to physical activity as a boon to learning.

I sensed that I really had to do something to get over the feeling that, short of a miracle, I might never become a good teacher. As a new teacher, this feeling visited me each time I reflected on my develop-ment. There was just so much to know. I couldn't gain a sense of the scope and depth of the knowledge foundation I needed, let alone grasp its entire breadth and meaning. My B.A. degree pointed out a few great thinkers and their patterns of thought, but nowhere could I find how the pieces fit together. Would I ever be able to teach beyond the frag-ments of knowledge if I couldn't get the whole picture? Still, there were steps I might take in order to develop competence in the concrete world at school. I could study each subject as best I could so that the children got something out of it all. I decided to add one more objective to my self-help plan. Concentrate on one subject for four years; devote the first to reading about it while attending after-school workshops on how to teach that particular subject; apply new aspects of what I learned about the subject the second year; incorporate an innovative instructional method or two, whether comfortable in it or not, by the third year; and in the fourth year, pull everything together.

I began with physical education, my least competent subject, as I saw it.

The Toughest Boys in the School

In the course of this plan I was destined to discover that children's temperaments include a broad range of behaviours. The year I began immersing myself in teaching physical education, I inherited "the toughest boys" of the school, a group of boys that had somehow ended up in the same classroom three years in a row. The principal, who assigned the children to their rooms at the beginning of the year, had been unable to separate them into different classrooms, now that split grades were the norm. Their collective behaviour, apparently, was entirely too distracting for regular classrooms where things were hard enough on teachers and learners. Their presence often dwarfed the other students' space in my mind.

With the nine o'clock bell blasting in my eardrums that September, I waited to see if the rumours held true. The boys filed into my classroom together. I looked them over as they walked past. They were tough all right, all seven of them. Here was the biggest grade-six student you ever saw; and here, too, the smallest. Each scowled as he affected a huge territorial air. I discovered soon enough that the boys had a human side to them—they hated to do what they were told.

Once settled in, I worked out a deal with them that would accommodate the whole class. While we discussed behavioural expectations, the other students divided themselves into three groups of six. In each gym period, the boys would learn one new skill. They'd practise this in the next gym period, when another new skill would be introduced. They would decide how to build and practise the skill. Such a deal might put the science of calisthenics at risk—a science I vaguely recalled from teachers college that meant exercising in logical sequence, from the top of the head down to the toes in a well-considered advance on bone and muscle. I knew the deal approach flouted rules of good classroom management, but I felt I had to meet the boys halfway in order to get anywhere with them. As for my part, I promised to intervene if they acted up. The basic rule agreed on was simple: keep the sweat rolling.

I shared my concerns with the physical education consultant at an inservice meeting. He assured me that actual contracts with pupils, if handled judiciously, can build a sense of co-operation among them. He showed me how to set up the gym, how to place selected pieces of equipment in corners, and to set out the mats strategically. The centre of the gym, he said, was best reserved for practising the skills learned and not for freewheeling nonsense.

Back in the classroom, I got that squared around with the boys. "This is no time for freewheeling nonsense, you understand," I said, and they nodded, exchanging glances.

From the first, they plunged into the work with gusto, manhandling the equipment as they huffed and puffed. On signal, they moved in orderly fashion to the next corner with its combination of equipment. As agreed, once they had the majority of steam out of their systems, I would demonstrate the skill of the week in three minutes. Now gym period was their show.

We had been warned in teachers college by a professor—the hard-minded Dr. Delmont—that technique and technique alone was everything. "Anyone teaching a skill without first mastering its rudiments ought to have his, or her, arm yanked out and be hit over the head with the bleeding stump," he said.

Dr. Delmont had flair. He was quick on his feet, and he had a way with words.

Today, I was on my own. I had practised dribbles with the basketball the evening before in the empty gym, Delmont's words big in my mind. Round and round the gym I went, bouncing the basketball in front of me, my fingers spread, their tips controlling the direction of the bounce. I succeeded in keeping my eye on an imaginary opponent ahead of me, too.

Next day, to my delight, the boys caught on instantly and set out across the gym on their way to perfecting yet another skill. A sense of relief swept over me. Boys soon to be men, I thought to myself. There was Jake dribbling down the red line with Teddy and Arnold close behind. Tomorrow's leaders! I was bursting with pride among the gym's echoing walls. If these boys had once been rude, I now saw only solid character and even refinement of manner. They had their oddities, but one could take them as they were, sweat pouring. I was pleased with myself. This was teaching at its finest, I surmised.

One day, a consultant newly assigned to our school rang up to say that he would come to observe and to help, if I wished. This was a regular duty for specialized consultants and it was always a pleasure to know help was on its way. He'd heard that I'd inherited a "mangy lot." I threw caution to the wind. I invited him to visit us immediately. Yes, this was perfectly all right. Yes, he could come that very afternoon, two o'clock sharp straight to the gym. I had great confidence in my boys, and I welcomed the opportunity to show them off. I thought it best not to forewarn the boys of our visitor, in case they got it in their heads to act up. The boys didn't like to feel self-conscious. They liked plunging into the heart of the action and then let momentum carry them along. At two o'clock sharp, they stormed the gym to begin warm-up stretches and running a few laps. Soon they'd head into their corners for, what I hoped would be, a dazzling display.

The consultant, a sculptor's dream of an athlete, stood inside the door of the gym. Muscular and alert to every move, he was ready to spring into action. I noticed Big Keith gave our newcomer the once over each time he ran past him. Big Keith appeared more and more like a huge cat loping across hunting fields. I didn't like the look of this, but I could only wait and see.

Big Keith was slowing down, muttering something to Jake. Next, he was off hurrying to catch up to little Normie Gossing, whispering an aside to him, too. I sensed trouble brewing but couldn't see what form it might take. Now it was time for the boys to enter their corners. One thing was clear: Big Keith resented the interloper and was trying to hatch something. I took a deep breath and blew the whistle.

"To your corners!"

Off they went, right on signal. Standing in his corner, Big Keith began physical contortions that defied description—the death of calisthenics, maybe. He twisted his body into an odd entanglement of limb and joint, science itself at risk. I caught his eye with an unspoken question in my gaze. Big Keith returned this with a look of his own: he was merely gearing up to do something astounding and needed a little time to mull it around. The boys were taking their cues from him. Instead of moving to the mat for a cascade of tumbles, Big Keith stood nonchalantly against the gym wall, one foot bracing himself. He was the centre of attention. He knew it and, in fact, was savouring the moment.

He did a slow slip-slop over to a mat, centre-stage, and like some huge drugged beast, flopped down. He proceeded to make himself comfortable, on his belly, and, with a wave of his hand in my direction, rolled his eyes and fell into a deep comatose "sleep." The others followed suit.

The consultant, seeing my mortification, sprang into action. Here and there among the boys lying on their mats, he bobbed up and down, trying to encourage at least one of them to get up and demonstrate the skill emphasized that month. I was horrified. This was like a nightmare on the night of the first day of school: I have lost control...the children are scraping each other off the ceiling...I stand there in numb shock...

The consultant carried on. I saw that his attention, though focused on the boys, took in the needs of the other students in their separate activity corners. He demonstrated a brilliant cluster of basketball skills for all, crisply executed in the centre of the gym. Arms and legs akimbo, the boys on the mats watched out of the corners of their eyes. I hoped it wasn't a myth that curiosity excited even sleeping cats to action. Not these lumps of indifference. They scarcely move their eyeballs. If they were being drawn in, they were not about to let it show.

When we got back to the classroom, with the consultant tagging along behind, I was seething. We'd soon to find out that cats, and cats alone, had nine lives. At the classroom door, before taking his leave and sensing my ire, the consultant shared some final words of consolation.

"I've run into this kind of thing before. Your boys were more interested than they let on. Next time, though," he added, "make sure you get them some plush cushions and a couple of cots."

When the boys settled into their desks, they tried to hide their embarrassment. I poured the coals to them. There was no excuse for their shameful behaviour. They had let us all down—themselves, the school and their teacher, not to mention our visitor, their parents, and the community. My frustration threatened to spiral into anger so I sat down at my desk and took some deep breaths.

Sitting there, trying to calm myself, I looked out the window. I was reminded of an incident a few years back when I was a child. Our teacher took us, his classroom of grades one to eight, to the field day in the town of Broadview. I recall this because of the letdown we children gave him. At the last minute, the school officials in town gave him a school yell, which the teacher now brought home to us to practise. He wrote on the board in big letters:

We've got the Go. We've got the Get.

We've got the gang that's got the Pep.

The Pep! The Get!

Yeah-h-h-h—Springside!

He could tell we were mystified. He didn't understand that we were embarrassed for him when he said that we'd be yelling this in town. Our families always insisted that yelling near people was impolite; raising your voice was as crude a behaviour as bragging about yourself. Yet here was our teacher, red in the face, telling us that we would be doing both.

"It's mandatory," he said authoritatively.

He made us practise, showing us how to raise our voices by half a notch until the volume satisfied him. That week, he took us into town and lined us up on the lawn with all the other schools in the district. We had never seen so many rows of children boiling in the sun. They were ready for something, you could tell.

El Cappo rural school, numbering about twelve pupils from grades one to eleven, was first. The boys and girls absolutely and triumphantly yelled at the top of their lungs! We knew them from having played baseball with them as a visiting school. As their guests, we let ourselves be beaten roundly. If our teacher was frustrated then, he was a sight to be seen on this field day. It was our turn to yell.

The megaphone blared out, "Springside Indian Day School!"

Our teacher leapt to our side and loosed a great and sudden shout from his throat! Startled, we accompanied him in a quiet, stately way; given that we had all just sung "God Save the Queen."

"We've got the go," we murmured solemnly. "We've got the get..." By the next line of verse the teacher had lowered the register in his voice, too. He finally caught on, albeit a little late, that it is rudeness itself to yell, especially during respectful occasions involving the Queen. Our teacher displayed a range of emotions as we caught his eye that day, but he remained our good encouraging coach, nonetheless.

Unlike me, that day as I looked from the window back to the boys sitting in their desks. I was still upset with their antics.

There are times when a teacher's righteous indignation gets the better of her, especially when her better judgement is contaminated by emotion and pride. I tried not to overreact in times of conflict. After all, children learn by example that righteous indignation has its place but that rampant emotionality does not. "One must never let negative emotion carry the day." Here they were, again, the aged professors pontificating at my door: "Revenge has no place in the classroom." That day, in front of those boys, I paid no heed.

"Next time I see you trying to cook up something, Keith, I'll make sure you can't sit down for a week. Are there no leaders among the Leos, Normans, and Jakes of this world, not to mention a disappointing Arnold, or two?" I was spluttering. My emotional reaction to the incident was taking away from the boys' need to reflect on their behaviour: "Gentle rebuke leads to introspection," one professor had said along time ago.

The boys knew they were in the wrong. It was obvious they were trying to make up for their behaviour by being extra good, hang-dog expressions and all. We sat at our desks, resigned to an uncertain fate. The room grew silent in the extreme. You could hear yourself think, the proverbial pin drop. The breeze outside brushed against the windowpane. The floor creaked in the hall beyond our door.

I wished we could get back to normal. I should have become a doctor, I mused dejectedly. That way I'd be out fixing bones instead of contemplating ways to break them. Better still, I should have become a dentist and moved down east. In my mind's eye I saw Goldie going about her tasks, her work so crisp, so straightforward, and clinical. Her schedule would anchor her day. Not me. Not my day. I recalled the notes we exchanged on the matter:

Goldie,

I admit your work has its good side though you may not believe I concede this. At least you can depend on your intentions, moment by moment. I can't depend on mine for trying.

Pillar of Effort,

You can't hope to know the difference between intention, per se, and good intentions unless you take a break from teaching. Where children are is bound to be noise and strain. You seem to be shifting gears constantly, poor thing. I control the angle of my instruments as I see fit. I tell you the road is paved...Call me as soon as you receive this, tonight. I mean it, pal.

I was brought back to the present by Norman standing at my elbow, his stringy brown hair a screen across his face. The whole class stopped working on their reading assignment to watch. "We're sorry for acting up. We won't do it again." With that he dove back into his desk. The boys sat ramrod straight, eyes fastened to their books. They wore expressions of scholarly concentration. Big Keith appeared to ponder the meaning of the universe. Jake and Arnold, brows deeply furrowed, worried about the plight of mortal man.

I heaved a sigh, "Well, I suppose nothing is really ever all lost. Confounded rascals, anyway!"

The room filled with laughter. We were back to normal. All that remained now was for the consultant to return and teach us the science of physical education, not to mention the art of self-management. As for pride in my teaching skills, I would save that for a rainy day.

I worried about those boys the year I had them. In times of disagreement, they were quick to throw their jackets to the ground and quick to spot the lay of the land and work the conflict to their personal advantage. They were quick to infect the entire tone of a room. I had to be on my toes, ever on the lookout for a telling sign. I was pretty quick on the draw myself. On occasion, underneath the boys' exterior and that street-wise swagger, I'd catch an odd glimpse of contentment. I savoured those rare moments.

I noticed, too, that toward they end of the year, they had begun to mature. They smiled real smiles, and easily. They didn't nurse grudges or seek revenge beyond a quick decisive exchange of blows when the situation appeared to warrant it. I hoped their true talents would someday come to the fore and last them a lifetime. They seemed to be on their way. As for me, I was beginning to see that the physical self, the mind, and the spirit, though difficult to keep integrated, at times, were most healthy when they worked in harmony. It didn't hurt to have the consultant's help either. On two subsequent visits the consultant taught us safety in the use of the new climbing apparatus. He emphasized good conduct as a feature of sportsmanship, which also raised my hopes as a phys. ed. teacher. Still, I knew I had to continue the search for true knowledge, knowledge to make me a real teacher.

I often wonder how neophyte teachers in the 1980s survived without the direct help of subject area specialists. Knowledge was expanding, the future seemed far less predictable and the curriculum was being drained of relevance. In the 1990s, school-based, peer support strategies were gradually defined. "Teachers teaching teachers" would be the main approach; all teachers would be learning in a continuous cycle about a revised curriculum and its meaning for teaching and learning. Expert help was built into the system and its availability planned for, despite changes in the level of funds.

A new teacher is something like a child on the first day of school. At least that was true for me, in part. Anticipation and excitement sprang up at the mere appearance of things. With paper and pencils, books and desks, there simply had to be a pony prancing somewhere in the wings! Excitement might be dashed, time and again, as a first true glimpse of might and mane failed to manifest itself. It was never that the pony had fled, one sensed at the end of each trying day those first few months, but that a teacher always had so much to learn. I certainly did, and I appreciated help.

For me, the best assistance came with the consultants and peers who valued joy and curiosity, and who didn't care a straw for the mistakes I made. With fellow teachers, in after-school sessions, there came another source of support. Here, a senior teacher would take the lead in a subject, say science or reading, and provide a hands-on demonstration for us. Discussions were lively and practical, with actual known cases in our school for reference. This way, we also discovered new things about the community, the school culture, and the students—all of which assisted our learning and made our extended days worth the effort.

Not long into the future, however, a new curriculum with its redefined and developed instructional objectives and practices would be the focus for all teachers now busier than ever after school, on weekends, and during holidays. With extra study, a teacher grew all the more cognizant of the theory and practice that might help even the toughest of cases among his or her students. I, too, learned to keep an eye out for the pony.

EIGHT.

CAPTIVE TO THE MANNER

FREEDOM OF MOVEMENT IS as important as stability. Stories told by new immigrants to Canada around the banquet table are uniquely interesting and always instructive. Being witness to such stories as a teacher, I found it more possible see into the heart of Canadians, old and new. In daily classroom interaction students would often reveal intimate connections between themselves and their family history, and I would often learn so much more while meeting with parents. From a First Nations teacher's perspective, thoughts of home always carry the hope for room for all at the inn. Stories of Aboriginal people and newcomers to Canada have much in common.

In Canada, since 1867, there were three major waves of immigration populated by different ethnicities, but there were also various policies on immigration with periods marked by certain groups being welcome and others not. The first wave began with the enactment of Canada's homesteading act, the Dominion Lands Act of 1872. An advertising campaign was conducted throughout western Europe and Scandinavia. A huge wave of immigrants arrived in

1885 with the completion of Canada's national CPR railway as an integral part of Sir John A. Macdonald's national policy. This first wave saw the settlement of the West, mainly by people from Great Britain. The second wave, in the 1920s after World War I, showed the arrival of British, American, and later, northern European and central European people. Later, in the Great Depression of the 1930s, Canada welcomed people of wealth.

History shows that not everyone received the same welcome. During World War II, Canadians of German and Japanese origin were deemed enemy aliens and had their property confiscated. In a similar manner, after the war, eastern Europeans who comprised the third wave were required to take certain jobs for two years in places Canada chose to send them. Teachers, doctors, and lawyers from eastern Europe ended up doing manual labour; they also worked in lumber camps and in the mines. By 1967, cultural background became less important and immigrants from developing countries began to arrive in the land of opportunity and security.

The feature of stability in the future continued to draw immigrants largely to Canada's cities. Their number included one of my professors and, a generation later, some of my students. Professor Colter, for example, arrived in Canada soon after World War II, while Diana, a student of mine, arrived in the mid-1960s. When I met Diana, I thought of Professor Colter not only because he was prone to confusing volcanoes with human hearts, but because, like Diana's parents, he came out of war-torn Europe to find a better life. The story of his life was unclear though he hinted at certain darkness. In a class lecture, he said that science, as a subject, included a history of evil as well as good. He told how IQ testing by the Nazis targeted slow learners who had reason to fear for their lives. I imagined him erasing his blackboard for the millionth time. I wondered why I felt aggravated by the doubts about fairness and justice that he raised in my mind. I wanted to believe in a rational and stable social order where the absolutes of goodness reigned. He said he was an immigrant who now wrote his name with a C. "Ks were cruel things in my time," he'd added.

Over the years, I learned much more about what he meant in conversation with my husband. Peter grew up in Berlin, which was bombed heavily during World War II. He witnessed, as a boy, what wars do to people. His mother renounced God the day her screams could not save a young Jewish girl from being beaten in the street before her eyes. Peter said that when community structures are flattened by war, their mediating influence dies and prejudices become weapons for survivors.

I compared this to my parent's situation. Our reserve, with its pastoral and idyllic scenes, was home to the ravages of two world wars, in their life experience. In World War II, my father joined the army and came home a stranger without the means to protect and nurture his family. In the second sense, our family remained in the grip of one of the greatest psychological wars of all time. From the 1800s onward, the systematic censure of a meaningful life continued behind the scenes: this silent war devoured people's names; it consumed culture and language; and it imbibed the essence of self-esteem. Predictably, the "inhabitants" (as textbooks referred to us), now on reserves boxed in by regulations, questioned their worth. Still, in some ways, I felt luckier than Diana.

In my first ten years of life free from institutionalized schooling, I retained an abiding sense of self. There was no school on the reserve during my early formative years. I also escaped removal from my home, unlike my brother Anthony who was forced to attend residential school, far from his family. I was too young to appreciate what this meant. Instead I desperately wanted to learn to read and write, and I begged to go with Anthony to the residential school in Brandon, Manitoba. My parents refused.

It was no wonder they kept me back. Anthony cried when he arrived back home that first Christmas. He told how the older boys would grab the younger ones and rub shoe polish on their genitals as punishment for any number of minor infractions while the headmaster stood by. Sometimes the headmaster helped.

My younger siblings and I became pawns in the people's fight to get a school on the reserve. The resulting ten-year reprieve from forced residential school meant that I was truly fortunate compared to my parents; and far more lucky than my brothers and sisters whose schooling began at an early age. Ever curious and motivated, I could sense liberation no matter the conditions. A wagonload of thunder rolling across the sky; a plane humming its way through the clouds; a poster on the wall at my grandmother's house of the Virgin Mary holding a shining heart of beams in her hands; or the sight of visitors coming from someplace else—these and other phenomena fired my imagination so intensely that it was possible to glimpse horizons beyond the confines of our shrunken boxed-in world. By comparison, though, Diana's world was even more subtly and tightly bound.

What was extraordinary to me, as a young teacher, was that wars affected the rest of a person's life as though he or she might still be living within them. Instability not only coloured a war-affected person's life but it also took a toll on the next generation. Postwar immigrant families and individuals fleeing wars or seeking livelihoods found new homes and economic security. Still, they brought their past with them. Their bodies might be safe from destruction, but their minds suffered even as new challenges had to be met.

DIANA

Diana was in my grade-five classroom. A product of modern times, her life was caught up in her parent's psychological world. I caught a glimpse of this the year she was in my room.

Diana's parents came out of postwar Germany and remembered the war well. Her father worked as a janitor for a string of stores in South Regina. He had been an engineer in pre-war Germany but was not yet proficient enough in English to take up his profession in Canada. Diana's mother was the homemaker. The parents were proud of their daughter and beamed with pleasure whenever I spoke of her academic ability. She was enrolled in piano, dance, and voice—she could sing like a bird. Diana seemed to have everything. Her future, it seemed, was assured.

Diana was a lanky twelve-year-old with a brilliant mind and a sense of order that was amazing. She thought and wrote clearly; she marshalled her facts and substantiated these with numbers in pin-neat rows. But she didn't wish to become a mathematician and be without friends in university, she told me. She wanted to be a model when she grew up. Diana was truly beautiful. She had fine balanced features and a bone structure that was also photogenic. I could well imagine her walking down a runway in some fashion house. Her clear skin, her wide calm gaze, her wonderful smile and graceful movements would capture attention anywhere.

It was a bright mid-December afternoon, just before the Christmas holidays, when Diana's mother phoned the school to ask if I could come over after school, bringing Diana with me, for "torte and kaffee." I said we be there five minutes after last bell. As we stumbled through the glare of snow, Diana confided that her parents really wished to talk about the school's Christmas concert.

Sure enough, they did. We settled down in the living room with its wood trimmed sofa and chairs in stripes of rose, yellow, and magenta, and a regional German cuckoo clock keeping time over the deeply carved piano. White Rosenthal porcelain lay on a black lacquer tray on the coffee table. The aromas of coffee and chocolate cake enticed nose and taste buds. But there was no easing into the conversation. The first utterance, in fact, set the tone.

"Diana won't be singing that solo about the Virgin Mary, or any such person, I'm afraid," the father declared.

He heard that I asked Diana to sing in the school concert.

"Well, then, so..." Mrs. Vogel added, nodding to Diana who left the room, looking heartsick. "We do not wish our Diana to be exposed to corruption and the opium of the people."

Her mother looked over at her husband in his chair, who sat drawing on his pipe. It was obvious she got it mostly right.

"I see..." I replied, not knowing what to make of this. Silence filled the room.

"You have to understand," Mr. Vogel continued as the furrows in his cheeks gathered animation, "we have lived through bombings and terrible things. Things that should never happen. Do you know why?"

I had the sense that this question was more of a command to respond than an invitation to voluntarily take part in the conversation.

"No," I said.

It occurred to me that I might also counter with "Just tell me." I bit my tongue. My own temperament rose in response to the brevity and sharpness of his cultural inflection. The light of my own cultural sensibility told me that the limits of polite exchange had just been ignored: never bark "why" at anybody.

"I'll tell you why," he said.

He glanced at his wife over his coffee cup, "Back home, many Germans got taken in by ideas, ideas that might have lost their power—Poof! just like that—if left to die. But no, they were made strong by religious thinking."

The clock ticked softly. Diana's parents nodded gravely at each other, then at me. I felt bound by hospitality; I was a guest. There would be no changing the subject. It was 4:15 by the clock. The winter sky darkened. We succeeded in pulling our minds onto open terrain, a mental field that was broad, indeed. It demanded definition. Yet I didn't wish to explore the looming topic. A short cut would have to do.

"So Diana shouldn't sing 'Silent Night,'" I said.

I had thought to accompany her on guitar, in honour of the time and circumstance of its composition and presentation.

"For certain, not," Mrs. Vogel confirmed. "Diana must be given the chance for real freedom in her mind. Nobody else's shadow should fall there, for sure."

She'd used the word *schatten* (German for shadow) and was corrected by her husband. Her cheeks turned crimson momentarily and then she continued, "Hitler's mind was bedecked with shadows." She proceeded once again, "That's what you get when you try to force perfection. Don't you think?"

Don't I think. I wasn't sure whether to respond with a decisive yes, or with a faint nod. That was best decided by deference, I sensed, and nodded.

"I'm saddened to think Diana won't be able to do her solo," I said. "She has so many other talents. Destined for the limelight..."

The sense of what I was trying to say was entangled in wool, so unexpected were the twists and turns in our conversation. I studied the little red and green house of the cuckoo clock above the piano.

The visit grew all the more charged now with talk about nations and ideologies and the power of ideas to build and destroy whole countries. The platter of torte, sugar, and cream changed hands with the coffee and spoons amidst my clichés and their quotes from the master thinkers, Marx and Machiavelli, marching side by side. Under pressure of the moment, I couldn't keep straight in my head what I'd read about these thinkers. Like old Professor Colter, I stood swaying in a doorway.

"More than buildings topple when ideas go astray," Diana's father said just as I thought we might consider the holidays as a topic of relief. I was tense with all that war talk and the thought of Diana not singing for us. The cuckoo clock sprang to life. A bird lurched out of the small door and sang its sharp half-hour note. It was 4:30. I thought more time had passed. Then, as if on signal, Diana entered the room and curled up in a chair, a textbook in hand. She smiled as I stood up to leave.

"For certain, good ideas are what people need," Mrs. Vogel said, as I struggled to slip my boots on. "But these better be correct."

Diana's father handed me my scarf. "The human mind is a wonderful thing," he declared, hints of no small accomplishment in his own. "It's the one and only thing we can count on. We must protect it."

I waved to Diana and turned to leave. Walking into the dark of winter, I felt a cold draft stroke my shoulder blades, sending a shiver through my mind. The logic of pure reason provides little solace to principles of the heart. To my ears and sensibilities, the energy, and perhaps the central attitude, in the discussion with Diana's parents seemed like a box of matches, ready to ignite.

As I trudged through the snow, I concentrated on the picture of Diana curled up in her cozy armchair, her sweater pulled up around her neck. I had to find a replacement for my best soloist. Never mind. Diana would play "Jingle Bells" on the piano, for the tableau. Her parents would like that. And true to form, on the night of the concert Diana played her piece with clarity and feeling.

But what really bothered me about Diana was the knowledge that she appeared to have everything, and yet she remained without. Diana's parents cared for her but so strongly that she was never left alone for a minute. Diana said so. It seemed odd, she said, when her classmates complained that they had to wait for their parents to get home after work. When Diana got home after school, one of her parents was always there. I could imagine them hovering over her each day commenting on her every action, though Diana never said so. Diana's complaint of having no personal time alone led me to suspect her parents were there for her but they inhibited her actions according to their fears.

Alas, theirs was a confining love. Her parents wanted Diana to be free, free to grow up to think her own thoughts, free from the constraints of religion, and free from fear. They were doting parents, but their own unresolved fears passed directly into Diana's life and learning. During school hours, Diana worked quietly at her desk, turning out impeccable assignments. She didn't seem to be unhappy, though I sometimes wondered why she rarely, if ever, took childish delight in the many little things that convulsed the less composed girls in the class. Diana would stop her work for a moment, look over at her classmates, smile, and turn back to her work. It was as if she harboured the temperament of a mature lady minding the business at hand. Years later, I had reason to believe that she might also have been biding her time for a dream of escape; she would run away from home.

Adapt and assimilate. These expectations, seen by Canada as ideal for Aboriginal and immigrant peoples, are practical requirements for all Canadians in the new global economy of the second millennium. The pressure to make adjustments in thinking and in behaviour is on the increase for human beings wherever they live.

In the 1960s and 1970s, there was reaction to a domestic economic and social order that seemed unresponsive to values of equality. Anti-authoritarianism and anti-capitalism became more than reactive concepts; they were social movements lead by creative thinkers and young idealists. However, the fervency of the 1960s became dormant at the close of the 1970s as a new generation turned its energies toward building its future while pressures on family life continued.

One spring morning, in 1975, about two years after Diana graduated to the next grade, I was up at the front of the room of my class of grade fives. The sun streamed in from our wall of southeast windows. I turned around and caught sight of little Tara Stills in the front row. The sunlight held her as if creating a photograph. The wide beam of light lit her face and outlined her white blouse with stunning clarity. Tara, a short boxy girl with a cap of black hair combed like a boy's, and a crooked front tooth, sat transformed into an icon, beautiful and rare. Her house key gleamed as it hung like an ornament from a black shoelace tied around her neck. She was a latch-key kid.

Tara was Generation X. She would see the fall of the Berlin Wall, the AIDS epidemic, and the arrival of personal computers. From the 1980s onward, she would be joined by Generation Y now entering the world of communications technologies and media saturation. Increasingly, they would see a hodge-podge of programs attempting to revive passing ideas of structure and stability, and to create fresh ideas about how people should live, and be allowed to live. Tara's world differed from Diana's; however, what they had in common was the childhood belief and feeling that the world was forever the same as they had found it. Yet all around each of them was change.

That sunny morning as the children filed past me out to the playground at recess, I wondered what kinds of changes life on the reserve would go through. Nothing, it seemed had changed there. Years later, while thinking about home on the reserve, it seemed to me that technology had the power to make "Indians" of everyone, inclusive of all Canadians, if they refused to step up and take stock. The parallels I saw were simple. First peoples of the Americas did not migrate to another world; instead, the world migrated to them and changed almost everything. In a similar vein, globalization and the Internet has brought the whole world to Canadian homes. It seems an exciting feast is laid before us; in fact, it is an exacting one. What's more, the menu is sumptuous and varied. A call to the table in the inn of the world shows room for multitudes. The family repast now seems to be taking place in a dining hall next to Beowulf's watch.

Recess was over and as I rose from my chair drinking the last of my cup of coffee, I realized that Diana's parents understood what was troubling about that. Familiar values, once reliable, are challenged by a plurality of perspectives. Parents may certainly try to control the exposure; others to define and prescribe their child's life plan. Diana's did. Mine did. And a professor, by the name of Colter, once said: "The psychological world of a child is a precious thing; a caring teacher takes that as a sacred trust." This was almost the same as saying a teacher's world was never exactly as she might come to expect from one year to the next.

NINE.

WILL I BE ME WHEN I GET THERE?

HOURS OF READING AND OBSERVING PEOPLE'S LIVES unfolding helped me see that the nature of truth is complex. Truth is powerful, I came to see; far more powerful than the awesome schemes and strategies that obfuscators like the influential Machiavelli exploited. While deception often won the day in his time, truth seemed to find its way back over the centuries to re-flood the plain with light and to this day remains present to those who seek it. No matter how a person defines truth, we are all, nonetheless, bound to it. However, it often seemed to me that spiritual truth was harder to define than truths pronounced by science and truth discussed in philosophy, in spite of what one read.

Writers, poets, artists, and other thinkers of the modern age were trying to impart, in understandable ways, that coming generations faced fundamental changes. People who grew up during the 1960s were also caught up in practical pressures. Few had time to confront the new reality in its entirety, to grasp it intellectually well enough to see that the Western world view, as we knew it, was losing its unity and meaning. Yeats forewarned that the world in which we felt at home was in danger of breaking apart. Gertrude Stein said that "in the 20th century nothing is in agreement with anything else." When Rebecca West, another twentieth-century writer, was asked in one of her last interviews to describe the dominant mood of our times, she characterized it as "a desperate search for a pattern."

In the late 1960s, those of us wishing to appear alive and sophisticated delighted in Dadaist images that led to, for example, the surrealist Claes Oldenburg's ceramic sculpture of disembodied hands with red fingernails poised above a crushed typewriter. This iconic image spoke volumes to the concurrent themes of feminism, industrial gridlock, materialism, and personal freedom. The nihilist's cry of "No more masterpieces!" had its appeal. It was difficult to appreciate this as a signal that the avante-garde as a literary and artistic movement was losing a sense of direction. Few had time to imagine, let alone contemplate, the fact that in an expanding global village people would have to seek community all over again; and that in a virtual world that search must also be for meaning itself.

In his book *Once Upon a Time in the West* (2005), Béla Szabados, a Regina philosopher, quotes Ludwig Wittgenstein who prefigured this shift from (seeking) truth to (seeking) meaning in his admission: "How hard I find it is to see what is right in front of my eyes." Szabados writes that "in the 60's and early 70's the programs show concerns with the Gettier-type [as per Edmund Gettier's paper, "Is Justified True Belief Knowledge?"] counter-examples to the traditional theory of knowledge as justified true belief, with topics such as memory, theories of perception and sense data, and the problem of induction, and skepticism in the foreground." He reports that at a meeting of the Canadian Western Philosophical Association at the University of Manitoba in the fall of 1977, one of the topics under discussion was personal identity. Professor Stan Cuthand became the conference's first Aboriginal speaker. Western Canadian philosophy had begun taking its long inheritance of thought and method a step toward exploring "flashpoints in Canadian society and culture." This included exploring cultural diversity, ethnicity, nationalism, and Aboriginal land claims beyond the traditional conceptual analysis available in the social sciences.

The search for meaning (let alone identity) wasn't a topic in any course of study back in teachers college. As a young teacher candidate, however, I became aware of the rift between the natural sciences and the social sciences, or more precisely between two of our courses: science and anthropology. This was evidenced in the behaviour of three fellow students who demonstrated a highly reactive bias for Christian fundamentalist truths as opposed to scientific principle and method. They sought to promote religious thought as the source of all truth and knowledge. Later, I came to appreciate that at the heart of fundamentalism lay the wish to protect certain truths, perhaps particularly, as absolutes. I stood in the path of coming intellectual discord.

My past experience with religion was mixed. Our small reserve was home to the politics of religion where different evangelists and religious institutions vied for durable purchase in the hearts of the people. These activities ultimately divided the integrity of ancient spirituality and created undercurrents of acrimony that moved from one home to another. My father would have none of it.

"Get those Holy Rollers the hell out of here!" he'd order my mother and her sisters, even if the visitors were Jehovah's Witnesses, or priests from the valley.

My siblings and I thought this unfair, because we especially liked one young priest who, whenever our father was gone, drove up from the valley into the yard to take us for short rides in his car. He'd tell us jokes and listen to ours and we'd all laugh. When my father came home unexpectedly one day, he walked up to the priest's battered Model-T. What he said ensured that we never saw our priest friend again. The priest was to take his mind back to the mission where it belonged.

When it came to choice of religion, my father reluctantly chose the United Church. I gleaned from his conversations with my mother that he did not like religions wherein people tried to save you, where they conducted Catholic ritual, and where people believed that Jonah actually lived in a whale. I found when I left home and moved to Regina that I liked going to a church where people sang hymns and didn't speak of seeing lights as though these were actually man-made lanterns. But I wanted to sing in the choir as I had done when I was a student boarding in various United Church members' homes.

After I moved to Regina, Peter and I wanted to get married in a church. We chose Carmichael United Church and then attended services at Knox Metropolitan, a church closer to home, where I then joined the choir. The years I attended, I noticed that people in my adopted church didn't expose one another's beliefs and then take a contradictory stance. In other churches, people openly struggled for religious grounding in almost any topic. However, in my mind, religious truth remained always a little out of reach.

One incident, though, that happened in teachers college seemed to offer a clearer perspective of an underlying issue. And I've hung on to that glimpse of truth for a long time. There was an unruly crowd on the bridge between science and religion.

In Dr. Heinrich's philosophy class, the concept of pure thought in relation to the human condition carried certain terrors for some of the students. It soon became clear to me that I, too, had more than a few things to learn. Like others, I was forced to confront my infatuation with a simple "knowing about," and I needed to work harder for depth of understanding. In one sense, truth meant freeing the mind from the shackles of narrow religious thought. Yet, truth and religion appeared to have so much in common. This apparent conundrum was not a source of easy answers for me.

Even though I paid attention to the ecumenical conferences being held throughout Canada, my ignorance about various religions and their intellectual stances remained practically intact. I listened to the reports in relation to my role as a teacher and the importance of religion in a teacher's life. Teaching, it seemed to me, was grounded in faith—from faith in humanity to faith in the future—and as such was probably pretty close to religious faith. I paid half-hearted attention to discussions on the radio and in the newspaper about religious differences. For the most part, the nature of the dialogue among religious leaders underlined what was common to all religious outlooks—for example, that all religions view the visible world as housed in an invisible world. But nothing scientific defined or proved an overall unity. Scientific truth remained paramount in my mind, as in most minds in the Western world. Yet in future decades, physicists developed theory and found evidence to show that, at the subatomic level, life is connected and that matter and energy appear as the same flow and cycle. There was a lot to sort out in the 1960s and a lot more in later years.

During my teaching career, I often thought about the incident in which Dr. Heinrich could easily have thrashed it out with the fundamentalist pupils, once and for all, when their ideas of truth were threatened and they baited him. He refused to rise to the bait. Instead, he chose quiet acceptance. Like the other professors, he left certain things for us to figure out. His was an introductory class filled from beginning to end with fascinating ideas. However, unlike the others, Dr. Heinrich taught without reference to accepted methods of instruction for teachers. Here, at last, was the opportunity to study humankind without the crutch of sentiment. I experienced an intoxicating sense of my mind being set free.

I was a bit in awe of this unusual professor who stood each day like a short pot-bellied cookstove in the front of the class. There was a convincing innocence in his manner as, day after day, he quietly dislodged our thinking from limited assumptions about time and space in the history of humankind. His description of the rise of the humanoids was startling. He talked about humans as though they had only recently emerged from the world of apes. He questioned that humankind had managed that disengagement, even now. The hairs on my arms bristled with the thought of our narrow escape unto a higher branch of consciousness. Now, as I contemplated Christian salvation in relation to Darwinian Theory, a cool piercing shunt of air rocketed its way through the corridors of yet unknown chambers in my mind.

It was the same cool current I felt but couldn't explain whenever I sat down to read the works of existential philosophers and poets. All that I could discern was that it had something to do with not being made in the image of God. As I listened to Dr. Heinrich, I looked at my fellow classmates with new eyes. Surely table manners signified. This wasn't exactly what some other classmates thought. Merciless truths, I was to discover, could make people upset. It certainly made a few pupils forget their manners that day.

The fundamentalist Christian pupils in Dr. Heinrich's class objected to all references to Darwin, and they decided to take matters into their own hands. It was plain to see that they had held meetings. How else could they hatch a plan so quickly? It happened on the morning that Dr. Heinrich explained the relationship of musculature and dentition to speech development in human beings. True to form, he stood in his spot talking in that characteristic unflappable manner of his. None of us were prepared for the scene that unfolded.

Up from his seat at the back of the room rose an older student. He called out that he wished to share a picture with the good professor, if he might. As he was already making his way up to the front, Dr. Heinrich nodded in agreement. The student marched up to Dr. Heinrich and stopped to unfold a sheet of paper to hold it up under the professor's eyes.

"So, what do you think?" the student demanded.

I glanced round the room to see if anyone could tell me what was going on. Others were doing the same. We were mystified, except for two female students seated in the back row. Their cheeks were aflame. They knew and were ready for something. Dr. Heinrich studied the sheet of paper.

"Yes, it's very picturesque. You have a talent for drawing."

The male student, greatly offended and puffed up with superiority, asked in ringing tones, "Is that all you can say?"

"Yes," Dr. Heinrich replied. "It's very nice."

"Ah, very nice, you say," mocking tones rang out. "Oh, ye of little faith!"

With that, the raging male swept up his books and marched out of the classroom, two triumphant females in tow. The rest of us sat there stunned. Dr. Heinrich hadn't even flinched.

He went on with the lesson as if nothing had happened. He continued to show us how the tight short muscles at the back of the neck of the modern-day ape prevented it from articulating words. It had to do with a seized jaw. He told us this as he physically demonstrated the impediment, in full profile, by pulling the skin at the back of his neck into a bunch and telling us to imagine his mouth packed full of huge teeth. I didn't like the look of it. He didn't look quite human with his hair smoothed flat back and his spectacles halfway down his nose. But the point stayed with me.

After class, a group of us gathered to determine who if anyone knew what the exchange was about. None could tell. Rusty Boulin, ever seeking direct action, insisted we co-operate to get to the bottom of it. We agreed to work in pairs. Eric Jones and I, "the superintendent and all-seeing mascot," were sent off along with the other pairs in search of the offending trio. Eric and I ran smack into them, conferring in the vestibule. Eric walked up and asked if we could take a look at the artwork they had shown Dr. Heinrich. The leader solemnly unfolded a sheet of paper.

We were even more mystified. Here was a simple black ink drawing of a bridge leading up from a garden skyward to white clouds. Across one cloud, a single word was printed: Heaven. The bridge bore a label, too: The True Way. At the base of the garden it said, Home of Mortal Man. This was just half the picture, however. To the right was another garden, this one full of weeds and a bridge broken in half. The broken-down bridge was labelled: Satan's Way: Darwin and the Doomed.

"The professor teaches temptations of the Devil," the male student explained. "This makes the mind ready for sin."

"They preach against God," one of the women vocalized.

Then, the male roared, becoming very red and pompous, "Our school board back home will be hearing about this!"

An ominous note hung in the air. A sense of dark disloyalty and abuse of trust threatened to swamp me with a wave of nausea. I understood that it was all right to disagree, but to go off to one's school board betrayed a deep lack of integrity. What was known was that school boards are often duty bound to respond to complaints. That board would now have to call our college president about our professor and his well-ordered thoughts. That was appalling; there was no rational explanation for such threats. It was now clear to me that even teaching was strung with the nettles of truth and politics.

Darwin and the Doomed. I didn't know whether to laugh or cry. That drawing and the self-important manner of the three students made their bias for blind faith seem terribly childish. Surely, learning implied a willingness to suspend one's beliefs momentarily, if only to explore another perspective with an open mind. No one had asked that the students give up their faith, least of all Dr. Heinrich.

Eric and I rounded up the rest of our search party to let them know. In our judgement, we said, there was a power struggle going on somewhere and those students complaining saw it as a fight between good and evil, between Heaven and Hell, to be exact.

"They don't like what Dr. Heinrich is teaching," Eric said. "And they mean to stop it."

Rusty halted our debate in his typical summary fashion, "To hell with the devil! Let us all stand up for learning."

The remark might have come in handy for Dr. Heinrich.

Doubtlessly, the fundamentalists had stood on guard. But I would not have known the underlying cause. The objective knowledge of science had butted heads with the subjective sincerity of religion, or more to the point, the empiricists had met the transcendentalists head on. In addition to that, the death of God, as an idea, was gaining ground in human consciousness. For the fundamentalist, the question was: could moral authority survive without religious authority?

For days, in the hallways just before class, knots of students debated the meaning of this little drama not knowing that our professors had long experienced the wrangling that we, too, would have to face in our life's chosen work. After all, ideas shape human relations and have done so for centuries and would continue to do so for centuries more. As it turned out, under the unblinking eyes of future-oriented professors in our tiny college, new and intimidating concepts such as evolution, were considered so that knowledge might grow.

To me, the episode lent immediacy to historic times that I had read about and now recognized as a kind of backdrop to an unspoken debate among us student teachers. I thought about the times when both wealth and pageantry bound the popes and the Medici to one another in a powerful coalition. It was not an uncommon association in that time of power-mongering and, as I was to understand, an association that would colour parallel events in our time.

Experience taught that out on the flat expanse of prairie, seeming devoid of opulence and spectacle, powerful forces nonetheless stalked the land, as they had in times past. Plainly, interpersonal tensions mounted as established cultures were dethroned under the pressures of change. Just as astronomy once had great difficulty extricating itself from religious authority in its transition from the geocentric to the heliocentric theory, closer to home, a contradiction in values arose from a plurality of perspectives. For example, the environment-protective stance as embedded in the traditional Aboriginal perspective was bound to clash with industrial thinking.

People reacted to the threat against their sense of truth and reality. In both behaviour and attitude, taboos and certain prejudices came to the fore. For instance, in teachers college in gym period, the fundamentalist students refused to take part in lessons that involved music or dance. They did not believe in square dancing, they said, because dancing had sinful roots. It seemed they were trying to forestall change by paying attention to details of personal conduct that the rest of us considered a straightforward cultural prerogative. At all gatherings and functions in teachers college, whenever there was music and dancing, the three sat at the edge of the dance floor waiting for the polite moment to leave. Not knowing what was at stake for them, I was very critical of the three self- righteous authorities on truth who had behaved so badly. Our little cookstove professor, Dr. Heinrich, on the other hand, managed a fine step and radiated real warmth at such events. He was bound to certain truths it seemed but maybe not necessarily to living them all at once. If the three students had made good on their threat to tattle on our professor, I couldn't tell for looking.

As the years went by, I found myself wondering about Rusty Boulin and Eric Jones. Rusty tended to reject all disquieting notions from the start while his counterpart, Eric, seemed content to stand on the fringes, waiting for answers. What's more, the two were from the same town. At the time, as understudies at college, Rusty hurried to the bedrock of his own counsel, Eric waited, and I promised myself that the day would come when all manner of doubts would flee before the bold mind of tomorrow's teachers. At least, these were the things I wrote a few years later when recalling the crisis of limited knowledge upon the crowded bridge to my wealth-bound friend, Goldie:

Goldie,
People don't fight over truth. They fight over pieces of it. Before I set foot in another classroom, I am going to learn as much as I can about Truth, Faith, Ethics and Justice and all kinds of other things. A teacher should know—and I am determined.

Never mind, Pillar of Society. You'll soon discover that these ideals alone may require the energy of a lifetime...

Even now, Goldie's practical blend of common sense and vision often eluded me, and I would do well to adopt that frame of mind. It seemed her reality had meaning, depth, and existential stability. In her mind, what a person did, big or small, day by day, mattered profoundly. It wasn't so much that she ignored human failings, whether in thought, word, or deed; she simply refused to get into a flap about others. She focused her mind and heart on a role that demanded of her consummate technical skill and specialized knowledge; yet she personally nurtured humour and calmness in her life. I, on the other hand, forever tested the ground I stood on. For me, things were not as they seemed and I often reacted with astonishment and, usually, a sense of trepidation.

TEN.

JUDGING THE PENDULUM'S MOMENTUM

EDUCATION IS AN EVOLVING STRUCTURE, a social construct founded on a system of beliefs that provide for a sense of permanence. Life as a teacher during the 1960s provided a unique opportunity to learn about the profession in a context of societal change. However, this did not mean that teachers were ready for deep fundamental changes.

Most of my fellow teachers, some new to the profession, seemed to think that life had always been a certain way and would remain so. I, however, held the opposite belief about what socio-political structures and policy could, and did, mean in my everyday life. My beliefs in this regard were based on solid experience.

As a fourteen-year-old, before leaving the reserve for good, I railed against a system of social structures that maintained our poverty. I'd pull up a chair at the kitchen table, as my mother and sister went about their chores, to express my outrage that the reserve had no gravelled roads to connect us to the highway that lead south into town and north to the mission in the valley. Reserve houses were made of logs and mud, I pointed out, instead of lumber and brick.

I had more grievances. I condemned the truckloads of berry pickers from town who slammed into our yard in their trucks, without a word of hello, and then stripped our berry bushes bare. I was outraged by the intrusion of land surveyors, too, who stuck ribboned stakes into the ground in front of our house with orders that they not be removed. I'd tell my mother and siblings, and anyone else who would listen, that this was an invasion of our property and that it was wrong-headed of our people to tolerate such behaviour. "It's not the surveyor's land. Kokum said the agreement said only so much off the top."

My mother ignored me at these times. That didn't deter me in the least. "And why should we sit around making lye soap when there's Lux and Ivory in town?"

The minute my mother sensed that I was becoming too loud and provocative she'd draw my attention to the possibility that I was just trying to get out of helping with the house work. And there was usually more than a pinch of truth in that observation.

A decade later, as a teacher who wanted to make a difference, I would attempt to put my observations of life into a practical perspective.

As a beginning, I set out to learn as much as I could about each of my pupils and their parents and what was unique in their lives. I also studied content and method in the subject areas I taught, and I took advantage of school division supports. Still, it would be years before a personal critical perspective would become clear enough for me to embark on any new avenue of personal development.

The 1960s taught that education in our province was a practical system, a system that adjusted itself to the vagaries of an agricultural economy. Good crops were never an assured thing and farmers couldn't depend on a steady cash supply. This reality impacted the financial picture of the province as a whole where the economy seemed, in over-all effect, largely a closed system of circulating income. I wanted to learn more about the realities affecting education but I didn't have enough money to go back to university then. For one thing, Peter and I tried to extend limited resources to my younger siblings who needed a temporary place to stay as they made their way in the world. Canadian laws precluded my financial support in education when I married a non-treaty Indian by taking away my treaty status. In time, I was able to obtain a loan from the provincial government and, over the next two years from 1967 to 1969, I worked a substitute teacher after the completion of each spring semester. I was glad that, in addition to university, there were other ways to try to keep learning.

As a teacher, I kept an eye out for higher order thinking seminars I might attend. I wanted to hear and participate in discussions about how organizations worked and why; but, apparently, organizational thinkers and communications theorists had yet to design informational packages for elementary-school teachers who were mostly female. These teachers rarely had opportunity to hear expert speakers on topics relative to the impact of socio-economic trends and impacts on learning. Male administrators and young male teachers got to go to unique seminars while female teachers in the elementary schools stayed home, you might say, in the classroom. Annual conventions, where any might attend, were limited to inspirational speakers who described trends only in the broadest of terms; they stopped short of describing how these trends drilled down into the lives of parents and children and how teachers might be expected to respond. Experience within the school helped make a good teacher, but it had its limits. To me, and I'm sure to other female teachers, the school often seemed like it had a boundary with an iron gated fence.

Despite our confinement to the school and schoolyard, young female teachers might-still try to judge the nature of change by studying a number of questions independently. From the perspective of my classroom, I observed, as best I could, the lives of pupils and parents in relation to obvious changes reported by the media. On the national scene, one read of families becoming less stable. Divorces were rising. Poverty grew. I was shocked to read of soup kitchens in Canada and in the United States. Were my pupils to ask me, I would not know what to tell them about this phenomenon.

I continued my trips to the public library where I read about global trends and their potential effects on the family and the school. When our daughter was old enough, she came along with me. Peter and I took turns watching her play with the books and toys for young readers-to-be in the children's section while the other read upstairs in the adult section. In addition to the works of social scientists of the day, the library had a good history section, newspapers, and magazines. One could also read reports that tried to make sense of the changes taking place.

Economists, for instance, spoke of the current model of wealth in North America as looking less and less like a triangle with the majority of the poor along its base. The model of the 1960s, they said, would be more of a diamond, with an expanded middle where the majority of people were exposed to the benefits of increasing wealth. It was predicted that, in a few years, the diamond would lose its lustre and begin to contract at its middle. The base of poverty would widen and the middle class would shrink. Over time, the diamond would come to look more like a potato sack, with its belt tightened and raised to the neck. But that was years away, and I knew nothing of its import then.

Instead, awareness of the emerging global society drew my attention away to international interests. Money seemed plentiful and possibilities beckoned everywhere. Momentum was building and it began to exert its pull on individuals. As inertia fell away, lives of ordinary domestic contentment seemed to place drag on the forward thrust and swing of the massive economic pendulum. The potential for personal independence loomed bright on the horizon as global trends made their marks in earnest.

As a teacher who read and then tried to apply what I read about in the classroom, I wished for the opportunity to at least join fellow teachers in round tables to discuss what the futurists pronounced. Fifteen-minute coffee breaks at recess disallowed in-depth discussion of a different world advancing upon us and our work. Hockey and football scores, new car models, and family events were all that comprised the hurried exchanges.

For instance, back in 1964 an article from *Fortune* magazine, "The Boundless Age of the Computer," resounded with Professor Baxter's ominous prediction that humans would one day eat all their food in the form of a single pill once daily. As young teacher candidates, we had laughed and called her a worry wart behind her back. In a review every bit as astounding, Gilbert Bourke's article told of computers and their impact on society:

> All information will be "on-line" or sent into a computer as soon as it is born; the whole operation will be "real time"—that is, data will be processed and fed back into the machine to control each "situation" as it develops the computer's great impact will come at a bad time. The labor force, owing to the wartime baby-boom, is increasing at a net rate of around a million a year, and by the end of the decade will increase by nearly two million a year. Owing to computerized automation and cybernation, the number of blue-collar jobs is likely to increase little if at all; and one has only to look at the computer's successful routine applications to see what it may do to white-collar employment.

Only five years later, in 1969, I read that in twenty years, ordinary individuals would have their own personal computer for about $25,000. At that time, I promised myself that I would sell house and home to get one and hoped my family would understand. The day couldn't come fast enough as far as I was concerned. Peter, little Gabrielle, and I could live in a one-room flat, if we must, and go to the library to keep body and soul together. "All we'd need," I told Peter, "would be a Persian rug, plants, and a big bookshelf full of books." That statement was never put to the test, of course!

In the mid-1960s, the global topics under discussion included global peacekeeping and social development. The Soviet Union and the Americans discussed nuclear weapon disarmament at the same time that ecumenical conferences began considering commonalities across the world's foremost religions. As well, new institutions such as the United Nations came into being. Papal leadership encouraged the re-examination of traditional attitudes of hostility and separateness. Pope Paul VI assured the UN Secretary General, in 1963, that the Holy See:

> ...considers the United Nations as the steadily developing and improving forms of the balanced and unified life of all humanity in its historical and earthly order. The ideologies of those who belong to the United Nations are certainly multiple and diverse, the Catholic Church regards them with due attention. But the convergence of so many peoples, so many races, so many states in a single organization, intended to avert the evils of war and to favour the good things of peace, is a fact which the Holy See considers as corresponding to its concept of humanity.

I couldn't help but compare this new state of the world to life on my reserve, that is, life as "...convergence of so many peoples, so many races, so many states in a single organization..." I fretted about what this lack of a common vision and vocabulary could mean on a larger scale in Canada among competing interests where reserve needs were already marginalized, among many people on a reserve of land in Saskatchewan. Back home, diverse groups such as the Cree, Saulteaux, Assiniboine, Sioux, and the Métis had been brought together by federal authorities to live on our reserve, an act that displaced the integrity and unity of the kinship system and its resources. The competition for scarce resources led to all kinds of stress and trouble. On the reserve people could no longer depend on others' generosity. There was little to share and few means by which to co-operate, establish, and maintain support among the different groups. My sense of insecurity rose once more.

Looking around me, I saw what seemed to be the beginnings of a reckless dismissal of conventional lifestyle and the instability this implied. People seemed bent on giving up old thinking for new insights but in the wrong way. Thinking and perception, themselves, had become objects of study in Saskatchewan. Studies of the effects of LSD, undertaken by local psychologists and university people were a matter of great excitement. Wherever one went, be it to spontaneous house parties or to planned social events, people discussed what a deepened LSD-induced reality could mean. To some, the mind was far more fascinating than had been ever imagined. I, too, read Aldous Huxley's *Doors of Perception* as the basic primer on mind-altering, psychotropic drugs. His book engendered a rising sense that I was likely failing to teach children how to think, let alone how to learn. Like everyone else, I felt tossed about by the turbulence of new ideas that hinted at an unfamiliar world.

These changes in thinking about personal commitment to common middle-class values stressed family life. It seemed that in all the excitement, people had increasing difficulty in distinguishing between personal needs and wants. The choices available to people were far more complex than I could have imagined five years previous. The everyday life of the children I taught was bound to be affected.

I had only half-listened to professorial sermons on moderation. Their unwanted advice was often a topic of discussion among those of us who yearned for sensual surroundings and other refinements. We argued with our professors. The professors, knowing better, warned about materialistic tendencies that might stand in the way of personal development. We countered that our basic intelligence would help us strike a balance between what was important in life and the pursuit of personal riches. It seemed that when the 1929 stock market crashed its effect remained palpable in the minds of our professors who had lived through its aftermath. We sat exchanging solemn nods, unaware that the ease of our remarks had a lot to do with the protective walls surrounding us, walls that had been built by the previous generation. Besides, the familiarity of the cafeteria allowed for the dreaming of dreams and the savouring of youth and its sense of freedom. I saw myself heading down an open road with money in my pocket.

Increasingly, in the mid- to late 1960s, people in our part of the world had money. It was certainly true of the families whose children I taught. In fact, during the boom years, it was possible for white-collar professionals to take several trips abroad and to come home with all sorts of unique objects such as African masks, oriental aromatic oils, jewellery from bazaars in South America, and fashionable clothing from Europe's capital cities. I realized that, as a school teacher, I might never be able to afford the fine Chanel suits and other designer clothes pictured in *Vogue*, which I drooled over. I tried to find solace in the thought that once I accepted the difference between an affinity for self-adornment and that insatiable search for ultimate apparel, I might wear any modest thing and feel elegant and luxurious both. It had to be a state of mind, after all. Yet I could not ignore the call of all the riches of the physical world. Even years later, I remained unconvinced that I could do without a lot of things. The allure of finery remained. Later still, I wanted a dozen or more of those pure jackets made by Giorgio Armani, in addition to the beautiful and stylish dresses designed by Diane von Furstenberg.

As a teacher trying to grow wise through reading, I began to suspect that an unchecked love of fashion might corrupt my soul but only if luxurious clothing became a substitute for self-esteem. It was one thing to wear a flower in one's hair as mere decoration and to paint bold stripes down the length of one's body as in tribal settings seen in *National Geographic*; but, it was quite another thing to be consumed by the lure of silks, ambrosial perfumes, fine lingerie, and wine served in the thinnest crystal. These were the "few things" I wanted, and now.

Often I had to give myself a good shake. Money did not grow on trees. Peter and I had a daughter to bring up, a house and car to pay off, and my student loans to pay back. A fondness for luxury beyond necessity hastens poverty of spirit, I intoned to myself, wondering if I were not beginning to sound like a couple of professors I knew. On top of all this, I was itching to go back to university after my B.A. Peter and I continued to read. Our living room and bedroom had books on the floor, on armchairs, on the sofa, all bookmarked and within immediate reach. Nothing proved all sufficient when the mind wanted to know and when the senses also had their demands. I shared my disquieting thoughts with Goldie:

I wish I knew for certain, Goldie, whether a good life requires that we seek the philosopher's stone instead of material things. So much of what philosophers write seems disconnected from the senses, senses that root people like me to the physical world. I feel the conflict. Perhaps there is nothing to be done but to sacrifice my life to good works. I have just finished reading Schopenhauer's statement that we forfeit three quarters of our lives trying to be like others. This comes as a shock—three-quarters of our lives! Here we are approaching our thirties already. In a few years turning I'll be seventy and maybe someone I won't even recognize. I'll be hard-pressed to explain my forfeiture at Heaven's gate. Still, the senses call.

Pillar of Poverty,
Have no fear. I will recognize you by the punishing lack of coin and mournful expression. I would say to come to your senses but I'm not sure how you'd interpret that. Schopenhauer, whom I have not read, prob-

ably suffered from a lack of good sense, such as what alternative is there? Anyway, one person's hemlock is another's anesthetic. At any rate, you do plan on going back to study. Material things come and go but learning stays.

In teachers college, sobering thoughts about surfeit and identity crowded the mind. Never assume that happiness and riches go hand in hand, the professors said. As untried consumers, we chalked this sentiment up to the Depression, the nine-year drought, and a world war that had wrung the last of youthful optimism out of that lost generation. How sad, we said among ourselves. For us, the world was an open door. At least it was an open classroom door. And for a brief time in my teaching career, I could believe in a world where learners, secure and content in their snug little homes, would never be exposed to anything that interfered with their growing minds and latent gifts. I was to find my worst fears realized in the life of an exceptionally talented boy.

Colin

It became ever so plain that when children are caught up in family breakdown, they begin to behave out of character. It's as though the sun dips behind a dark cloud, there to remain. It took a while for me to see how delicate the ties are that link home and the child to self-esteem.

I remember Colin. His family and he had only recently arrived from England. His father was a doctor and his mother a homemaker. I adored Colin with his sun-yellow hair, his pudgy swagger, and his brilliant wit. He was a perceptive boy, had a nose for characterization and stepped in and out of various characters with effortless fidelity. He didn't especially like to display the entertaining side of himself, but once he cut loose, the boys said, "It could split your gut."

In fact, Colin was a small version of Peter Ustinov, the great Russian-born English actor of considerable proportion, genius, and wit. According to the boys, Colin was a maniac for Ustinov films. He watched these and sought to perfect a repertoire of characters and their peculiarities to the extent that, now in class, everyone was fair game. Whether involved in group work indoors or playing outdoors, Colin suddenly sprang to life as one of us, mannerisms, voice, and little vanities down pat. What's more, he put words in your mouth.

I remember the first time I caught a glimpse of this side of him. At first, I worried that this ruddy-faced chunky boy who seemed so aloof might be fated to be a loner, perhaps by preference. Yet this picture didn't quite fit. Despite his closed-mouthed demeanour, Colin swarmed with friends. He was the first to be picked for team sports and was popular in mixed groups. Ever on automatic alert whenever there was a newcomer to our classroom, I found myself breathing easier. Colin was getting along just fine.

One morning, out of the blue, Colin turned his talents on me. I went over to a group of children who working on a science lesson. Their project was to test various bits of foodstuffs for their fat content by rubbing tiny food samples onto squares of white paper. They were to view these against the light from the window to check for telltale grease stains. They were then to make notes on their observations. The exercise involved recording the information and their ratings in chart form.

Colin led the investigation. This morning, he studied a peanut. He held it up to the light, turning it round and about and commenting on its usefulness to "apes, lemurs, bats, and moles of awesome hue." His characterization of a mad scientist was beyond anything I'd seen in a young boy. His act was electrifying. The effect was more than the accent, more than the staccato movements, more than his facial expressions. In a total, yet subtle, way Colin had become someone else, and I found myself looking into the brilliant blue gaze of a scientist.

"As for the fat content of this specimen," he said, "nothing must be left to guess work."

Absorbed in his character, I didn't realize right away that he was referring to my fat content. The children were beside themselves.

Looking at me, he intoned, "Just grip it. And flip it onto its less burdensome side..."

When the truth of the moment hit me, I burst out laughing. But now Colin was already just Colin. Over the course of the year, his moments of spontaneous characterization enlivened our minds. He was a tonic for everyone and every situation.

Colin's abilities didn't end there. He loved to paint. Indeed, the first of his little watercolours breathed with resplendent hues; it touched the heart. His was a painting of trees along a highway, their filmy branches reaching toward the sky. The composition was simple and yet remarkable in its liveliness. Colin captured the spirit of green and purplish trees reaching up through a shaft of golden light. He had unusual gifts, and such gifts need nurturing. I decided to speak to his parents at the earliest possible moment. If they recognized and supported his talents, he'd go far in their development. He might be a great actor some day or an artist. There was nothing, in fact, he wouldn't be able to accomplish. I was certain of that. On the night of the school's open house I waited for my chance to speak to his parents.

Colin shyly pointed out their arrival in the crowded room. His picture of trees hung on the wall, shown to advantage. But this was not the immediate object of interest to his parents this evening. They stood at the back of the room studying the art work above the lockers, seeming to enjoy what they looked at. I made my way over to them. Dr. Buxton, tall and urbane, remarked that he liked our little studies and would like to know how they were done. I told him that these were our practise portraits.

I explained that the exercise helped children learn how to make portraits, and what went into them.

"The children found colourful full-view faces in magazines and then cut these in half, vertically. Then they use pastels, crayons, and watercolours to duplicate the missing half of the face. The photograph side acts as a guide."

Mrs. Buxton, short and plump like Colin, nodded wisely.

"Which is Colin's?" she asked.

Dr. Buxton scanned the faces. "There it is!"

Colin had managed, as usual, to put a quirk in his portrait. He took half the original photograph of a wide-eyed fashion model, all right, but then he had added a wink to the side under his control. Dr. Buxton burst out laughing.

"He's got it absolutely right. Just look at her. Caught it perfectly," he said.

"Caught what?" Mrs. Buxton, on tiptoe, searched the face.

"That look in her eye—any man would recognize that."

Colin and a group of his pals gathered round.

"Yeah," Colin said, giggling. "Got it from *Playboy*."

Dr. Buxton laughed conspiratorially, joined the boys and asked them to point out their "gals" to him.

Mrs. Buxton looked at me, visibly upset, "Men! Honestly! When will they grow up? It's no wonder little boys..."

A shadow crossed her face. But in a twinkling, she caught herself and began to talk about other things. In fact, we said that we'd set up a meeting to talk about Colin as soon as Dr. Buxton was able to arrange it.

One day, the light went out in Colin's eyes. The crazy little ditties that once filled the air when he was around fell silent. Colin had grown oddly mute and now behaved in a distracted way. This was unusual. I noticed that when it came to his work, he persevered but nothing came easily to him anymore. I knew I should call his parents; there had to be something to his behaviour. The very next day, his mother came to see me. She wasted no time, in fact.

Her outpouring was shocking. Amidst short intakes of breath, she said that she had to find a job now. She had no skills, she said, and very little money. She really couldn't return to England, just now.

"It will be hard on Colin who loves his friends and his school. Colin's father, you see, has gone to South America with his nineteen-year-old secretary. They're to be married. Indeed, they colluded before my very eyes on the dance floor one Saturday night, about a month ago."

I sat blinking at her. At first, I missed the full sense of what she was trying to tell me.

"That girl," she said, choking on her words, "is very pretty, very slim, compared to me. She wore a white dress with cap sleeves. They've gone to live in Buenos Aires. Her dark hair is short with bangs, even now I see."

She sobbed as she sat trying to describe her loss. "He has a new job in a research hospital," she said. "Everything is beyond help. Everything Colin and I have ever known as a family is erased, lost. A letter of explanation, if you can call it that, arrived the other day. It was very brief, very killing, 'I know things will turn out for you and Colin. I need her. Take care then, goodbye.' This is all he wrote, not a word more. Not a single word."

I was shocked and saddened to see Colin's mother, at the end of the day, sitting at our little round table fighting to hold back tears and running arthritis-widened fingers through her lifeless straw hair. She wept in a way that said everything from bitterness to grief would be hers to suffer, to endure alone, for a long, long time.

"I'm so ashamed," she said, "because on top of everything, I'm going through my change of life and it's exceedingly difficult for me to concentrate. This doesn't help when I apply for jobs. Interviews are not going well. Hot flashes make reams of perspiration run down. It's all a horrible confusion!"

As Colin's mother struggled to her feet, ready to go, she patted my arm distractedly, her mind fixed on terrors that awaited her.

"I'll be going, now," she said, and left.

And there it was. Those were the times when it was deemed romantic to think about running away with lovers to islands in the sun. It was then also possible to go and live there, at the drop of a hat, with a nineteen-year-old, at the ripe old age of fifty-five.

Like so many cases of family break-up that came flooding into the classroom those years, Colin and his mother were swept away before the end of term. His mother found a job in Winnipeg, though no one could say exactly how and where Colin was. Their house on their old street was now empty.

As I drove past the deserted place on the way home from school, one evening, I looked at the stand of trees in Colin's yard, their long branches reaching up. They seemed strange yet familiar, somehow. I stopped the car for a closer look. And there they were, Colin's purply green trees! Yes, there was no mistaking. No mistaking that he had painted and transplanted the trees to the open highway in his imagination. These were the very ones he'd transformed with the softest rays of gold and magenta glowing through them. And here I was seeing them exactly as he had seen them, at sundown, when he brought them into his little painting. Colin's trees swayed gently in the empty yard with no eyes but mine to see. They took my breath away and I sat in my car trying to gather up the pieces of my heart.

Back at school, I raged. It wasn't fair that Colin's future was swallowed up by circumstance. All he had needed was time and security for his talents to grow and to shine. It wasn't fair that his mother was cast aside at this time in her life. As a young teacher I struggled with emotions that threatened to overwhelm me.

"You're not a social worker. You are a teacher!" fellow teachers reminded me. It was their way of saying that I had a duty to perform and that I needed to save heart for the others.

I had to admit that, at times like this, my old professors could never have prepared us for certain realities. There is no help for some things. Even boys like Colin had to find their way alone, down long-abandoned trails. The crucial link between home and latent talent, once severed, wrested from children their gifts, maybe forever. In my worst moments, thankfully, a sixth sense said no, not necessarily forever. And I tried to keep that hope alive.

Families began splitting up in growing numbers. *Statistics Canada: Canada Year Book 1976–77* shows that, between 1961 and 1971, the divorces in Canada increased from 7,723 to 29,672. Popular songs about the fountain of youth and freedom, along with the availability of money, made anything seem possible. For so many, these were heady times. The economy was buoyant and some adults yielded to the fantasies that their pocketbooks could now support. One need only be under thirty, or at least behave and think young so as to fit in with the new and rising influential age group. Their freedom found expression everywhere: mini-skirts, long strings of beads, and even bare feet were noticeable at public gatherings. It was also possible to reinvent aspects of the past in convincing new ways. For example, bygone fashions were the rage. Pin-stripe designer suits, granny-gowns, wire-rimmed glasses, and leather boots made their proud wearers secure in the belief that money provided real choices. If anyone was hungry, it was a hunger that was hard to define.

Some parents, too, sought to embrace the possibilities for an unconventional life of personal freedom. For many, there was the sense that this could be accomplished quickly, as a cultural revolution was at hand. A way to begin, for some, was to look the part. Next, was to forget one had obligations, like one's children.

JUSTIN

Clothes make the man. Foibles of the heart do not. Discontent now made its presence known at school. More families were giving way to the best and the worst of times. I have only to think of Justin Whittaker to see the effects.

Justin was courteous by temperament and tense in demeanour. He was the sort of boy who went out of his way to protect the feelings of others, and when you stopped to think about it, his father could have learned a lot from him. The difference in their characters, however, was plain to see.

One day, at school, I began a series of lessons on how to research and write a report. The students were to decide upon a topic they wished to explore. Each child would have a choice, not only to capitalize on each child's individual interest but also to ensure there wouldn't be a mad last-minute scramble for the same few books or encyclopedia. Importantly, each child had an opportunity to take on the challenges of narrowing down a topic. A teacher learned a lot about her pupils' thinking skills and thought processes by observing how each defined solutions to a research challenge or task.

One afternoon shortly thereafter, in library period, Justin's eyes lit up. He walked up and down the rows of books, looking at titles. He came to my table and told me that he wanted to write a report on the diseases of the human body. Could he, please?

"Most certainly," I replied.

He soon assembled a heap of books on his table. In the next period, he gathered even more books and pamphlets. I wondered if he recognized his dilemma, if indeed this was one, and what he would do about it, or did he want my help? I thought it best not to interfere just yet as he was learning more about his broad area of interest just by working through book titles and jacket summaries. In the next period, his pile of books began to dwindle. Back to the shelves they went. Then, one day, he came over to see me.

"There are just too many diseases. It would take me my whole life to write a report on them. I've decided to look at regions of the body."

"Is that helping to narrow down your topic?" I asked.

"I know what I want to about write now," he replied.

"Good, let's see if I can guess. In what region of the body is it?"

He glanced at the girls sitting at my table, engrossed in their reading, and said quietly, "I can't say it out loud. May I whisper it to you?"

I inclined my head and he whispered, "It's in the region of the loins."

"Oh," I said, nodding and trying not to show my amusement. "Good for you, Justin."

Even as he worked, bent over his books, there was strain and nervous tension in his manner. In fact, tension filled his days no matter what he worked on. I tried to imagine him just being a boy playing in the sun, as lines of verse might describe boyhood; but, try as one might, it was impossible to picture Justin Whittaker gamboling in the fields. Something was wrong.

The Whitakers were a good-looking couple; especially, one would have to say, the father. His dark chiselled features were perfectly sculpted for magazine advertisements, no less. The mother, fair colouring and slim figure, was sophistication itself. The bones of her face were strong, yet there was something fragile in her expression that made her seem small and delicate. Both parents dressed elegantly and expensively and shared apparent concern for Justin's progress. It was easy to think of Justin's home life as secure.

According to his schoolmates, Justin's family was wealthy; they had three cars, a sailboat, and a motor home. Mr. Whittaker loved driving his high-powered sports car, the envy of the boys. Mrs. Whittaker had a car of her own and drove the family's station wagon, as well. Theirs was the biggest house on the street, the girls said, and it was from a third floor that Justin waved when he couldn't come out to play. One could see the broad high roof of the Whittaker home from the school.

"They're real strict," the children said. This innocent observation gave no hint that there was trouble at home.

It was hard to imagine Justin ever having to suffer the same embarrassments that the less well off children often had to endure. When the poor and the wealthy share a neighborhood and the same school, as is often the case during the transitional life of a community, less wealthy children take on certain postures to appear financially equal to their classmates. They fib, saying they have lots of skates at home; so many pairs, in fact, that mom mistakenly gave away the last pair that fit. And, yes, they have mittens, fur-lined leather ones, gone missing. Their imagined belongings come encrusted with jewels of every sort. Considering this, and guarding against children having to go without, teachers kept extra skates in a box in the basement just in case someone "forgot" again. The box also held an assortment of mittens, toques, and scarves.

When our class decided to go skating, it was surprising how Justin ran for cover the way he did that wintry day. We were on the point of heading out the door when Justin said he had forgotten to bring his skates. His face was bright red.

"You practically live next door, Justin. Run home and get them. We'll wait," I said.

My assumption was that money took care of all the simple wants in a child's life. This was about to be tested. So was my idea that money could buy protection from the pain of embarrassment.

The air grew tense. Justin's friends exchanged glances. It was taking the boys longer to line up at the door. The girls were in line, eager to leave. The boys nudged Justin and he reddened.

"I don't have any skates," he muttered.

His high colour was the shame of the dispossessed that I had come to recognize. I'd trained myself not to blink an eye and hoped I hadn't at that moment.

"We can fix that," I said. "Go get a pair from the storage room downstairs. Gerald, help him find some. And hurry, boys, we don't want to miss a minute of ice time."

In a minute or two, we were heading outdoors and on our way to the rink. Justin brought along the only pair of skates remaining in the box. We arrived at the rink and he put them on. They were miles too big. He stood up and his skates turned out as his ankles turned in. He pretended not to notice, nor to care, and set off struggling across the ice. Bless his friends; they didn't fly away on their perfectly fitted skates solely intent on their own fun; they didn't leave Justin floundering on his own. Instead, they huddled round, shielding him, lending the lie that Justin Whittaker was a great skater on solid skates. A motley crew crowded in behind him as he made his way to the far side of the rink. Justin, with desperate gaze, struggled out in front as his friends followed along in exaggerated nonchalance. I minded my own business. So did the girls.

Once again, the gracious spirit of children manifested itself in their actions. They protected their wounded, instinctively offering a shield against further discomfort.

Toward mid-June one day, Justin came into the classroom obviously distressed. He went straight to his desk and sat there. His eyes were red; emotion threatened to give him away. I wasn't sure if I should intrude.

"Justin?"

He quickly put his head down on his desk. I glanced at Gerald, his friend who explained, "Tramp got killed in a car accident. He's dead."

This was unthinkable. Tramp, that small yellow mutt who followed Justin to school practically every day, gone? The sight of Tramp sitting in the middle of the playground savouring the breeze and waiting for his master livened many a day for us. The dog seemed to know exactly when to come, too—one hour before final bell. There he'd sit, among the swaying dandelions and tall grasses beside the basketball tarmac, nose pointing south, waiting for Justin, his beloved master.

This was going to be one long sad afternoon. The children and I could do nothing but let Justin feel his grief. We worked quietly at our desks. Two girls got up to place notes on his desk. He scarcely raised his head. Other notes followed. Justin had lost even more than his faithful dog that day, but he and Gerald were not saying anything about it, at least not yet.

A minute before final bell, Gerald came to my desk to say that Justin felt ashamed; his mother sent word with him that she was coming to see me right after school. Justin had asked Gerald to help tell it. Now Gerald stood beside me trying to find the right words.

"Justin's dad left home for good."

Now, Mrs. Whittaker and I sat in the quiet of the room, the children gone for the day.

"It's just as well," she said.

Mrs. Whittaker's pallor was warmed by the soft glow of a pink and butter yellow scarf tied in a bow at her throat. "There was always so much tension in the house," she said. "It was exhausting, really, and there never seemed to be any way out of it."

She paused. "Justin has always been very perceptive, and he felt the tension, even as a toddler. I'm sure of it. He's been so good, never demanding, the man of the family, really." Her gaze was steady. There was sadness without anger there. It was as though she had accepted a certain reality a long time ago.

"Justin's father is not a wicked man, really. It's just that his interests are solely his own and his ambitions lie elsewhere. He doesn't want what Justin and I want and need, snug rooms, the dog, feeling free to be ourselves..."

She gathered up her thoughts, "Our house is more than anyone might wish for. It has charm and beauty. The neighbourhood isn't one I grew up in, however, and I'll be glad to get back to something I understand."

"We'll miss Justin," I said.

Mrs. Whittaker smiled. "We'll be fine. He wakes up in the middle of the night crying...the divorce...His father's presence, such as it was, meant something to him..." Her voice caught in her throat but she smiled and continued, "We'll be fine. My parents are being wonderful about it. And I want to thank you for everything. Justin really looked forward to coming to school, you know. You made him laugh, he said."

After Justin left, a palpable emptiness hung in the room. The empty desk that once held a living breathing boy was a painful reminder. His friend, Gerald, concentrated all the harder on his work. It was as though he sensed a vast hollowness would fill him the minute he stopped working. His face was solemn, his cheeks red with the exertion of trying not to remember. It would begin to seem soon enough, that Tramp, too, had only been a dream.

One midsummer evening, while out for a stroll, I saw Mr. Whittaker and his girlfriend. They looked happy and pleased with themselves. She was a stunning young woman with long blond hair. She wore a pale taupe dress that set off a wonderful tan. There was a look of physical perfection about the two, as if they had just stepped out of the pages of a glamour magazine, a red sports car as a backdrop, the road ahead wide open. It made me think of Justin struggling to narrow down his research topic that one afternoon. Later, he would only say that he did not wish me to see his report. In the end, I did not get to see it.

Throughout my career as a teacher, I found it impossible to intrude on a child's privacy, even if it involved an assignment that had somehow changed into private property. Personal reflections, especially, had a habit of running away and the page would suddenly contain thoughts over which the young writer grew protective. Justin's report might have been like that. It was one he didn't wish to hand in, he said, having completed the report on his chosen body part. I agreed. Justin would have finished his work, I knew. And he would have done it well; his deep sense of courtesy and respect would have seen to it.

I worried about Justin after he left. I hoped his mother and grandparents, between them, might prepare him for a new world. It was a future that was coming closer, though its shape was hard to tell. For now, coming to terms with another broken bond between a father and son was about all I could manage.

Marital bonds were often stretched to the breaking point. There seemed to be a false sense of security at play, as though there was the promise that as long as you fulfilled your individuality, all else would be taken care of, including the next generation. This fallacy in thinking led some people to experiment with their relationships in pursuit of fantasy or personal ideal. Likely, no one intended actual harm. Justin's father, it seemed, merely followed the dream while his mother remained wide awake to the pain of her own, and her son's, reality.

Still, I felt I had little right to stand in complete and utter judgement.

My material excesses, like everyone else's, were a part of a greater struggle, I could see. Despite my protestations for others, I was hardly immune to the lure of worldly goods. Hence, I, too, became a member of the unthinking materialistic bourgeoisie that I had read about. As well, there was the worrisome fact that I was fast approaching maturity with no font of wisdom in sight. Despite growing realities, people of my generation let themselves be led into temptations of all kinds. It seemed few of us gave thought to the implications of our materialistic tendencies, although we like to listen to songs decrying this. I understood the hypocrisy all too well when I met Jamie.

JAMIE

As a teacher, you wonder what becomes of a child who leaves the school before the year is over. Sometimes they send plaintive messages of a longing to return as though from way across a distant sea. Gradually these fade away. Sometimes, nothing is heard. At other times, you wish you knew less about the children who stay; their struggle is so evident. At times, I found myself wishing to be able to teach without feelings. But this was like trying to build up the heart's tolerance for a sea of broken homes. It couldn't be done.

Consider the time a young mother walked out of house and home, leaving her two-week-old baby behind. The abandoned husband came to see me. His face was ravaged with pain and raw with too much smoking. This was Jamie's father. He was in a terrible state of nerves. He sat there, running nicotine-stained fingers through hair that needed washing.

"She left without a word," he said. "She isn't going to come back. She moved in with some guy on Hill Avenue. She took Amy, our daughter. She doesn't want either of our sons. Not Jamie, not the baby. They have a real big house, too. One she always wanted. One I couldn't afford."

We sat in silence. I was appalled. Jamie was only nine years old, a sweet-mannered boy whom anyone would love, and now with a baby to mind. I asked his father how they were going to manage since a baby needs tending, day and night. I knew the father was not in a position to pay a full-time sitter. He was a mechanic who worked long evenings for a second-hand car dealership, after having rid himself of a decrepit farm a couple of years back.

"Jamie and I will bring the baby up. We can do it. Jamie's a good kid," he said. "He's doing good looking after the baby. Gets up nights and feeds him, like the nurse told him. They come around, those nurses. Social Services probably sends them to check on us. Yeah, he's good at changing the baby. Keeps him clean. I try to cook but I don't have time. Jamie and me, we have a system. We eat all our suppers out. Otherwise, it's everyone for himself, except for the baby, of course. I told his mother she could come help with the feeding if she wanted, but she said no dice."

"She doesn't want to help with the baby?"

"Nope, they're off to Europe for a holiday. Main thing is, though, she doesn't want to see the boys. Amy is all she took. She's satisfied, I guess."

"Is there anything I can do for Jamie?"

"Oh, no, just send him home if he's too tired. We've had some rough nights already."

"I'll keep a watch," I promised as he turned to go.

These were anxious times for Jamie, I could tell. Every noon hour, he ran home to make sure the part-time babysitter was looking after his baby brother "the right way." He seemed to take comfort in following what he thought must be the rules for bringing up a baby. Already he was an anxious "parent."

Jamie's difficult situation called to mind a family back home. There, both parents left home. They left an eight-year-old boy and a one-year-old girl in the care of their maternal grandfather. The old man was blind. Eight-year-old Morley told us his secret out in the schoolyard, where the teacher couldn't overhear. He was alone now, he said, because his grandfather had to go to the hospital, for a couple of days. Morley left his baby sister alone and came to school, saying that if he didn't the welfare people might find out and take him and his little sister to jail. His grandfather told him. Everyday now, Morley left a piece of bannock on the floor and water in a jam can for his little sister before he ran to school. I'd see his haunted face across the room during class and I'd watch him race home at recesses to check if the baby was choking on things. In the end, he was found out and he and his little sister were taken away.

Now here was Jamie in difficult circumstances. He would come to school chewing on chocolate bars. Dark circles grew under his eyes, and he began to put on weight around his middle. The fresh energetic boy with glossy hair and big bright eyes was replaced with weight and weariness. Neither he, nor his father, seemed to be following basic rules of good nutrition. But how could they find time to cook, too? Both held down full-time jobs and they were bringing up a baby.

Jamie told me bout the baby's progress, now and then, and how he and his father dealt with things like getting the baby new clothes and a good salve "to keep his bum from getting chapped." As time passed, they seemed to get better at these things. Jamie held his own with his school work now, too, and over the next few months he seemed to get a bounce back in his step. I asked him, one day, how things were going.

"The baby sleeps through the night," he beamed. "If he wakes up, he just gurgles and goes back to sleep. But guess what?"

I couldn't guess. Jamie's eyes shone so very bright—dare one hope his fortunes had changed? Could it be a word from his mother, at last? There was such joy welling up in his face.

"Jamie, I give up," I said, laughing. "What is it, for Heaven's sake?"

"The baby has a tooth," he breathed. "He's teething."

Jamie shone from head to toe! He did everything the nurse told him: gave the baby its drops, rubbed numbing gel on his itching gums, gave him plenty of boiled water to drink, "I held him a lot, and the tooth popped."

So what if his schoolwork slides, I thought to myself, seeing that Jamie's unwavering sense of responsibility was matched by a sense of wonder. These gifts would stay with him. They'd see him through. This I knew.

I wanted to make sure Jamie's final report card, that year, reflected passing grades in everything. His report card should help, not hinder, his progress in the coming years, I reminded myself. Here was a boy who deserved more than the C he had managed to achieve. In fact, this could be a B. And if you really thought about it, I would say to myself, an A. Two more As would hardly be stretching it. Sitting with Jamie's report card open on my desk, I came to the truth of things: this pen of mine was really a boy and his life.

According to his father, Jamie thought only of the baby now and no longer cried for his mother at night when he thought his father was asleep. He was growing up. I saw now, too, that tough times can be endured if the spirit can remain unbowed. Jamie was living proof of that. It followed that this was even more the case when good parenting remained a cornerstone of home and society. A question that loomed large on the horizon: whose responsibility was it to nurture the ties that bind?

The social revolution, full blown or not, had carved out a permanent niche in traditional culture. Every aspect of life seemed touched by the ideal of liberation. Home and family underwent changes as roles began to be redefined. Women, standing for equality at work and in their personal relationships, confronted dogmatic beliefs that seemed based entirely on arbitrary assumption—that she should stay home and keep house, for instance. This added stress in the traditional home. It was impossible to judge, particularly as a young teacher, whether marriages that broke down were destined to survive in the first place because other families flourished through role reversal. From what was said and from what I saw, I drew my own conclusions. Building a stable home life for children was not the main goal for some people, and the current ethos became a useful tool for them. Just maybe, in the case of Justin and Jamie, this was the tip of the iceberg.

ELEVEN.

TRUE NORTH, DUE SOUTH, AND NO COMPASS

IT SEEMED THAT SOME PEOPLE in my chosen profession had the habit of interpreting the master thinkers to their own advantage, as the moment demanded. Even as an untried idealist whose thinking was tempered by a little professional experience, I perceived equivocation and hypocrisy in the affairs of the school system. These were no mild indiscretions either. Each gave me occasion to reflect on my adequacy as a teacher.

A basic tenet of the profession, for example, was that only specialists should teach special subjects. Integrating the visual arts, dance, and drama was one thing, I discovered, but the teaching of music as a subject in its own right required the mastery of musicians, some of whom might also be teachers. Books I read about the topic pointed to the wisdom in this. The school's insistence on specialist consultants bore out this belief. However, I was too naïve to understand that inexperience itself can sometimes help society meet its goals–such an understanding would come with time.

For now, I was left to ponder how to teach any number of subjects well. In my struggle to prepare myself, I searched out the wisdom of more experienced teachers and read scholarly articles in professional journals whenever I could. If, now and again, there proved to be some misinterpretation of scholarly thought by the educational leadership of the day and therefore a threat of its misapplication in the classroom, I would just have to tend to my own lamp. This is what I told myself. Being yet fairly new to the profession, I believed in the existence of master teachers who would always be there to help. The possibility of an unequal compromise between competence and mastery would not be my concern, I thought, and, for a time it I sat on a comfortable perch.

In August 1966 a new principal to our school announced that I would be teaching music in the coming year. In spite of telling him that this would only be my fourth year of teaching, he persisted in slating me to teach this specialty, not full time but hardly only when the spirit moved me. I would teach music to the grade eights, all twenty-eight of them, even if my actual job that year was a grade-six class of twenty-six pupils. No one else was available to teach music, I was told. I would have to carry grade-eight music as a complete subject for the entire year. I couldn't believe my ears. Could it be that in this highly specialized area, anyone might do? What a startling admission for the profession! I found it hard to swallow. Yet, here was one of many such admissions to be made about the true workings of a school division with cost-savings in mind.

"How was I selected?" I asked. I was informed that it was a well-known fact at the board office that I sang in the choir at Knox Metropolitan Church and could hold my own beautifully—this, according to a respected school official who sat in the first pew, directly in front of the choir loft, every Sunday. Although I knew the futility of it, I objected. I countered that I could sing on key, but little more, and that my voice was not altogether clear when hitting the high notes. I agreed that I could hold my own in the alto section but only because the choir was shored up by the genius of our organist, and composer, Mr. Ernest Moore (not to mention Miss Ruby Flexman and Mrs. Olga McKinnon who sang like angels). Besides, I reminded them, Mr. Ken Jenkin's tenor covered all error with arresting beauty. His help wouldn't be available to me in the bright glare of a classroom full of grade-eight pupils.

The principal reminded me that "good teachers are able to teach all subjects equally well" at the elementary level, particularly, where teachers know how to correlate the arts with other subjects. It was an art, he said. The wisdom had much to do with theory, I said, and a teacher ought to teach specialized subjects based on her knowledge and on her talent, and not just at the high-school level either. I was simply not a credible emissary for the gracious territory of the music masters, I argued. You'll do fine, the cheerful smiles of fellow teachers said. So, despite protestation, the field where giants stride was foisted on me.

Another chunk of reality to digest, I thought. I had yet to learn, that in times of wealth, when the arts became a flourishing industry, there seemed to be a great buying and selling of songbooks and musical instruments and the hiring of male teachers, as experts, in the ranks of female elementary-school teachers. My old professor's warning about scarcity and the arts came to mind, a warning as clear as a clashing cymbal. And since there was no help for it, I accepted my situation. I would teach music. Economic realities of the time did not allow otherwise.

Great reluctance is overcome by seeking the greater truth, I told myself. I clung to the hope that some philosopher of enduring good-ness had made that assertion long ago for the benefit of struggling non-specialist teachers like me. Music is like visual art, I told myself. Taking this as a first principle brought some consolation and provided a starting point from which to encourage myself along the journey of teaching so wonderful and fine a subject as music.

A few weeks later, as I considered my plight, other facts rang out loud and clear. Not many teachers liked teaching music. Some gave it short shrift. Others made deals to swap subjects. Many sized up their situa-tion and had talks with the principal to get out of the assignment, while

I was silly enough to think a specialist would be at the school again that year doing justice to music as an important subject. Money or lack thereof was one reason female elementary-school teachers had to teach all of the subjects as best they could. I complained to my confidante, Vania, who taught down the hall from me.

"It appears only high-school teachers have choices," I railed.

Vania shook her head, replying that, in her country, occurrences of this nature had something to do with the war of the sexes. Males won, hands down. This seemed a reality in Regina, we agreed, since most elementary-school teachers were females who taught specialist subjects, as well.

Goldie should know about this, I decided. I wrote to her complaining that it was true that in poor times there was scarcely a single itinerant music teacher in sight for miles around. During times of wealth, I wrote, underlining the word "wealth" with a triple stroke, there were great attempts to give equal status to all subject areas, music included, even at the elementary-school level. In the heat of the moment, I dashed off the point I wished to make. As usual, Goldie's response reflected her singular self-possession in the midst of her own busy life.

Goldie,

Music teachers in elementary schools seem to be female from one end of the city to the other and out into the countryside. High-school teachers have the advantage—not to ignore the theory of male superiority. Word has it that males earn $1,000 more than females for the same work in the system! Recently, when a female colleague took the issue up with the board, her salary was raised by $1,000—but then, so were all the males' salaries. Disparity is blatant, and I am furious!

Pillar of Song,
So sing bass.

I called her that night, as she knew I would, and we had it out. She laughed, saying she had to get my attention on this matter. She pictured me at school, locked away in my classroom, marking books till Heaven knew when. There had been no time to write a decent reply. She said that an option she aimed to pursue was to open her own business as a matter of course. It was an option I didn't want, even if it might be had. In 1968 The Teachers' Salary Agreement Act was passed. It would establish area bargaining for teachers and trustees. But even years later, gender-based inequality in take-home pay prevailed to a certain extent.

In 1970 The Royal Commission on the Status of Women Report showed that women now rejected the stereotype that, as wives and mothers, they were dependent on their husband's incomes. Years later, still, women activists who were able to gain access to careers in law, medicine, and academia soon confronted the "glass ceiling." The salary grid of organized work in the 1990s gave clear evidence of intended equality, but factors of interpretation, such as experience, qualifications, educational level, and social background, still permitted a varied and unfair application of policy.

No sense of progress was available to me as a beginning teacher. If I loved my profession, I hoped to honour it and to exact its principles. I faithfully paid my dues to the Regina Public School Teachers Association. However, reality said, at the time, that I was stuck with having to teach grade-eight music even though that year I had a regular grade six class to teach all subjects. A few weeks later, I inquired of the board whether a general music consultant had been hired and if there were plans to hold any workshops. I was told that, in time, a music consultant would be available. Time, however, waits for no one. The children were practically at the door and there was no one to lend a hand. In desperation, when school began, I brought my guitar to school and taught the folksongs I knew. These were mainly old French and English ballads of love and courtly manners and patriotism that I had learned in my spare time, as a personal hobby, ballads I now hoped the children would like as much as I did. Songs like "Mary Hamilton," "Barbara Allen," "Plasir d'Amour," and "Un Canadien Errant" bared our hearts to the ages. My repertoire, although large enough for a few lessons in a row half an hour at a time, was much too limited to think in terms the requirements of an entire year of grade-eight curriculum. This was worrying, to say the least. I worried about what to do when my ballads and folksongs ran out.

I hunted for contemporary songs that I might learn and then teach. Pop music for preteens hadn't come into being yet, at least not in a big way. I listened for new songs on the radio as I drove back and forth to school. Songs of the 1960s filled the airwaves but many dwelt on the subject of personal alienation. My pupils were practically brand new to life and wouldn't be able to identify with these. Besides, the subtext of many songs seemed to say that society was unable to find solace in the forms of beauty that existed naturally in the world. I thought that children ought to see and know beauty before they sang of loss and alienation.

As I listened to popular music with renewed purpose, it pained me to think that, in contrast to many artists who sang of an increasingly impersonal world, my concerns were basically conservative. Now, I recall a question: what did we prefer, a lifetime of intellectual riches or material wealth? The quick answer was "Intellectual riches, of course." My final answer was "Both." This after confirming in my own mind that poverty makes materialists of us all. I had escaped a world where no money meant no books. The original question was rooted in ideal middle-class circumstances, which had not been part of my childhood experience.

Sometimes, I wondered if I should just give up and abandon everything in pursuit of the so-called greater truths of the modern age. Apparently some of these were to be found only through the medium of drugs. A lot of the music pointed to that. But it frightened me to think that I might have to give up my mind, or at least control of it, for truth. I steered clear of songs for my little pupils that led the mind on "trips" that were "far out."

I clung to the idea that the clearest and brightest vision of the future was attainable through the ordinary pursuits of work and recreation. Even so, I found myself doubting the power of the intellect as the sole guide to modern thought, so strong was the messaging of the day. Current writers and thinkers, like the influential Aldous Huxley and the popular Timothy Leary, had me on a string. After all, the times we lived in, as I saw it, had as precursors intellectual giants like Francis Bacon who painted the "Man in the Box," an image that captured the horror of the cornered intellect and spirit, an image that always made me shiver with cold. Samuel Beckett had kept us all *Waiting for Godot*. Did psychedelic reality really lead to greater truth?

As an antidote to this personal crisis, I read the works of German existential writers who tended to return the mind to concrete reality no matter how chilling a picture they painted. English language poets, like Emily Dickenson, William Butler Yeats, and T.S. Eliot, pointed to the human being as the author of his or her own humanity, often without reference to direct concepts of God. Hart Crane, in his poem "The Broken Tower," exemplifies the attitude:

And so it was I entered the broken world
To trace the visionary company of love, its voice
An instant to the wind (I know not whither hurled)
But not for long to hold each desperate choice.

I felt the power of what seemed a perverse sense of personal choice and control. My prayer was that I be allowed to study in a bright broad light. Part of me was afraid to grow discouraged, to give up teaching and to join the hippies who claimed to live the reality reflected in the songs written and sung by Buffy Sainte-Marie, Bob Dylan, Leonard Cohen, and other artists who clearly wanted to bring an end to modern plagues such as war. Horrifying pictures of a ravaged Vietnam were everywhere. The hippies' world of truth and peace seemed only a step away. Yet part of the hippy reality consisted of an internal psychological world brought on by drugs, a world wherein brambles grew in deserts of diminished choice. I lacked the courage to leave the confines of my own mind, such as it was. Besides, I didn't think I looked like me with my hair down, in a long floral dress with a long string of beads. A guitar might have completed the picture. But my guitar went well enough with my regular teacher's apparel. For me, enlightenment would remain not only a goal, but a life struggle.

Everywhere, in the 1960s and into the 1970s, there grew a deep longing for a new vision and identity. Flowers versus wars, free love versus monogamy, personal belief versus conventional thought. I couldn't say for certain whether values were to be found within, or without. The songs of the balladeers of old hinted that these dwelt within the heart. However, I could see that, in contrast to our world, the musicians of old had lived sequestered lives. Feeling perilously close to the edge of an abyss, I stayed with the time-worn ballads of universal themes of stability to teach in the classroom, as long as these lasted.

I tried not to think that ours was a world in which we humans might assume that moral codes and ethical precepts can be easily abandoned in favour of a false idea of freedom. I did not wish to dwell on the fact that the roots of identity grow slowly over time; they are not deliberately forged at some new cultural foundry. In all of this, I pondered what music I would teach once my repertoire of ballads was exhausted.

LITTLE MUSICIANS

I prepared myself to teach music to my regular class as best I could. After school and on weekends, I studied the mechanics of the auto harp, the five-line musical blackboard, and the dust-covered boxes of instruments that I found stashed behind floor-hockey nets in the corner of the equipment closet in the school gym. I pulled the boxes out of their hiding place, dusted off each instrument, and subjected this treasure trove to exacting scrutiny. Hauling everything to my classroom down the hall, after school, I practised tapping and strumming rhythms. I listened to the timbre as I tried to figure out the characteristics and possibilities of each instrument. I wished the janitor would quit stopping by my classroom to express feigned sympathy for the new teacher who refused to admit that all the stamping, beating, and humming in the world would not turn an ordinary person into a musician, least of all for tomorrow's class.

"Let me know if there's anything I can do to help," he said the first time he stopped by. He shook his head as he swished his broom down the hall. "That nasty old Batch and Bee-thoven."

I taught myself the rudiments of each small instrument. In time, the children and I devised ways to learn these together and to synchronize our efforts. Within weeks, we became a band and a chorus. I taught the children how to play the recorder first, using this as a way to introduce the basics of music and to encourage the reading of music, and of course, the work of practising it. During noon hours, I drew musical bars on the blackboard and numbered these. Through the use of various symbols, I indicated where the instruments, including the percussion instruments, came in the melodic line. I taught each child the little I knew of the instruments that interested them, and in turn they taught others. Cindy learned the rudiments of the drum and she taught her classmates what she knew. Soon, Brad learned more about the cymbals and taught them to Bobby. Then, Mika tried out the possibilities of the auto harp and taught others.

In addition to listening to recordings of the past and to modern composers, I found no better way to teach the love of music than to let the children experiment and learn from each other. Our classroom windowsills and counters were covered in music sheets and instruments. The "rule" was that a student might arise from his seat anytime during the course of the day to figure out, or to practise, a piece of music using an instrument of choice. A consideration was that each student had to finish his or her regular class assignments first. Often, two or three children would get up from their seats; on signal with guitar, autoharp, and recorder they would fill our working hour with sweet melodic pieces. Fellow teachers thought my approach to music instruction cumbersome since it was not neatly scheduled and, hence, fundamentally distracting. But the children and I decided it could be done, and with regard for others. Here was no exaggeration. It was all fabulous music to us.

By the end of term, the children grew so confident in their abilities that we decided to put on a concert for the whole school. I was well into my fourth year of teaching at this point. Each of my 1966 pupils was either singing or playing an instrument in a solo, a duet, or in a group. We waited for that day with great anticipation. We were bold. We even asked Kirsten to bring her bagpipes. She would play a piece of music on her own. She agreed to prepare her piece at home.

Now, after practising at school and at home, our musical solos, duets, trios, and other group combos were ready. The big day finally arrived.

The whole school sat in rows on the floor in the cool of the gym this hot June afternoon; grade eights in the back row, kindergarten and grade ones, in front. Paul and Daniel, mops of dark hair and confident smiles, walked to the front of the assembly. Their performance would set the tone. The boys would sing to their own accompaniment on guitars they had learned to play themselves. I held my breath. They began their duet, a folksong called "Hush-a-Bye My Little Baby." Their voices blended perfectly; the twins looked as though they'd been performing all their lives. They captured their audience. The tone of the room was warm and focused. A loud burst of applause followed their singing.

Our master of ceremonies, a volunteer from our classroom, grinned from ear to ear. She nodded to me at the back of the room, and I motioned to the class that they were to take their position in the front of the room. So now the class sang a hearty rendition of "In the Merry Month of June." More applause! Then groups of two or three students played recorders and harpsichord pieces from music books that containing simplified versions of the old master composers. This was followed by a class orchestral piece in chorus with marimbas and other percussion instruments. Our audience sat smiling in obvious enjoyment.

Then, without giving me a moment to collect my thoughts, Janet gave Kirsten, who was waiting in the hall, the signal to fill her bagpipes with air. Kirsten stood tall in her tartans and began. The start-up alone of the bagpipe, I was to find, clatters to the very ends of the earth, scattering huge hippos in its wake. We were on a course and there was no turning back. I grossly underestimated the volume of the bagpipes indoors, in the basement, where solid bare walls amplify sound so amply.

I motioned Janet to close the door behind Kirsten the second she entered the room, thinking that her playing out in the hall awaiting her signal to enter was likely disturbing the principal on the phone upstairs. Janet mistook my signal to mean shut the door, period, and she slammed it shut in Kirsten's face.

"I mean, after she comes in!" I whispered so fiercely that the whole room heard and burst into laughter.

Janet opened the door and Kirsten strode in, her bagpipes scrolling out a bandwagon of rousing sound with hair-raising trills. That sound, I knew, called a Scotsman to arms as surely as its melodic line soothed his ire. Kirsten's arm squeezed the bag and her tiny fingers flew up and down the length of the pipe. She finished her piece brilliantly, her little face red with exertion. But the bagpipe's final lethal tone died away all too slowly, like a lone cow tangled on a piece of receding pasture. Silence filled the room. I grew concerned that Kirsten's bagpipes had erased from our minds all the peace and joy our concert had created, thus far. The sound stirred wide-awake sensations in every living thing. I motioned the children to stand and take a bow. I wanted to rush over to Kirsten and give her a big hug.

The room burst into applause. There were whistles and loud hurrahs. The teachers gave us a standing ovation. At the back of the room, the janitor gave us the victory sign. I was glad he came as he had only recently ceased teasing me when I'd arrive at school right after supper, to figure out another aspect of this thing called teaching music. He'd quit referring to my study time as "Batch and Botch Night" and now he only swished his mop dexterously as he passed by my door. I gave him the thumbs up in return. Somewhere between the bagpipes and the hippos and the solemn pride of the children bowing to thunderous applause, we glimpsed mastery in ourselves.

Over time, I came to appreciate that each subject—be it music or physical education—captured and helped to develop an excitement for learning. It depended on whether the teacher knew enough about the subject and its subject matter to bring out its features in interesting ways for children. Professor Delmont, our physical education instructor, had known what he was talking about. So had our music professor, Professor O'Connell.

Dear, kind Professor O'Connell! He was forever insisting that music brings the breath of life to learning. "It lightens the heart, focuses the mind, and connects the soul to the mystery of being," he'd said. There, in the midst of his tips and techniques, his lengths of soda straws, combs and papers and variously filled pop bottles, all laid out on the table as substitute for real musical instruments, I saw how strongly he felt about this. "The world of the classroom doesn't abound in material riches," he explained with eyes glistening, his face flushed with great and sudden feeling, unmistakable under the fluorescent glare of the classroom lights. "But you must teach to the ideal anyway."

"Never short-change any type of music, be it Mozart, American Indian, or Gershwin," he said. "Wherever there are children, there should be music. Creation itself has rhythmical significance that brims with profound meaning. Humanity responds deeply to music and will do so for all time."

I saw that his tears were for the music he played, that day, for example, a Negro spiritual about home and dreams of freedom. There was more than the beauty of the music that brought tears to Professor O'Connell's eyes. I listened carefully for what he said he loved so that I, too, might sense the grief for lost liberty and lost democracy remembered by black Canadians. I, too, might sense stories behind the South American celebratory songs and rhythms. I, too, could almost imagine myself wandering along the Andes Mountains looking down: dwellings hug the valley floors; jungles blanket the hills; deep green rivers lace their way around deep rooted trees; Mayans read the stars. I wished to travel there, to find out things for myself, instead of sitting here in class with a professor who tried to impart thoughts and feelings too big for young hearts. My own tears threatened, sometimes, but I was never sure for what.

True teacher that he was, Professor O'Connell played his vast record collection for us each and every period. It was as though he knew something we could not. When we went to say our goodbyes at the end of the year he said, "Where there is music, poverty is only a state of mind. Let us hope for at least one musician on your school board."

We paid no mind. Somebody else would teach music. We were going to teach only teachable subjects, the subjects we were most comfortable with. This was a new age after all, an age of plenty. Professor O'Connell was a son of the Depression. He told how his parents couldn't afford a radio, let alone send him to high school.

As young idealists, my classmates and I were certain that we had been born into perfect times, particularly after we added up the tales of struggle that haunted the old generation. Theirs was an inheritance of dust, thirst, and unending anxiety. Theirs was the aftermath of war, of unemployment, of rural isolation. In contrast, we had hope, we had ourselves, and we had grit.

Soon, we would have to re-visit our beliefs, once we saw how it really was.

Professor O'Connell had been trying to make his protégés understand that even in the schools of our day in the 1960s, wealth was not distributed equally. It took me about ten years of actual teaching in the system to see that some urban schools had more financial resources than some rural schools. There were hints of a provincial North–South imbalance. In addition, the notion that men made higher salaries than women was soon to become evident. I gradually came to realize that it was going to take a tough-minded generation of professionals to insist on equal pay for equal work with equitable conditions right across the system. That was to be the hard work of the 1970s and beyond.

Do more with less! There were inequalities to be set aright. Over time, the tenacity of the few won us music consultants, musical instruments, and record players throughout the system. Professor O'Connell would have been pleased.

Miracles also occurred in rural Saskatchewan. Children won music and drama festivals throughout the province, despite circumstances. Also, despite the lack of teaching materials, new research said children learned better if they studied and played a musical instrument. The wonder was that I could teach music, too, after a fashion, at least to the extent that it pleased me to no end that the children actually enjoyed their lessons—with apologies to Bach and Beethoven. There was no doubt in my mind that music prompted learning beyond passive appreciation. That was just fine by me. Apparently, there were no musicians on the school board when I was struggling with teaching the subject, a notion that would have come as no surprise to Professor O'Connell.

In fairness, in times of disparity, school boards are left with bad choices. Biased decisions in resource allocation result in negative bias against female teachers or, as I witnessed, against the arts. School board members could not know the extent to which learning is mediated by the arts. For one thing, most are not trained in the field. Importantly, the sciences then were in the very early stages of brain studies and the theoretical understandings of, for example, neurobiologists regarding left brain and right brain thinking were not yet linked to educational thought about how we learn. It wasn't obvious either, apparently, that the arts actually nurture the sciences, and vice versa. Each field invigorates the other's domain of thought by certain qualities of intuition and perception that break the grip of traditional mono-mindedness. This, in turn, sharpens thinking and strengthens the interpretation of reality. DaVinci's artistic and scientific inventions speak to this.

Where there is a scarcity of resources, children can become society's victims. Today, in the second millennium, the appearance of socially sensitive programs in "community schools" owes much to school board members who understand how deeply their decisions affect the minds of succeeding generations. As a young teacher, I knew little of this struggle. I only saw that a child like Rico and his once struggling family might benefit from a little extra help.

Rico

When Rico was my student, I came to realize that society's hypocrisy comes in different disguises. This became most evident when Rico got the strap. I found out more about these disguises when I met Rico; and, later that same year, Ryan. Just as there are have-not schools, there are have-not families, despite all appearances.

Rico's parents were trying to establish a future for their son and daughter. However, the family's unique circumstances and their anxiety about resources compelled them to put the real needs of the children second. Newly immigrated, they no longer had the support of their extended family left behind in the old country. In their country of origin, Rico's parents had worked day and night to earn a living, but there was always someone at home to mind the children. Here, in Canada, there was no such help. Arrangements had to be worked out, all of which drained away more money than the family could spare. Things were not going well for Rico, that year. It seemed Rico's parents had all but forgotten about him.

He came to school that first day with his mother and aunt, the only other member of the family to accompany them to Canada. When I first saw him, Rico gave the impression of a nine-year-old boy who had been held upside down in a barrel of water, scrubbed, dipped once again, and combed—hard. His face had dried to a shiny tightness and his rooster tail remained determined. What bothered me about Rico, a regular kind of boy in every other respect, was his deep sense of resignation. There was a deadness to the air around him. Maybe he had not had a good night's sleep. He was pale. There was a lost expression on his face.

The three of them came into the room, a little girl trailing behind. Rico was pushed in ahead of the women, unwillingly it appeared, from the way he stood, his mouth tight, a small fist gripping an imaginary object. I smiled. He looked away. In contrast, his little sister Angelina radiated pure energy. Her ponytail flew this way and that as she surveyed the room with big blue eyes. The women spoke of Angelina's many friends and claimed that Rico was getting ready to make new friends, too. Rico wanted to leave, I could tell.

His Aunt Celina was quick to spot his tension, "Rico, you smile for your teacher. What she gonna think?"

Then it was his mother, "Rico, listen to Celina. She your aunt."

Rico's mother looked at me, her grey-blue eyes making me think of Rico's. "He not good. Angelina, she good."

The aunt nodded in agreement and Angelina grinned. They spoke in broken English, their words carrying their concern for the reality of the boy under discussion. I changed the topic to the family itself, though I learned little more by this approach. Rico, who stood quietly, kept out of his family's critical eye for the time being. At the end of the visit, he managed a bit of a smile for me. It had been a good visit for all but Rico.

In subsequent days, I kept an eye out for signs of playfulness in him. There were none. Instead, he got into squabbles when out of sight on the playground; these sometimes turned into fist fights. The playground supervisor grew impatient. There was bound to be trouble.

I couldn't put my finger on what was bothering Rico. He averted his eyes when spoken to and refused to respond to my questions. I noticed that he came to school wearing the same torn blue jeans and blue-jean jacket, day after day, his little rooster tail still standing on end. His face was clean but the rest of him had begun to take on a greyish hue and an even more tired demeanour. Surely his mother must have noticed. But she still hadn't made him change his clothes and get at that neck of his.

"If there's any trouble with that Enrico boy," the vice-principal said on more than one occasion, "let me know. He'll find out a thing or two."

Well now, even the grown-ups were intimidated. Talk had got around. Still, Rico only shrugged his shoulders and shook his head. No, he would say, there was no trouble. No, he had no problems with anyone.

"Rico, if you have any trouble let me know, all right?" And he'd nod.

It was clear that Rico wasn't working up to his potential either. He was as bright as anyone but he put no real effort into his work, and he began failing. Finally, I called his mother. Could we talk about Rico and his schoolwork? She came the same day.

She had dyed her hair. It was now a shade of red, something like carrot curls in a vat of wine. Delighted, she laughed at my description. Dying one's hair was not done in her part of the old country. We laughed again, enjoying our notions of modern women. Rico, who came with her, at her insistence, looked pained by the interchange. Our discussion was frank. Rico needed a good night's rest and a good breakfast, I began. He needed to ask for help when there was something he didn't understand. I'd help him with any problem as best I could but I had to know where to begin. Rico's mother said that he was learning lots at the restaurant. Rico said nothing to this. And when he and his mother left, I sensed he was as unconvinced as ever.

The weeks flew by. Rico didn't change, in fact he only looked more unkempt and tired. Dark circles hung beneath his grey-blue eyes. Something had to be done. I shared my concerns with his sister's teacher down the hall; she might know more from Angelina who was far more outgoing than Rico and far more talkative. According to Angelina's teacher, Rico and his little sister neither slept nor ate at home. It appeared the family didn't own their own home outright. They sublet the house to an older couple who took turns sharing the space with Rico's aunt. So on certain days, a storage space at the back of the restaurant was home for Rico. His parents tried to make a go of things and Rico helped out in their restaurant. There was no time for homework. There was no time for play.

One day, things took a turn for the worse. Little Angelina ran into the school during recess screaming for her teacher to come outside. Rico was going to cut a boy! Teachers in the staff room rushed to the playground. It was true. Rico had a kitchen knife and was circling another boy with it. By the time we got to the scene the scuffle was over. The vice-principal intervened, just in time, but he was furious. There was to be absolutely no violence on his playground, he yelled. Rico appeared unmoved.

That day marked the first time I witnessed a strapping. It was my duty to witness this. The vice-principal was thorough, "No. Don't cup your hands, Enrico. Hold them flat. Any hairs or sand? No? Right."

The strap cracked through the air. There were to be three on each hand. I braced myself. Rico didn't move or flinch. His eyes were steady. Blank, really. He held out his hands, small and callused. Crack! Rico held steady. Crack! I vowed to myself, then, that I would never mete out punishment in this calm ritualistic way. No, and no again. I might say terrible things, scream, and swear outright—a boy would understand that. But there was something about making a study of small hands, about turning them over in the light of the principal's office, before doing this violence to them that was stark beyond belief. Crack!

My mind fled; it was all there under my nose: the witnessing, the bright lights, and the scrupulous care when laying on the strap. Crack! My thoughts struggled to give meaning to what I was seeing: this is surely a technical matter...legal protection...observable damage...children not withstanding...Crack!

I had no real idea what I was trying to think. Little Rico walked stiffly out the door and the vice-principal asked me the question, "Are you all right?"

"What?"

"Are you all right? You should go sit in the office for a while, you're pale."

"I'm all right," I said.

While trying to recall Rico's face, I knew I was not all right. But I couldn't put the numbness I felt into words. For certain, Rico was a have-not boy. Here, too, was an authority figure making sure that a value of society held firm. But I was having difficulty remembering what it was.

After Rico's strapping, I found myself trying to think more deeply about materialistic lives. What was truly necessary to have led a good life? Tolstoy had given everything away, including his study and its entire contents. I saw pictures of his remarkable room, large and amply furnished in the grand style, bearing a heavy oak desk that I coveted. Potted plants with huge fronds stood in the corner of that room. Most telling, though, was a photograph of him, in a flowing white beard and gown, a prodigal son leaning on a cane, on the road to somewhere else. The hippies of our day would admire that and would believe that they, too, had relinquished materialism on their way to a better world. But I could not believe the claims counted where drugs could be a substitute for almost anything, including Tolstoy's study. I was ashamed to think that I wanted so very many things from the tangible world and saw no end to my wants. Tolstoy's desk would only be a beginning. And there were other confusions. It took good money to dress up and, increasingly as the years sped by, the same amount of money to dress down. Designer jeans competed with ordinary jeans in the market place. Society's pursuit of its vanities lacked dignity in the light of Rico's immediate needs. It was going to take time to understand Rico's story, and others like his.

Throughout my teaching career, I tried to recall when, and if, we were told outright in teachers college that, in our world of plenty, children suffered cruelty and isolation, not to mention humiliation and misfortune. Our English professor once told us about three-year-old chimney sweeps in industrial London immortalized in William Blake's poetry. Soot-covered, but otherwise naked toddlers, reportedly, were prodded with pointed sticks sharp enough and long enough to force the child to climb up through dark narrow smothery interiors of chimneys all over London. Industrial Britain was hard on its children, he said. Its chimney sweeps had to be toddlers, he claimed, because slightly older children were already too big to get through the chimney openings, prod or not. The toddlers worked the hours before dawn.

"You'll be relieved to know that England outlawed child labour and that children are now free there," our professor said.

I was relieved to know that I would never ever have to hear little voices calling in the streets, at dawn, as Blake had. "Weep! Weep!" our professor mimicked their voices for us. "They were just too young to say 'sweep.'"

I couldn't look at him when he repeated the word "weep" again in that high little voice because I could see how a child's parched mouth might look like a tiny black and dying rose.

A decade into teaching I was aware of dangers on all sides. I saw that the work of teaching most certainly had to include the concerns of social workers. But I obtained few satisfactory answers from my colleagues as to the extent of my role and responsibility and where to go for guidance. More and more, the worth of having at least one parent at home to bring up babies and preschoolers was overshadowed by the economic reality that both parents had to work outside the home in order to maintain the identical lifestyle that had been enjoyed in the 1950s. There was scarcely anyone left now to attend to the needs of the child at home.

I wrote to Goldie telling her of discussions increasing among my fellow teachers regarding our common struggle to keep the duties of teaching and the demands of social work and parental guidance separate and apart.

Goldie,
I know that a child can't help coming to school with all of him, or all of her. The totality of needs confronts me more times than I wish. I can't seem to compartmentalize teaching and social work. I can't keep my mind anchored in Reason while my heart sways with Emotion. Yet, some of my colleagues speak of mastery over such awful reality...

Pillar of Equivocation,
I have said, in fact more times than I can count, that rushing out into reality with only "the ideal" as a guide is like pulling teeth without anesthetic. Last month, when we telephoned, you said you wished to go back to

university to learn more about teaching. I bit my tongue, then. But now I say: Come to the molar capital of the east. Or else seek the difference between teaching and holy roller-ing. You'd think there'd be a manual about your true job. If there isn't, shouldn't you be asking why not?

This letter, too, found a place on my little round hallway table. Dearest Goldie, I would think, forever precise; there could be no final manual for these matters. I hadn't realized, until she wrote, that I was harbouring unrelenting thoughts about going back to university for a second degree.

The pressure of my ignorance mounted, yet I stayed teaching, now, too, out of necessity. My husband and I had a little girl to bring up; there was also the matter of my student loan and our wish to pay off our house as soon as possible. Lacking a support system, with my parents on the reserve and my husband's parents in Germany—when they were there at all—I insisted that our little Gabrielle's future depended on the stability of both our jobs and incomes. Anxiety for the future had become a permanent fixture in my psyche. Certain events in my childhood had demonstrated to me how fragile an Aboriginal person's life was. More than anything, my parents' and their parents' life stories shaped my outlook and my deep sense of insecurity.

When my father came back from Europe at the end of World War II, he began to farm right away. He worked hard at it and had every hope of success. Like all farmers, he rose at the crack of dawn and stayed out on the fields well after dark. He often said that the only time he felt good was when he worked up a sweat and could sense his strength. Whenever he had free time, which was rare, he'd take us all into town for small supplies. On these occasions, cars roared past our team of horses. By the time we'd arrive in town, we'd be thirsty and dusty from head to foot.

My father's sense of pride arose not only from his life as a soldier but also because his farming skills were admired and won him a place of respect in town. Like everyone else, he waited until it was his turn at the till, money in hand. He was never forced to let others be served ahead of him, though, many people from the reserve were, including my maternal grandmother. This happened whenever my father was not with us, I noted. Still, our mother told us we were getting ahead.

Farming might have gained us a happy life, but hope of this died. The big red barrels of gasoline could not be counted on to arrive as needed. The Indian agent's quota system limited the quantity of grain to be sold. The Indian Act prohibited commercial ventures that touched natural resources on the reserve. My father could sell neither gravel nor straw, nor even hay to raise money for seed. His fields, though ploughed and disked, lay exposed to the elements. He might have been able to sell firewood, but so many of the trees on the reserve had been cut down to help the war effort in previous years that there were few left standing. Now, only scrub brush and saplings stood. During the war years, the Indian people hauled wagonloads of wood into town as their donation to the war effort. Years later, I saw photos in the Saskatchewan Archives in Regina of their teams and wagonloads of wood on what was likely the main street of a nearby town.

It looked as if there was no way out, but my father's hopes rose once again when Ottawa offered a new income scheme. Reserve land would be cleared of brush, ploughed, and set to seed as a community venture. The Indian agent persuaded the younger men from Cowessess and Kahkewistahaw to agree on clearing land that stretched between the two reserves. The older people did not want to see the natural flora and fauna disturbed. The land to be cleared and tilled stretched to the edge of the hills leading into the valley. The Indian agent, a middle-aged man with light reddish hair, a paunch, and arms covered in liver spots, came out to set things in motion. His friendliness had a forced quality, however, when it came to cutting down the trees. He apparently spoke with Ottawa's authority and backing.

That spring, the people set up a work camp in a field near our home. Crews began cutting down scrub brush and stray poplars while the women stayed in camp tidying their tents, cooking meals around campfires, washing clothes in zinc washtubs and visiting. Evenings, a friendly din surrounded the campfire. Games and speech-making went on till well after dark in this hopeful temporary community. My mother said that, in a way, it was like the pow-wow where people met to celebrate life. However, over time, people involved in the project grew tired and wanted to go home. They finally cleared, plowed, disked, and seeded the broad field, and put a fence around it.

At last they could take down the tents, re-load the wagons, settle the children in for the ride, turn the teams around and head for home. It seemed that hope for the future had been granted.

Later that fall, the crop was harvested and hauled into town. However, when the grain was sold and the accounts drawn up, no one was to receive so very much. Men heading a family received about twenty dollars. My father looked embarrassed as he told us. The lowest cheque was fourteen cents, he reported. I was glad it wasn't meant for us.

My father angrily stated that this situation was like the reversal his own father had experienced several years back. Apparently, at that time, the townspeople of Broadview had sent a petition to Ottawa requesting expropriation of the reserve's moneymaking haying fields, ostensibly because these stood in the way of agricultural progress of the settlers. This, too, I was to find in an archive file.

"It's just so damned intentional," my father said.

My mother replied that there was no use thinking that way. After the land expropriation, my father's family and the people on Cowessess began an even greater downward economic spiral.

Now here I was, a few years later, teaching and living with hope but also dogged by an inherited fear of possible external obstruction in my own career and my undying wish to learn. This personal outlook instilled in me a sense of protection toward the wish to learn in all children. A few times, I had to rein in a quickness to overstep the boundaries between a teacher and other relevant professions.

RYAN

I was constantly astonished by the readiness with which children learned to cope with difficult circumstances. Cold, hunger, sickness, and stress visited them, but the power of their curiosity and sense of wonder almost always shone through, as if polar mental states were programmed to have equal time in their conscious selves, no matter the basic conditions. Children seemed able to seize fleeting moments of joy and not dwell on times of suffering. The end to misery seemed to come with even a single good cry.

I saw a lot of this in my new school at the end of the 1970s. This was my first school in a transition area where economic and social stability gave way to a new community life taking hold. There were tensions as people moved away and new people came to find homes and to reinvent themselves and their adopted community. Family life was in various states of success and failure.

All the same, Ryan's case proved difficult. No matter what happened, good or bad, he kept smiling. Now and again, Ryan spoke of difficulty in his life, but he'd immediately get on with whatever caught his attention. His ready smile gave me hope that he would naturally seek the good and go with it. But smiles can mean many things, I was to discover, and in certain grown-ups they may even be perverse. Ryan's father was the sole breadwinner of the family. He came to the school for a talk about Ryan, one day.

I turned around to see a well-mannered urban cowboy in blue jeans standing in the classroom doorway. I introduced myself and asked him to sit down. He eased his tall frame into the chair at the round table at the back of the room and assessed me through half-closed eyes. I told him about Ryan's progress. However, before I could say very much he declared that, come what may, the teacher's word was the law, in his house.

"I'll back you up as far as Ryan goes. He needs straightening up."

I was startled by his heightened colour. It didn't match the soft-ness of his voice. I explained that Ryan's inconsistency in his daily work was likely what affected his ability to read at his grade level. I began to think that a pleasant meeting with the promise of problem-solving had got off the ground. Ryan's father, every so often, smiled a big warm smile at me. I couldn't define the intru-sive quality in his manner, it was as though he talked not about Ryan at all but instead tried to reveal something of himself, some-thing of which I should perhaps approve. Not knowing what to make of this, I mentioned his fine leather boots. He'd been holding his foot up in a peculiar way, and it occurred to me that his boots were likely brand new and he merely wished to show these off. His face reddened with pleasure as he pointed out their solidly sewn seams. I was glad to have taken the time to make mention of them, for doubtlessly, they were his pride and joy.

"Yeah. Picked them up in the States," he said.

"They're certainly well made."

"Yeah, they got the workmanship down there..."

"That's obvious," I said. "Ryan must like them."

I tried to turn his attention toward the meeting we were suppose to be having.

"Yup," he said, holding my gaze.

A self-centred man, I thought to myself. I closed the meeting by describing how I planned to work with Ryan to bring his reading level up. I told him that he might help Ryan select books from the public library. Finally, he ambled out the classroom door and turned around to give me what was probably his best huge mouth-watering smile.

"You leave Ryan to me," he said, his voice husky with feeling.

When he closed the door behind him, I wasn't sure I liked the man, nor what it was that made it seem to matter.

Ryan enjoyed school. There were reports of absenteeism in previous grades, but he rarely missed a day. He came to school uncombed and rumpled, but clean. His cheerful nature shone through his big brown eyes. For a youngster who had to get himself off to school each day, he was doing fine, until the winter months arrived.

The days entered the cold grip of an early winter that year, and the children got into their heavier jackets, fortified by scarves, toques, and mitts, in record time. Snow had yet to arrive but a bitter wind already raked the dead grasses in the yard and whipped them across to the fence in and around the perimeter of the school where they stuck, enmeshed with other weeds and bits of paper left there after a summer of carelessness. Ryan, I observed, continued coming to school in a T-shirt.

"Ryan!" I hollered the first time I saw him standing out in the yard, his arms blue and ears red. "You'll catch your death of cold! What are you thinking? Where on earth is your jacket? You get on home and get yourself dressed, right now."

Ryan laughed at my consternation, saying he couldn't go home. The house was locked and his father would "freak out" if he were to be called at work. I insisted Ryan come in for a jacket from the big box.

"Aw, it's all right," he said. He grinned from ear to ear, "I don't feel the cold, besides I never dress up when it's this warm out. No way. You're getting upset for nothing."

"Then at least get into the building and out of the wind," I said, herding him indoors. "I want to see you in your jacket tomorrow, young man."

As a busy teacher with so many things to do at once, I assumed that a child's good sense prevailed when the conscious mind took over. In other words, I told Ryan but I didn't check to see that he was properly dressed the next day.

By mid-November, the snow had still not arrived but a knife-sharp wind cut through our jackets and reminded us to put on winter boots, thicker socks, lined mitts, and toques. Despite the cold, our class would walk to the indoor skating rink for a workout, as promised. I invited anyone needing skates or wanting extra clothing to get these from the big box downstairs. No one accepted. Another quick glance and we made ready to leave. But, now, where was Ryan? None of the children had seen him at noon hour. He always came into the yard just before the bell, the children said, but these last couple of days he stayed home until the very last minute. There was nothing to be done but to leave without him. I left a message with the school secretary to try to track him down and to tell him to come to the rink. We started out, a merry troop of skaters, soon caught up in a sudden squall of light snow. With a half block yet to go, one of the children hollered above the wind, "Here comes Ryan!"

It was Ryan, all right. He came hurrying along, smiling broadly in the grip of winter's icy breath, in a T-shirt. He chuckled at my scolding and reminded me that it was quicker for him to go directly to the rink than to turn around and go back home. I had to admit the logic in that. Still, he might freeze to near death inside the rink. He shook his head. All that skating, he insisted, made a person warm up fast, "A guy can get enough heat in him to last all the way back," he reasoned. "I know, trust me."

Trust me. I was reminded of his dad. I hurried the children into the building and considered our predicament. Patrick could lend him an extra sweater; Jodi, extra gloves; Jackie, a scarf; and Bruce, a vest. Ryan absolutely refused these, insisting that he wished to "stay cool." I suggested we call his father then and ask him to bring round a jacket. But Ryan resisted saying it would only make his dad mad; besides, he said his father let him go just the way he was, lots of times.

Before heading back to school, I gave Ryan a stern warning that if he refused to wear the things we offered him he'd have to share my old fur coat with me. He smiled, put on the sweater and the gloves and wrapped his head in the scarf, laughing all the while. We set out. It had grown bitterly cold. The wind was stronger now. It dashed ice pellets into our faces as we trundled down the street, heads lowered. I turned around. Poor Ryan. His lips were blue.

"Ryan McRory," I commanded, "you come right here and share my coat!"

He must have been terribly cold. He ran up and I unfurled what I could of my coat around his shoulders. We stumbled along reaching the school just as the entire street turned white in a raging blizzard. Ryan promised he'd wear his winter things from now on. I said I'd be waiting, and I was.

He came to school the next morning wearing warmer clothing, all right, but these were at least three sizes too small for him. His jacket pulled his shoulders up in a way that hampered his movements. Worse, Ryan wore a look of shame. He'd rather die than have it known he had no winter clothes. He didn't want his classmates to see he was poor, at least not that poor. As it turned out, there was a whole lot more he didn't want us to know.

Take the time he came to school, huge red welts on both his arms.

"Look," he said, showing me red welts that went up one side of his arm and down the other. Some were flat, others were puffed up, still others had turned green and blue. I looked at the welts with a growing sense of alarm. Getting them must have hurt horribly.

Questions formed in my mind but before I could ask, Ryan smiled, "Aw, it's just my dad. He got mad again and walked up and down on my arms in his boots. Leastwise, he didn't punch me in the face. I told him I never want to get a black eye."

My mind reeled. Never want to get a black eye! Never want to get a black eye! My thoughts ran in every direction at once. Ryan smiled and said that it was a pretty good deal, if his dad kept his word.

I practically ran to the principal's office where I found myself trying to answer a battery of rapid-fire questions:

No. Ryan has never come to school with black eyes.

No. Ryan isn't trying to make a scene, again.

No. He isn't just crying and carrying on.

No. This is not the central business of the school.

Well, then?

Fellow teachers gathered around, "Here, in this neighborhood, you get that all the time," they counselled. "Monitor it. There might be another side to the story. Ryan could be taken away by Social Services if you raise a fuss. God knows where he might end up. See how he's enjoying school, lately? Think about it."

Think about it. I was overcome with nausea thinking about those boots and Ryan having to live with a parent whose mind was so warped. The principal and my colleagues warned that I could over-step my boundaries if I chose to interfere. I decided not to confront the father. It would be better if he never came to the school again, I thought. He didn't, and although I was grateful, my view of the professional role of the school had been let down.

Still, I, too, had no idea of the extent of things. I considered Ryan's abuse an aberration, a one-time incident, a single family problem that time was sure to heal. Knowledge of child abuse, child neglect, and child pornography was a long way off in time; or, perhaps it was so well hidden that the education profession had not yet trained its eyes to see.

We got through the winter with Ryan and his ever shrinking jacket, all of us shored up by his humour. He was the sort of boy who smiled, forgave, and avoided getting into trouble on the play-ground. I took pains to be thorough and positive in the report cards I sent home with him. I sent the best samples of his schoolwork, too.

When I saw Ryan a few years later, his outgoing cheerful manner was intact. He hurried toward me from across Thirteenth Avenue, one Thursday evening, calling my name. Peering toward the figure in the gathering dusk, I waited near the steps of the drug store. He strode into the full light of the street lamp, a tall strapping teenager in a black leather jacket. I knew right away from that smile that it could be no other.

"Ryan Andrew McRory! Can it be you?"

As usual, he was smiling as if he had a good story to tell and his eyes shone bright with its happy containment. He had grown to the size of a broad-shouldered man. I could see that he wouldn't have to suffer wrongful punishments anymore. He was in high school now, which was okay, he said. He didn't know if he was going to stay there long, though, he remarked, as he looked at me out of the corner of his eye. My heart sank.

He burst out laughing, "Aw, don't look so disappointed. I'm not gonna quit."

He hadn't forgotten how to tease me. Ryan was proud of his black leather jacket. I told him he looked great in it. He was better at looking after himself now he said, "No more T-shirts in blizzards. And none of that old fur coat, either." We both laughed. He was doing pretty well in school, he said. His dad was on the road a lot with his new job and was seeing a girl in some town.

As we parted, I felt new hope that Ryan would be all right. He had pride of presence. And, I hoped that his father might leave him alone now. Ryan, I knew, would likely try on a few character roles before truly settling into his own strengths. He wouldn't end up mean. I sensed that in my bones. Like their fathers before them, some boys grew into bitter men and took their anger out on others, but Ryan seemed to have an ability to rid himself of negativity. He had a sincere smile that I hoped reflected his take on the future. I said a silent prayer, anyway, just in case.

TWELVE.

A Way to the Clearing Imagined

I REACHED THE STAGE in my development where the answers I found about what makes for good teaching were only about as good as the questions I asked. I realized that it was taking me longer than I expected to learn my profession. Still, I got better at asking some of the right questions: what is important to teach? What makes it so? How does a teacher stay in tune with a child's reality? What is truth? However, I had yet to learn the art of asking such questions of myself. It would take a few more children caught up in a swirl of peculiar incidents before I began to see more deeply into the heart of a teacher's role in defining true knowledge for children. An incident, early in my career, would teach me another needed lesson on measuring one's own depth and clarity of thought.

Tatiana and Ivan

Two of my pupils came in after recess to tell me that some grade fours were teasing Tatiana and Ivan, the little Andropov twins in grade three. The older children had said to others on the playground that Russians put their mothers to the plow. Children were pointing fingers at the twins during recess chanting, "Plow girl! Plow boy!" Apparently, their teasing persisted even when the grade-eight monitor asked them to be quiet and everyone could see the twins were crying. I told the children I'd look into it, and went to see their grade-four teacher.

Miss Smith recounted that in social studies period that morning, she had briefly pointed out a picture in the schools' authorized grade-four textbook that showed Doukhobor women hitched to a plow set in an open field of newly made furrows.

"Nobody made anything of it. Besides, it's in their approved textbook," she said defensively. "All I said was that they're a hard-working people. I didn't say they were Russians."

She grew angry. I assured her that I didn't think she'd done anything wrong intentionally. However, the children took a false idea onto the playground and, as a consequence, feelings were running high. I left her to deal with the situation, her eyes boring into mine, and returned to my classroom.

So it was true. What teachers left unsaid perpetuated mistaken beliefs. Score one for professors of critical thinking. It was plain that some children didn't, or couldn't, read beyond pictures. It would take a thousand words, and a lot more, to set things aright with the innocent Andropov twins. None of the children had developed an understanding of history enough to realize that it had taken all kinds of people, including Russians, to build the province we shared as everyday citizens. How could they? They were eight years old!

I rounded up my friend, Vania, and told her that teachers might be neglecting to point out to their pupils that the Russians, Germans, Ukrainians, Cree, Black Canadians, Poles, Norwegians, Ojibwas, Métis, Pakistanis, Jews, Chinese, English, Scots, Irish, Sioux, Dene,

Italians, Jamaicans, Chileans, and Finns belonged here. Saskatchewan is home to all of them and they had all contributed, was what I meant. However, I presented my recitation to her with a know-it-all fervor. "Teachers," I pointed out passionately, "need to become judicious purveyors of the neglected realities of our common heritage!" I had mounted my high horse and threatened to gallop onto even higher ground. "Sins of omission do nothing for grade fours," I added, ending my impressive litany.

Vania looked at me long and hard. "And, what about the Armenians?" she asked. "Or don't you give them the time of day?"

In an instant, Vania exposed the thinness of my knowledge.

In the manner of good friends, she had pushed me off my high horse. I had embarrassed myself by showing off and then bumbling so horribly. Vania didn't give me a moment to reply. She closed the door to her room after the children filed in and rolled her eyes as she laughed that silent irksome laugh of hers. So there it was. I was as ignorant as any grade four about Saskatchewan history. It was hard to accept that I had fooled myself. The litany of nationalities I delivered to Vania was an incomplete one. There was no real depth to the so-called knowledge I flaunted. Well then, I would have to do something about it. I knew books were only part of the answer.

That was when I began a search at yet another stage of my development as a teacher. I intensified my regimen of reading and studying on weekends. During summer holidays I surrounded myself with piles of old photographs, maps, letters, and memoirs from the provincial archives. The archives was a place where citizens fortunate enough to discover its quiet sanctuary might review their shared history and inherited social contract. I often hummed the hymn "Faith of our Fathers" in my mind while I worked.

The archives proved to be a unique place. It marked a time of new insights for me and an appreciation for hidden truths among primary sources. "Some people have the mistaken idea that an archive is a place where boring musty documents are stored," an archivist commented the summer morning I first arrived there. "But as they begin their exploration, they can scarcely contain themselves."

She gathered up a pile of old school registers to take to the table where a group of seniors chatted excitedly. They had come in to find their names written down in old records. Then she put another box of files I had requested on my table. A treasure trove: all manner of letters, photos, and diaries began to fill out gaps in my knowledge. Exciting! There was no other word for it.

One day, I overheard an archivist tell a researcher of an event in the late 1800s. A settler had swum across a stream in the pouring rain; clothes bundled on top of his head as he bit down on a billfold for fear of getting his papers wet. His teeth were chatter-locked when he reached shore. Papers? What kind of papers would these be in 1889, I wondered? And my curiosity sent me on yet another quest. As it turned out, the papers were land deeds. Turn that corner and there was more to know. If I looked hard enough I knew that I'd find all kinds of information for my pupils. Stories about their grandparents and their parents' grandparents waited to be found and shared. I knew I would not be able to collect these single hand-edly. I'd need help. Volunteer mothers would have to be called in at once.

It seemed that every time I turned around at school, I found myself asking parents to volunteer for something. What a pest I must be, I'd think; but I couldn't help myself. On the other hand, the parents of the children I taught, as well as people whose children were grown up now and gone, were more than willing to assist our projects, each and every time. I called on a couple of stay-at-home moms (an increasing rarity) and told them that the archives had cartons full of letters containing stories that the children should know about. These were first-hand accounts with photographs of historical events, such as the Regina Cyclone, the Regina Riot, and the construction of our legislature. These personal accounts simply cried out to be shared, I told my eager volunteers. Would they be willing to research personal stories related to major events for us? Would they be willing to transcribe tape recordings of people reviewing their past? Of course they would! I warned the archivist that there would be more of us coming. She ran her fingers through her short curls and smiled knowingly.

I was proud of this project. So proud, in fact, that along the way I picked up a true case of archives fever. I decided I needed to write a letter for posterity, too. I would design the perfect letter and send it to my dentist friend down east. This way, when I died there would be a small memento of me and my classroom of children. I decided to write it in such a way that Goldie would grasp its historical significance. She might treasure it for a few years and then turn it over to an archive so that future generations, upon finding it, would hold it up to the light to study its watermark to assure themselves of its authenticity.

I composed the letter in the quiet of my classroom after school on the day I conceived of the idea. In fact, no sooner said than done. Now, however, as I reviewed my letter, a peculiar tone of self-consciousness bothered me. Never mind, I reasoned, friends just skip over things like that, forever going straight to the point. I decided not to let this minor flaw worry me because in reading this letter, I reasoned, future historians would marvel at its timelessness. I was careful to date my letter in a clear hand. My archives-bound letter, via Goldie, described our project:

Soon mothers and archivists together were piling over materials there on the fifth floor of the university library building, temporary quarters of the archives. Six months later our collection was ready. We called in the school librarian, who grew so amazed at the quality of our product that she said she would be pleased to catalogue it for the school library. She expressed delight, her eyes glowing, with her new-found treasure in hand. When we told her that fellow teachers and principals in neighbouring schools had said they'd be willing to pay for copies of this unique collection, she offered to deliver the copies to the schools that very week, to save us the trouble. The children's mothers were proud that we could now begin our real mission of teaching an in-depth history of our province.

I wasn't so sure, when I re-read my letter, that it was necessary to mention the "glowing eyes" of the school librarian, but I had a stack of books to mark and I hated to start the letter over. Besides, her eyes did glow as though calculating the true personal worth of something. I couldn't wait to get a response from Goldie. Her note arrived about three weeks later:

Pillar of Posterity,
I intend to treasure this missive in its entirety. You do not describe the antics of your cat, this time, however. Pity, I love the authentic life in that beast. I don't think I've shared this with anyone, but, Pillar, when I die I want to go to archives.

She had signed her full name, dated it carefully and put a double stroke under A.D.

Friends are like that, I told myself; high-blown schemes never work with them. They return you firmly to the ground every time. I knew this much, however: as a friend, she would not send my letter off to archives. Nor would she save it for the next generation that might find it brittle and streaked with age, its ink faded. I was glad. It was just possible one could grow ashamed, posthumously.

As for Tatiana and Ivan's difficult situation, the principal called in the twin's parents and the parents of the offending students for a closed-door discussion. As a result, the twins and their tormentors were able to throw off the mantle of distress and get on with the joy of being children on the playground. As for the offending textbook, its presence on classroom desks remained a few years more. Vania said she could see why my classroom's archival project was good; it was to be a source of fresh information on people's lives and relationships. In fact, she cheered the work on so enthusiastically I thought it destined to improve knowledge and thinking in all society. I had a hunch it would benefit me in the same way.

I often felt, as a teacher, that I was the soul of ignorance. I could recall a storehouse of facts but this was never enough. It was apparent to me that people had always known how to string facts together meaningfully, but the magnitude of the things they did not know escaped conscious analysis. This is why one studies Shakespeare, I would think. Great writers prepare the mind and then corner it adroitly so that the reader comes to understand the nature of things left unsaid. This should become a habit of mind, I would think, sensing the need to reach this point in my own thinking. Yes, true understanding meant going beyond connecting apparent facts that, in the end, only hint at reality beyond the observable. Getting the big picture right meant searching for the less obvious, but crucial, connections between ideas and events. And to do this, I had to see how my mind was tied and then determine how it might become untied. A first step was to try to make sense of reality by making a distinction between my idea of it and the new reality on its way. But then the 1990s was still twenty years away.

My mind was tied all right. I became aware of this only too well after I met and taught Praheed.

Praheed

I learned something about myself, which, as a professional, was almost too humiliating to admit when I taught Praheed. Ignorance was one thing, applied ignorance another. Praheed made my short-coming very clear to me.

Praheed had recently arrived with his family from India. He was tall for his age. His movements about the room were like a swan gliding across a silvery lake. The key problem for Praheed, and for me as his teacher, however, was his almost limitless tenacity. His parents came to the school to tell me about it.

"He works very hard, but very slowly," his mother said. "And we think that it's all right for him to take his time. Perhaps he tries too hard to absorb everything all at once. I hope you'll not think Praheed a rude boy, but we must warn you, we cannot get him to hurry."

"Does he get loaded down with homework a lot?" I asked. I tried to guess the extent to which his approach might affect his output, never mind his input.

"Ah yes," his father confirmed, "but he is accustomed to it and stays up late, till ten and sometimes eleven o'clock at night. What's more, if there are exams he stays up later."

"What seems to be his main concern? Does he read slowly, or is it his handwriting? In time, things may pick up for him."

"I'm afraid it's both," his father said, smiling self-consciously. "And this might well be a burden for him but he never complains. It's not like him to complain."

"Is there anything I should do?" I wondered if they wished to discuss strategy, past, present, or future.

"We don't think so," his mother replied. "We feel you should know in advance, however, that Praheed has been raised in the Indian tradition. He meditates if things get too much for him, which can be often."

Meditate. I tried to recall what I knew about meditation, if anything, and realized that my knowledge was limited. Further-more, my knowledge of India was almost zero. I had only fleeting thoughts of saris, jars carried on the head, crowded streets, Kipling's Kim—those sorts of image.

"A child in a state of profound voluntary restfulness doesn't sound bad to me," I finally said.

We laughed together and agreed that if any problems arose we'd call each other immediately. We sat awhile visiting, feeling a bit more comfortable with the challenge of Praheed. I relaxed enough to absorb and enjoy the beauty of their apparel, the lovely muted green sari and the fine herringbone jacket. I thought how good it would be to travel, expand my horizons, and truly learn. It would do me a world of good.

Praheed had the temperament and manner of a prince. He bore a kind of remoteness that you couldn't mistake for shyness, so strong was his sense of self. His parents hadn't understated his slowness. Praheed approached his schoolwork as if in the grip of a sea-bound dream where he was captain of a most solitary and singular treasure-laden ship. It was frustrating to watch him write. Each letter, shaped according to the ancient laws of sculpting stone, was laid down by this scribe, exact to the last miniscule detail. He crossed every "t" and dotted every "i" as if he were carving a slab of marble. His rate of reading, if one could describe it as a rate, was a slow rounding of waves on a distant shore.

Praheed never answered questions thoughtlessly; he'd fan his long eyelashes in slow graceful arcs and share his opinion with great deliberation. And, when he spoke, he enunciated each syllable and letter with a purity of sound an actor might take years to perfect. It was abundantly clear to me that our classroom of boisterous children was hardly the place for Praheed. But he stayed close to his helm, only sweeping his dark eyes once or twice over the world of noise and bustle. I had to admire his steadfastness.

It was one of those sunny but windy mornings in early October when children are bound to be as unruly as the weather. Sure enough, they were. In windy weather children become about as manageable as skiffs in a leaping sea. I knew what to expect and tried to prepare for the worst. On those days, I had to settle the children down the minute they walked through the door. One of my personal strategies was to wear quiet colours like soft grey, pale fawn, or faint rose—certainly nothing red—to dampen my rushing about in mindless urgency. I spoke in modulated tones. For added measure, I tried to begin the day's instruction with those subjects that allowed me to keep my eyes peeled. "Hold your horses!" was a well-rehearsed phrase meant to head the genuinely agitated off at the pass, often to no avail.

A real remedy was to send the unruly rascals on a run of several laps around the gym. Gymnasiums, however, were hard to come by on short notice as they tend to be in use at all times. Gym periods are tightly scheduled and often dominated by hard-minded teachers unwilling to trade periods, windy weather or not. Lucky is the teacher, indeed, whose gym period falls on the same morning as the arrival of a wild dust-pitted wind. Gym days rarely, if ever, fell open on the day I needed one.

Never mind, I'd say to myself, we can always sing. I learned that it was shrewd to accompany all song with a stern expression, too, as the weather bore down on us. Despite this, the children often ignored the gentle expression I tried to project and would launch into song with boisterous intention. Thank heavens they knew when I said something I meant it. It's a wise teacher who cultivates that virtue from the start, I'd remind myself, thinking of some old professor. For instance, if I said in tones uncompromising that we were to sing, we'd sing. And the children sang lustily that day, with the same gusto as the dust devils that spun and whirled outside our window.

That is, all except Praheed.

There was something in the way he remained seated at his desk that I found unusual and highly disturbing. He sat with his eyes closed, swaying from side to side, as if in the grip of an external force. Was he about to faint? In a flash, I was at his side.

"Praheed?" I heard myself say. "Praheed, is anything the matter?"

The children fell silent.

I grabbed Praheed's his shoulder and shook him vigorously. His eyes rolled back in his head as he turned his face to the ceiling and then flopped forward onto his desk. The tension in the room rose as a wave of horror swept over me. Was he dying?

"Praheed! Praheed!" I called. "Answer me. Answer me. Are you all right?"

"I'm oomm," he said. His voice was muffled as his head lolled on his arms. He repeated something that I could barely make out, "I'm...itating."

I could not believe my ears! "You're what?" I cried. "You're levitating?"

The second I said it, my mind saw it: How high would he..? How would I get him down? Where was the principal? All reason had fled. What would I do with a levitating child? Who would bring him back down? I was caught in a swirl of dizzying thought and stupefying images, my stomach in a knot, my mind a cascade of ignorance.

"Don't do it, Praheed." I heard myself call out in tones completely unmoored, "Don't you dare levitate!" The class stood there in stunned silence.

"I said meditate." Praheed was sitting up looking at me. Something in that steady gaze settled me right down. The children watched in silence. I came to earth fast.

Some days teachers feel foolish beyond words, and I wished that day that children didn't see right through things, as plainly as they did now.

"All right, then," I said lamely, straightening up and returning unsteadily to the front of the room. Ignorance of people and history was likely written all over my flushed face, I knew. No wonder. Confronted by my own ignorance and in sheer panic my mind had reduced reality to a stereotype. A flash of emotion exposed my ignorance. My face grew hotter and hotter as I realized that I was likely as red as that primate's face I once saw on the cover of *National Geographic*. Somehow, evolution had caught that face unaware: a face full of self-consciousness, on its way to shame.

I forced myself to go on with the lesson.

"Let's take it from the top. One and two, and..."

The children burst into song. Praheed pursed his lips, and I had the distinct impression he was looking right through me.

Whenever I did anything extraordinarily foolish, such as display my ignorance, I tried to console myself with the belief that teachers college had given me and my fellow classmates too brief an introduction to teaching. They might have tried harder, gone out of their way, but they had not! Still, I knew our professors had done as much as they humanly could to prepare us. In later years, I had to admit that it must have been like trying to teach life itself. My mind was a veritable Gordian Knot of ignorance and it was going to take hard work to untie it. There was no question. I had to get on with learning more about Canadians, the world, and me.

Our professors in teachers college were fond of repeating one truth: "Every child is unique." We students maintained a kind of running theory that this pet phrase had grown the longest of beards, right next to: "You can never know too much." The professors were also fond of saying that deeper knowledge would be a great comfort to us one day. "You'll never be bored in your calling. When it comes to knowledge, you must never rest on your oars."

Even as late as the 1970s, it was impossible to predict the speed and the extent to which change would occur in our province, as in the rest of Canada. I read about telecommunication technologies but did not know that an information explosion would result in a global network of spin-off economies. "Reality isn't what it used to be!" was what people heard. Whatever the reality, I learned that I was ill prepared for a child whose family kept faith in me and in the school I represented; Praheed was a star pupil whose uniqueness taught me that I had better give my full attention to the depths of my ignorance.

In the 1960s and 1970s, as a teacher I saw myself a "keeper of the faith." In the 1990s I would wonder what that could mean. I pinned my hopes on finding the best of wisdom in the way teaching was organized and delivered. I tried to fit in by putting into practice the "tried and true" of instruction in my daily classroom lessons. However, sometimes in the back of my mind, there appeared some anomaly, some glimmer of truth that cast a light, however yet dim, on a changing horizon. As for keeping the faith, I would wonder just what that would mean in the 1990s. The moral sentiment no longer seemed to carry the same meaning in the rapidly changing conditions of contemporary life.

THIRTEEN.

RAISING THE BAR

THERE WAS SO MUCH MORE TO LEARN in this highly creative time. I tried to understand what contemporary writers wrote, what new singers sang about, and what artists unveiled. Artists presented us with the most extraordinary images. Colour combinations that "didn't go together" pierced the eye and excited the nervous system. Geometric shapes, in a kaleidoscope of hues, leapt from canvasses that held both immediate and infinite space in startling ways. Artists and groups of artists, such as the Regina Five, stretched the aesthetic vision beyond anything I had ever witnessed in even those boundaries crossed by modern masterworks of Picasso and Chagall. Picasso and Chagall had taken the earlier artistic traditions of Europe and America beyond static realism in landscape and portraiture. The Regina Five went further. Rules of space, form, and colour served as supports to their visionary innovations. In the atmosphere of creativity and exuberance, it felt good to be young and, as we felt in our bones, so very true to ourselves as we basked in the works of those who invented our times even as we lived them. Along with eager friends, Peter and I would head off to the Mackenzie Art Gallery on College Avenue to become caught up in even more sculptures and images that cried out "never before." Many of our artists, using the elements of colour and light available to all, created extraordinary effects and went on to world fame. When I first laid eyes on Ted Godwin's painting, "A Tartan for Winter," its quality of woven light touched me deeply.

Peter helped me accept that we could not afford to buy the Godwin piece, that, by the time we might have sufficient means, it would be residing with a worthy art lover, somewhere, forever. It was a painting I would mourn for all my life. I mourned the loss of other paintings, too, through the years, but never in the same way as that tartan.

I also made it my business to learn from new writers. Ken Mitchell wrote about life in Saskatchewan. It came as a kind of shock; an eye-opener that one's local city and province could be the stuff of a writer's work. Regina: a setting! Thanks to *Wandering Rafferty*, I felt mentally alive because I could see, for the first time, the city I thought I knew. This was a gift. And, so it was all very wonderful to be able to attend gatherings where creative men and women presented prairie lives in a light that was both unique and universal. Those who opened eyes and ears had a rare opportunity to get a glimpse of bigger realities and their nature. I sensed I had best get ready for a new take on reality.

I longed to study beyond my B.A. I had to keep reminding myself that my pupils and my life as a teacher provided more than enough timeless insights. After all, I'd tell myself, school was the pulse of the future. I didn't dare think that in my search I was duty-bound to leave the classroom. For now, personal circumstances constrained my will. My salary hovered around three thousand dollars a year, which barely covered expenses, let alone my ambitions.

At the time, I didn't know that in a few years, at the close of the 1970s, I would return to university on a sabbatical and then return to my school division to fulfill a three-year obligation. I did not know either that I would have the opportunity to teach in a transition school at that point. Socio-economic changes were taking place in the core area of the city and, increasingly, the school was being seen as the centre for strengthening school-community relations on behalf of children and their growing needs. First Nations and Métis families were moving into the city at this time.

At the end of the 1970s I could not long ignore my growing sense of discomfort with my progress. I was teaching, purportedly by all who taught there, in one of the best schools in the city. And I had more than ten years experience. Yet, I felt trapped. In years prior, the feeling came and went. I always managed to make myself think this was a feeling a neophyte might suffer in a profession that must forever withhold a final blessing. My sense of personal ignorance did not diminish with time. In fact, it seemed to deepen. Goldie and I had a longer than usual exchange on the matter. I tried to face the truth of my situation and so sent a note off to Goldie whose patience had to be as steady and reliable as the hands that worked the very nerve buds of people's teeth.

Goldie,
I feel a growing dullness of the brain, or something. I should have studied philosophy, mathematics, and the arts and the sciences in depth. But, somehow, that would still be only a starting point. The reality of children means I should have studied sociology, anthropology, and economics—all the social sciences, in fact, along with psychology and religion. Yet, I feel this wouldn't be the answer—not all of the answer anyway. I believe I'd still feel inadequate: I know this in my heart, Goldie. Maybe this is what all teachers must think forever. I know you've studied for years to carry out the work you do. But do you ever feel dissatisfied professionally?

Pillar of Doubt,
The way I see it, preparation can rarely cover all the bases for kids. They ask impossible questions without even thinking. This doesn't mean you could know the answer. Any philosopher can tell you that. You ask about

me. Well, my hands know whereof I speak. They, alone, are precise and founded on laws of exactness. I believe you to be an earnest teacher, Pillar, but you are definitely one who could do with a break. You've been at this for—what?—10 or more years! I promise you, if you make the effort to do something constructive about your doubts, I vow to become more of a poet in my life.

Here is my first line—as proof of the scope and exactness that is the way of all dentists:

Behold the summer hills encircled with a necklace of fair pelicans! Chin up, Faltering Pillar. Pack up everything and move down east. (Note considerable wit in this.)

More of a poet, indeed! She was teasing again. Yet Goldie's words left me with some hope of resolve, a resolve that might rise full-blown one day. We would see what we would see. For now, humour and wit like Goldie's would have to do. As for me, it was still "go west young man."

One day, at school, I overheard our principal in conversation with a superintendent from the public school board office. "A lot should be happening in Aboriginal Education," he said, quietly under his breath, "but there's no leadership in the system."

There came the reply, "We spend hoards of money sending people to all these fan-dangled studies and nothing comes of it."

Walking past them, I wanted to stop briefly to ask what they meant, exactly. But in those days, men, particularly when in groups of two or three, tended to behave officiously toward women, especially those who taught elementary school. A pecking order was kept in check at all times. Considering this, I made a mental note and walked on.

But that overheard conversation triggered another "crisis of the limits" in my head. On my way back into my classroom I recalled an earlier incident that had touched a nerve. My daughter, Gabrielle, was about ten years old then. Her teachers taught with great skill and innovation.

Still, I was concerned that she wasn't learning anything new about the first peoples on this continent, her ancestors. It was a pleasant surprise when her grade five teacher demonstrated a change of approach, or so I thought. Gabrielle came home, one day, excited that her class was going to have show and tell about family backgrounds. I was very glad that Peter and I had had the foresight to take her with us to the reserve, to pow-wows, family reunions, and cultural feasts as often as we were able. She had been with us to Germany to see her other homeland, too, thanks to the generosity of Peter's parents.

Along with a full-colour magazine and show-and-tell articles from Germany, I excitedly selected a small willow basket that had been made by her maternal great-grandmother. Inside, I placed a beaded medallion that my mother had made for me. I added a small braid of sweet grass handed down to me through my mother from her mother, a "medicine woman."

Things didn't turn out. Why, I could only guess. It might have been because the other children had brought store-bought articles for show and tell, which was a likely case. Perhaps someone had made a hurtful remark about Aboriginal people. Whatever happened, Gabrielle chose not to share her materials. The minute she came home after school, she put the basket and contents up on the piano and slipped outside. She didn't seem to want to talk about it. I thought perhaps she didn't want to be on display as someone not "the same." But surely her classmates knew that every culture is different. Gabrielle refused to say. Her father and I were left to wonder why the teacher had been unable to build a bridge of appreciation for everyone's heritage, to everyone's show and tell. I asked myself if such omission was still possible in a growing global world.

There had been other reminders. It wasn't as though people of vision weren't trying.

It was back in the summer of 1978; I brought the subject up once with Goldie and Vania both of whom I had invited to my home. Their travel plans and schedules allowed them, at last, to get together and finally meet in person and to catch up with events in my life. As to the issue of a kindred spirit among people in the global village, Goldie thought a challenge might be that people lacked organization to handle the unusual development of a shrinking world. Vania agreed; she thought that when people made a commitment, organization followed. Goldie's and Vania's lives seemed so full and vibrant to me, especially as they sat in my living room in their pastel summer dresses of buttercup yellow and periwinkle blue. I wished I had their experience of big city life, like Vania living near Vancouver and Goldie in Toronto. It seemed multi-ethnic environments built confidence and sophistication in people, generally. I, on the other hand, had doubts to contend with and feelings of real constraint. I was dressed in grey but thanks to our discussions, my fledgling vision re-affirmed itself as a high-colour banner.

I felt newly committed to change. Such was the way of summer visits with friends who understood. They gave me energy. But then I was alone, again.

I recalled that as far back as my fourth year of teaching (1967), I received a telephone call one evening from a community activist, the lovely and gracious Mrs. Clipsham whose reputation, along with her husband's, was known to me. I had heard about her early work on the board of the YWCA. In collaboration with friends, such as Walter and Inez Deiter, she worked tirelessly in the mid 1950s to help found the Friendship Centre. The centre provided support to First Nations people who began moving from the reserves to the city early that decade. She also chaired a co-ordinating group that maintained a rooms-registry for the accommodation of travellers to the city. I learned that she was now also in the process of trying to stop the spread of stereotypical information about Aboriginal people found in school textbooks. At the time, I was teaching days and taking night classes, and I was also trying to make time for my husband and daughter. I knew that with my having to study on weekends, I would have to decline the offer to join Mrs. Clipsham's group that was evaluating instructional materials for bias. I grew very interested in the topic and checked out the school library to see if teachers were receiving benefit of her Mrs. Clipsham's work. A search through the school's library pamphlets and books revealed nothing yet. However, her work was to have implications for new and better instructional materials; and the department of education was to play a big part in the development, ultimately. Her influence remains strong, as seen in the community development work of her son, Fred Clipsham, city councillor in Regina for many years.

As professional and personal reminders gathered in my mind, I grew all the more determined to go back to university. This time, I told myself, I'd study First Nations and Métis history at the Saskatchewan Indian Federated College on the University of Regina campus. There, I reasoned, I might be able to read Canadian history with a clear head, certainly without the fog of imported bias. As a starting point, I would find out what scholars were saying about Aboriginal history, today. Having seen archival documents that helped clarify a few thoughts for me, I now wished to know Saskatchewan history in its totality. The 1980s were drawing up to the classroom door and I came to understand that something fundamental had to change; that meant a change in me, too. I made a few calls.

At my own behest, I found myself meeting with Mr. Garry Wouters at the Department of Education on College Avenue across the street from where the old teachers college building once stood and where professors shared their knowledge of the arts and sciences with young know-it-alls, as I had certainly been.

"What can I do for you?"

Mr. Wouters sat behind a desk in the middle of an office with filing cabinets lined down one side. His welcoming smile was genuine. This was in contrast to some of the men at the public school's central office where the code was to don an authoritative manner with which to address, it seemed, a good many important issues at once, and where a friendly smile was an option.

"I'd like to talk about a curriculum for schools that includes Indian people," I said.

He told me that discussion on a major curriculum revision was underway.

"I am ready and willing to help," I said. "I'm an archives buff, you know, and a tolerable teacher."

I could see his mind at work. "When would you be ready to start?" Apparently, an inclusive curriculum was not an alien idea to him.

This was Friday. "Monday," I said.

He threw his head back and laughed.

"All right, the week after," I said, thinking that I had been too forward.

He laughed even harder. "What I mean is—it takes time to establish branches, people, and programs."

"How long?" I asked.

"We have to go through a number of levels of approval; hiring takes time. Preparations can take up to three years, realistically. You should be able to apply for a position two to three years from now. I'd watch the newspaper for ads around then."

Three years was a long time, I knew. So much could happen in the interval. But there it was. I had enjoyed my discussion with Mr. Wouters. His firm handshake and his clear focused expression told me he knew his business well and that matters would be dealt with starting now.

Years later, I would learn from experience that it takes time to work through government process and through a department's internal politics when establishing a branch. If I knew then what I would learn later, I would have told Mr. Wouters that I'd see him in five years. In the meantime, as I waited, I kept busy studying on my own in the archives and at the university and public libraries, summers and weekends.

In the meantime, I formulated a plan. I would apply to the Regina Public School Division for a sabbatical leave. I had received my B.A. with distinction, back in 1969, and had prepared for my finals in the German language for a goodly number of classes; there could be little question I would be a strong student if given the opportunity. I was told that I would be awarded leave on the condition I return to teach in the division for three years. I would receive a percentage of my salary, as a student and was free to explore the possibility of federal funding, as well. I nearly fell out of my chair. For the first time in my life I could study without fear of disabling poverty. I signed the agreement with a flourish and a rush of happiness.

My plan of study focused on the story of Saskatchewan. This included self-directed study of primary documents at the Saskatchewan Archives, in addition to fulfilling the class requirements for the year.

Dr. Oliver Brass, a Saulteaux scholar born in Fort Qu'Appelle, was one of my professors at the college. He was a fine teacher. He taught classes on First Nations history using interesting illustrative materials. He interpreted the present conditions of Aboriginal peoples with what he knew about oral history, as well as with contemporary research.

I first met him through my teachers college companion, Sheila Scott, when he and she were undergraduates. She brought him round to meet Peter and me at our new apartment. She introduced me as "the gal who kicked her high heels off in a snow bank and had to be saved." Her preposterous exaggeration broke the ice and we had a delightful visit together. Sheila and Oliver invited Peter and me to their wedding the summer of 1965. It was wonderful to see my old teachers college friend so happy.

Dr. Brass cared about his students and took pains to encourage us. He told me I was a budding writer, a sign that I was a clear thinker. This pleased me no end. I liked to be thought of as having a clear mind. Most of my superiors through the years had a fondness for saying that I was "articulate." By contrast, this made ability sound incidental, even accidental.

Dr. Brass took an interest in our limited financial resources as students and told us about a funding program for urban Indian and Métis students to which we might apply. I nervously asked him if he thought I qualified and he assured me I would. Unable to access federal funding, I applied for and received partial funding as an "urban Indian" in the last quarter of my final year. This helped round out the percentage of the salary I drew as a teacher on leave. I was very thankful.

Dr. Brass was a good teacher and a visionary who went on to develop the Saskatchewan Indian Federated College as an independent university.

Here was something new. At the college, I could openly lay claim to my identity whenever I was asked about my background and nationality. This gave me a rare sense of freedom. A weight had lifted. Now I could tell anyone who asked me that my father was Cree and my mother Saulteaux without having to overexplain myself, without having my companion withdraw in a sudden grip of self-consciousness. I didn't have to absorb pangs of that old inheritance of colonial guilt and embarrassment here. Nor would I have to hear it said that I was a credit to my race (rather than the human race). Instead I heard from those who spoke of parents and grandparents having survived residential school and the capricious brutalities of the Indian Act. I also participated in the cultural rituals and ceremonies appropriate for women. Furthermore, I was able to take the classes I wanted.

Oddly enough, having a German name and a degree in German language and literature, meant my identity was questioned by some of the First Nations students. These were my classmates who felt a strong cultural bond with one another and their reserves. They had not left home at age fourteen, as I had. I recognized that what might seem odd to others suited my life just fine. I'd studied German for more reasons than I gave; I often said that I wanted to understand my European in-laws better. Thrilled to be studying again, I made sure I also took a class in Aboriginal visual arts. The class in art history was a symbolic psychological homecoming and a permanent home to all "voluntary" exiles. The voluntary part came in exercising the choice to leave one's cultural home. One's new "home" was the visual arts that encoded cultural memory as one unbroken line of development in an otherwise fragmented history. To finally see that story was a homecoming.

A Cree-speaking professor of renown, Bob Boyer, remarked that the artistic life of the Aboriginal people was the only tradition that survived as a continuous expression of their history, values, and culture wherein people embraced change, as they always had. I found his remark stunning in its significance. I thought everything in the people's past lay in fragments, severed completely from its origins, its historical roots and context shut off from academic inquiry that might lead to a recovery of ancient truths. Instead, the arts had remained a gateway to that truth.

What I learned at the Saskatchewan Indian Federated College prepared me to think more deeply about an inclusive curriculum for schools. I knew it would take time to formulate my ideas and maybe have these accepted. The college didn't have a curriculum studies department; neither did it have an on-campus-teacher preparation program, let alone a comprehensive library. I wondered how questions of Aboriginal pedagogy might be addressed by the college. Aside from the elders, there was little by which to begin defining levels of knowledge and levels of learning in Aboriginal education. Nonetheless, some things were clear to me. The knowledge base of public school teachers in this area was terribly inadequate, as was mine, through no fault of our own. Yet, the picture of failing Aboriginal children in schools was everybody's business.

I was astounded to find that the more I read of primary documents, texts, and literature the louder grew the deafening silence. I wondered how I, as a teacher, might even begin to address the issues that were of interest to me and my classroom. Basic understandings had to come first. It seemed that defining a new synthesis for Canada's identity from a colony to a nation with Aboriginal perspectives in mind was complex, to say the least.

Yet a new synthesis, to be made known, had to include Canada's diverse Indian nations, the French Canadians, English Canada, and a plurality of other immigrant groups. Each history, except for the silence surrounding Black Canadian history, seemed straight ahead in its telling. But, the larger story of all people's relationships at home on Canadian soil was defined by policies that complicated the vision of a shared future. Supremacy of identity was a mirage and policy was badly conflicted on that point. Teachers didn't have enough information to decide whether Canada was an American-type melting pot or a Canadian boiling pot.

Tensions centred on continuity of sovereignty. The French, like the British, had won a home on Canadian soil using European conventions for land acquisition. The French had established a continuing right to a separate identity. The British maintained important links to England. As for the Indian Nations, their treaties with the British Crown enabled the release of land and resources to the settlers for generations to come. The treaties provided early settlers (as they continue to do for today's immigrants) security of tenure, a deep and rare human right, for as long "as the sun shines." Why were we not teaching that First Nations and the British Crown had a permanent relationship that benefits all Canadians? Part of the answer lay in the barrenness of the provincial curriculum. Little actual content, let alone instructional guidelines were available to teachers. Textbooks provided only dry, uninspired, stereotypical, and inaccurate information to work with. Educational leaders had not yet done their part; it might even be said there was deadwood in the system.

Students at the Saskatchewan Indian Federated College, with whom I discussed this matter, said it was odd that First Nations signatories to the treaties, momentous as these documents remain, had not yet earned the title "founding fathers." The harder question for them was why Aboriginal people continued to suffer exclusion from anything relevant to the power of decision, particularly over their own lives. Power was an issue prominent in the minds of students particularly as Canada struggled to define its constitutional identity. I would often recall Dr. Brass saying to his students, "Nothing leads like legislation."

Prime Minister Pierre Trudeau, young and brimming with energy and optimism, led the patriation of the constitution, a cornerstone to Canada as a nation. His vision, arguably sensitive to anomalies such as special rights, defined Canada as a bilingual and multicultural country. However, his analysis regarding Canada's relationship to Aboriginal peoples was circumspect and problematic, especially in terms of related policy. The 1969 White Paper passed through our student hands like wild fire. That policy document on Indians sounded the death knell of Indian identity in the legal sense. For example, discriminatory marriage legislation had removed my legal identity thus robbing me of the right by treaty to educational financial support. It appeared now that any, and all rights, could be systematically removed from treaty Indians. Canada's answer to its "Indian problem" appeared to lack a rational foundation, let alone a moral one.

Basically, the 1969 White Paper sought to dismantle the Indian Act, the only federal statute that defines "Indians." Under the guise of bringing an end to the Indian Act, Canadian legislation known internationally as the world's most oppressive document, the government would destroy treaty promises and obligations. Students at the college were stunned.

To the many students who went through immense personal difficulty to get to university, the 1969 White Paper was a travesty. More often than not, the students were single moms with children, or young people living on their own, or caretakers and guardians in charge of their siblings and ailing relatives who depended on them to succeed. Most were barely scraping by. Many were forced to take out government loans to cover the basic costs of living, as I had done. I was lucky by comparison because I had a job to go back to after my studies.

My job meant teaching "Canada." Yet the more I learned, the more difficult seemed the task of teaching young children the bigger story of their country. I felt it was my job to nurture pride of democracy, love for the best country in the world, and appreciation for our common past. Little of this could be achieved by hiding Canada's past. As is well understood, families with big secrets fall apart. Countries with unexamined pasts rot from within. I looked at my pupils and saw the face of a new generation. I felt responsible.

I also felt helpless. There was no one to ask. There was no curriculum guide or textbook to show me how I might begin. School board consultants lacked training in the area of Aboriginal education. There was no one to help me try to teach the history of Canada to the depth of knowledge each child in my classroom deserved. High-school students debated issues; though most high-school teachers lacked the knowledge necessary to knowledgeably guide classroom discussions on Canadian–Aboriginal relations. The classroom debate, a popular teaching method, remained an intellectual mess waiting to happen. For instance, a common statement for debate would be: "Aboriginal people should pay taxes." However, in the first instance, Bill C31 people, like me, pay taxes on income, on property, and on purchases. So do Métis people. So do enfranchised Indians. So do First Nations people working off reserve. Teachers failed the test of truth in the very method meant to clarify truths within the classroom debate. Pure and simple, teachers college had failed in this department.

Teachers college, however, was not solely responsible. That much I could say in defense of my professors. Organizations composed of trustees and school administrators, for instance, might have called for a new provincial curriculum long before they actually did. A curriculum guide ought to have been available that explained to teachers how they might go about teaching unique identity. Instead, misinformation remained an obstacle. In the 1960s and 1970s, and even today, people tend to speak of First Nations as though they are one group—this mistake is akin to stating that the English and the Portuguese form a single culture and language. First Nations consist of many cultures and they are multicultural and multilingual. A teacher, knowing this, might conclude that First Nations identity can be taught under the concept of multiculturalism, a concept in its own right. However, First Nations parents could object, and do. Multiculturalism, as defined by the constitution, narrows the meaning of identity to concepts of ethnicity. The First Nations see their identities in terms of nation, beyond ethnicity and other immigration concepts. Nations make treaties. The question remained how to teach a sound understanding of Canadian–Aboriginal relations. Policy that would lead to a new curriculum was badly needed.

I remember the sense of rising excitement at school when the idea of defining Canada's identity ignited people's imagination. Interest began with the 1963 Royal Commission on Bilingualism and Biculturalism. A few staffroom conversations centred on French–English relations. I was astonished that Aboriginal people and the treaties didn't come up in these discussions. Being new to the profession and mindful of my situation, I was nervous about speaking up about this. All I knew about treaties, at that time, was that our people and Queen Victoria struck a deal about the land that was fair for all Canada's immigrants and the Aboriginal people. I didn't speak up and I didn't find out more, at the time. I was most concerned with my ability to maintain parental and collegial confidence in me as a teacher, first and foremost.

Oftentimes I wished to say something, my heart thumping in my chest, but a sixth sense warned no, not yet. It felt, when I look back now, not unlike a person would feel in Orwell's 1984 where government officers pitched historical papers and other memoranda into a memory hole set up to obliterate evidence for the thinking mind. The Thought Police thus erased identity. The policy of 1971, Multiculturalism with a Bilingual Framework, omitted discussion of Aboriginal relations. The omission went unnoticed by teachers and principals, who, if they did notice its absence, opted for silence, as I did.

The good thing was that I could teach a multicultural identity and be confident that I was covering the bases for most children in my classroom. No curriculum guide, though, provided a way to teach the identity of a First Nations girl who came to my classroom from northern

Saskatchewan. And no such document "explained" Vincent, a First Nations boy, either.

VINCENT

I was nervous about teaching in a transitional school because I'd heard that it was extremely challenging to teach in a school where social conditions, economic realities, and local culture were changing. Such factors added unseen layers of tension that could erupt among the children, anytime. I arrived at the school in August to look things over. My classroom windows looked onto a wind-blown scarred lawn edged in pavement with tufts of dried grass and stringy dandelions trembling in stony soil. Soon it would be September. I saw a box of new chalk open on my desk and made an important observation; the chalk was as good as any classroom's anywhere.

There I met Vincent. When I saw him, that first day of school, I thought how undemanding a presence he made. Generally speaking, the behaviour of boys, especially boys under stress, is highly visible. They tend to act out their feelings more vigorously than girls who can usually go on with their lives, quietly, despite their burdens. Vincent was a calm even-tempered boy, although his life's circumstances might have caused him to be otherwise. He was well mannered. Many would say he was shy. However, shyness had little to do with it. Vincent, I could tell, was brought up in the tradition of his people; that meant tending to life and its circumstances in the quiet manner. By cultural code, his remained an undemanding presence. I knew from my own childhood what these expectations for behaviour were. My grandmothers' calming ways curbed many a thoughtless word or gesture and affirmed even my minor courtesies. Now, I saw the tradition—and I saw the boy.

He loved to draw. The little pictures he drew were of scenes around his home on the reserve. He missed the roads, the trees, and the walks with his dog, he said, so he drew them. His family had come to the city toward the end of summer because his parents needed to find work. He liked school, he said, and I could tell he did. I kept an eye out for him, though, because I knew that children coming in from rural areas sometimes took a while to feel comfortable in their new city surroundings. Vincent was doing fine by the end of the first day. He made friends easily and worked hard.

He told me in a quiet moment, after school one day, that the hardest thing for his family right now was finding a big enough place to live in. His parents told him that city people were cautious about having strangers come up to their house, and they might slam the door in their face but that he was not to get upset about it. That never happened, Vincent said, with a smile. They were finally lucky to get a little house. The landlady, who showed them the inside, Vincent said, was not backward about strangers. In fact, she gave his mom the key right away and told her, "No dogs, no relatives, and no paint."

According to Vincent, the landlady insisted the walls of the house were to remain off-white though Vincent's mother wished for soft rosy walls and a yellow kitchen. Vincent's mom and dad were glad that they could concentrate on finding jobs now, he added. Vincent smiled, saying how his mother wanted pink drop-earrings like the landlady's and "red plastic high-heels like hers, too."

According to Vincent, his mother and father started out each morning together. They'd split up when they got downtown to look for work and catch the bus back from the bus stop on Eleventh Avenue in time to make supper. While his parents were getting established, Vincent settled into the life of the school.

It was about a month into the school year when I noticed a subtle difference in Vincent. His tone and manner changed. His quietness was more like silence now, so I began to pay closer attention to him. He came to school in rumpled shirts and tired jeans, a dramatic shift from his once ironed shirts and creased pants. He remained diligent about handing in his work, but he was slowing down. One day after school, I went over to his desk to talk to him.

"Vincent, is everything all right?"

"Yeah, I guess so."

He packed and unpacked the books in his school bag, showing no signs of wanting to leave.

"Trouble at home?"

"Yes."

"Do you want me to talk to your mom, or anyone?"

He hesitated a moment and replied, "Dad brought home another woman."

Vincent did not have to say anymore; his mother wouldn't want to talk to anyone, just yet.

"Are you and your mom living some place else, then?"

He nodded. "We're living with my Auntie Lilly."

I understood now why he was sometimes late and why he wore the same clothes everyday. A sudden thought of winter sent a chill through me.

"Does your auntie live far from school?"

"Yeah, kinda, but I don't mind walking."

He stopped; he sensed what I was thinking.

"Mom doesn't have a key to the house," he explained, "so we can't go in for our winter clothes."

"There's always a way around that," I said. "Lots of kids just take coats and things from the big sharing-box in the storage room downstairs."

"Yeah," he replied. His downcast eyes said he wouldn't want this.

"Things will turn out, Vincent. In the meantime, be good to your mom. And let's you and me talk some more. Anytime. Okay?"

At that, he smiled and quietly walked out the door—into a world of dwindling hope, I thought to myself.

With the children dismissed and gone home, I sat at my desk wondering about Vincent and his mother. With another woman walking in through the door of her home, she couldn't stay and pretend nothing happened. She had no choice but to leave. Nor would she be asked to come back any time soon. Being a good mother meant more than swallowing her pride and putting up with these things. She had to find a place to stay and was lucky to have a sister in town who would let her move in for a while, children and all. Vincent struggled. His parents were caught up in separate worlds and would have no real time for him.

I began to feel a mounting sense of urgency. I wanted to give Vincent something before he left our school for good because he surely would leave now. Almost all broken families ended up leaving. I wanted to give this boy something that no one could take from him, something he might treasure as his own. But what? A book of stories perhaps, stories of courage, stories of heroes, stories of his people's inventions and of their many contributions to the growth of the Western world. This would see him through. I was fairly humming: Vincent, you be here come Monday.

I began my search among the books on the shelves in our class-room. There were no books of the kind I thought about. Puzzled, I hung my coat back up on its hook in the room and, master key in hand, hurried down the hall to the locked library. Suppose I go through all the titles, I thought. An evening's exploration of these dear old book shelves was not a new experience for me, and I was gripped by a familiar sense of anticipation, the thrill of hunting down the right book for the right child, at the right time. This was a quest for treasure, after all, real treasure: Let there be pirates on every sea. There are fish in the ocean...fragments of verse formed themselves inside my head, crowding my excited mind, whether they made sense or not.

Alas, the evening wore into darkness and the coldness of the floor had seeped into my bones. I was exhausted. Among the heaps of books piled up beside me, not a single one was written with a thought for Vincent in mind. They seemed written by people who believed the earth was only recently made round and that only half the world's inhabitants had had a hand in its forming; the other half scarcely figured at all. Apparently, "uncivilized people" on this side of the world were busy warring. They were preoccupied with chasing down mastodons. They were intent on sacrificial rites. This was the state of affairs in school books, then.

A book on pre-Columbian surgery gave momentary hope. Momentary, since its description of ancient surgical knowledge and methods was ample. However, the portrayals dwelt heavily on notions of trial and error. The subtext was that whenever a mindless scraping at the head of a patient with a sharpened bone did not immediately result in corrective surgery of the brain, the medicine man (not a surgeon, mind you!) might consider casting this aside for a really sharp-pointed stick, nearby. According to such historians, successful surgery just happened when the serendipitous coincided with an immediate need; nothing was ever planned. These fictitious accounts didn't connect with the photographs I had seen of recently excavated skulls that had been buried thousands of years ago, their cleanly fused trepanation obvious to the naked eye. The historical writings didn't explain the pre-contact existence of advanced dentistry on this continent, either. The time when an emperor, or whatever his high ranking title would be, could have his teeth implanted with decorative gems of agate, lapis lazuli, and diamonds, painlessly, too, one had to imagine if the myth were true that emperors always extract vexation's due. Nothing was told of the great international trading days of the plains people either, at least not in the language a boy would understand. There was not a single story for young Vincent, who was now badly in need of an identity rooted in his people's great and wonderful past.

Vincent left without saying goodbye. He didn't even come to pick up his things. It was as if he had vanished into thin air. The house was empty, the children said, and there was no one living at his aunt's place, either. When they called on him the last couple of nights, they said, all the lights were off and no one came to answer the door. The children were upset.

"Vincent will be fine," I assured them. "His family probably went back to the reserve. He'll be glad to see his dog. And his mom is bound to find work there." The children were not receptive, however; they pretended to be engrossed in their reading. There would be no coming back for Vincent, we knew. And it would take a long time to accept how things really were.

Over the years, it had grown more and more difficult to admit that a child, any child, was unable to pick up a book that told the extraordinary tale of his or her people. It seemed that the longer I taught, the more I had to face the truth of it all. Teachers could be keepers of half-truths or seekers of the full truth. I would have to choose between the two, and soon.

I was thinking more often of Vincent now and about the books he might one day read. There was no getting him out of my mind. In truth, Vincent's life was an outcome of countless unexplored facts of his peoples' history. I mentally reviewed the many books that I had studied as a teacher. Some depicted Vincent's people in a damaging way, and pupils at all grade levels read these books. Here, for example, was a picture of a starving "Indian" wrapped in a Hudson Bay blanket; he appears to be trying to sell buffalo skulls to settlers who hang out of a train window at a whistle stop, with the dry open prairie all around. Nothing in the accompanying text explains the plight of the man nor his state of mind. A federal government official letter of the time stated that people on the Cowessess Reserve in the 1880s, "...are to be kept on starvation allowances..." It could be my family member who stood there, gaunt, isolated, an historical image only.

Sterile depictions rob all minds. And all children. I despaired that certain photographs did not engage the heart and mind like those of the European settlers of the same period. Pictures of European women dressed up in lace gowns and parasols, needing little more than the borrowed hats and finery of a photographer's trunk of props to depict signs of social status and hope. Many a pioneer woman smiled girlishly from these photographs; "Wish you were here," they seemed to be saying. School children wouldn't notice that several different women for miles around might be wearing the same dress. In contrast, they could see the hungry searing eyes of desperate Indian people wearing clothes that were never anybody's. In a few years turning, with concepts of trade and commerce in school curricula beginning to take shape, pictures would say a great deal more. Photos of Indian people working behind counters in department stores, for example, did not exist in textbooks, if they existed anywhere in the first place. The absence of such images added to the stereotype that only non-Aboriginal people worked. But there was no text to explain why.

It seemed the real story of human development might have begun to take on the idea of a rounded Earth, a completed orb at last, when Columbus arrived. But the new storytellers, the modern historians of the days, wrote that story in terms of half-globe thinking. Indeed, this was to be a habit of mind, a tradition. Instead of recording that the world was now aware of itself as whole and teeming with new-found neighbours who had fascinating customs and technologies for mutual benefit, reality was narrowed down. What was unforgivable was that Vincent was forced to remain a stranger even to himself because of a fundamental flaw that shaped centuries of thinking. He and his classmates were being asked to learn a one-sided history of this immense continent they called home. One would think the Mayans dead and gone. One would think the indigenous farmers and coastal trading peoples all nomads. One would think there were no libraries on the American continent before Columbus. And this, in my classroom! I was beginning to see that my thinking had been tied for some time. I was not a real teacher, even yet. I was a keeper of half-truths.

I went for long walks. I wanted to become a good teacher. It was another thing altogether to leave teaching in order to work on curriculum revision at the provincial level. Yet, that reality was on its way. The 1970s had beckoned, rolled up to my door in fact, and then unrolled a path I couldn't ignore. The opportunity to inquire into the heart of teaching entered my professional thoughts more and more.

Existing textbooks and media of all kinds in the 1970s presented inaccurate, negative views of First Nations and Métis identity. These views were taught by people I admired, in a profession I respected. It began in teachers college, in fact, with Professor Palmer, a compact white-haired man who taught Canadian history. It was his firm belief, he said, that the five senses and one's emotions were the best teachers. He read aloud in class the more telling passages from Arthur Lower's textbook, *Canadians in the Making*. Like the writer-historian before him, Professor Palmer presented readings of horrific description and interpretation without a sense of personal analysis and ownership: "The Jesuit priest had been tortured the long night through by the Indians who tore at his flesh and raked his body with burning sticks from the fires he was forced to dance around..."

Professor Palmer had read without malice and left without answers. Questions remained. It seemed I was being told I would continue to teach from works that bowled you over with the biases of the past.

This jarred the teacher in me in ways difficult to ignore. It was as if I could not turn off the alarm clock in hope of returning to a dream of hope. Still, a nine o'clock bell rang out somewhere and I grew determined not to be late for school.

I set aside time to think a few things through. Change was something I could not effect alone. History demonstrates that deep change rarely turns on a single issue, however complex. Fundamentally, education was on a collision course with a new generation. I could do my part, the first step of which was to learn what I could about the reality behind popular portrayals. I would study the statistics, archival documents, recorded oral histories, and what the social commentators were saying. When I found a document that looked closely at the history of my reserve, I could see why its story lay buried. The big question suddenly became: how could teachers, or any other educational leaders, take up teaching Canada's history of Aboriginal education without feeling they had been traitors to the teaching profession? For starters, teachers appeared to have failed their profession's hard-won time-tested and universal principles of teaching and learning. Between 1965 and 1972, First Nations people were migrating from reserve to city at an accelerating pace. The percentage living off reserve increased from 25 per cent to 36 per cent. As far as teaching and learning went, about 90 per cent of students in rural and urban Saskatchewan failed to reach grade twelve. That was in the 1970s. The failure didn't stop there. If the school had failed Aboriginal students, it also deprived non-Aboriginal students of important knowledge: how we learn from our past; how we live together; and how we hold responsibility for the state of our social contract. That is a lot of learning.

In today's world, now reaching beyond Marshall McLuhan's global village, boundaries are beginning to mean less and less. In his book, *The Truth about the Truth: De-confusing and Re-constructing the Postmodern World* (1995), Walter Truett Anderson characterizes this as a time of "rebuilding all the foundations of civilization"; we are "emerging from the security of our tribes, traditions, religions, and worldviews." In such a world, relationships are the very foundation to a country's security. As today's teachers begin the task of discovering and de-confusing Canada's past to benefit its succeeding generations, school administrators and trustees can assist them in their search; for it is society's teachers who are entrusted to "keep the faith."

In order for me to keep the faith, I would have to learn more about teaching a complete account of Canadian history and culture to all my students, I would have to make an effort try to understand the past and see ahead into the future without the help of a clear picture like the one painted by thinkers like Walter Truett Anderson and others. I asked myself, for instance, why Canada's approved education programs failed Aboriginal people. This was true for members of my family through the generations. Clearly, I was in pursuit of knowledge that wasn't available to me in the public education system of the 1970s. Professionally speaking, though, I felt an obligation to learn how to teach Aboriginal history like a mature and thinking person.

The story of schooling for my grandparents and my parents is a profoundly sad one. Family members, returning home from residential school, had a haunted look about them. In contrast, I often saw contentment in the schools where I taught. The children there were taught by caring teachers. If I had learned anything about being a teacher worth its name, I knew and understood that teachers and school administrators have only to obey the guidelines of the human heart.

In the early part of the 1970s, I attended evening seminars on a range of contemporary topics offered by one of the Catholic churches in Regina. In a particular session, the topic centred on Viktor E. Frankl's book, *Man's Search for Meaning* (1959). The group discussed Frankl's therapeutic model and his thesis on man's search for meaning as the prime motivator in human beings. Frankl asserted that the will to meaning goes beyond the will to power, as defined by Adler, and beyond the will to pleasure, as proposed by Freud. Frankl wrote that he understood and appreciated fully Nietzsche's claim, "He who has a why to live for can bear almost any how." Frankl understood this because he suffered the tortures of the concentration camp and survived all of its horrors and privation.

I was still teaching and still deeply inhibited about my life story when this special seminar took place. I finally had a better understanding of the domination and resultant apathy and related socials ills that were rampant on our reserve.

I recall my distress in realizing that, at the seminar discussions, none of the priests and parishioners, among whom were a couple of teachers, said anything that reflected conscious thought about Indian people in Saskatchewan and how their life's meaning had been broken. Instead, the discussion was hermetically sealed in a time and place. It was as though the problem of inhumanity belonged only to Europe's past. Frankl's stunning and important story was circumscribed; his breakthrough in the field of human psychology drastically abbreviated. I couldn't make myself speak up. For one thing, if I as much as uttered the words "my grandparents" in public my emotions would overtake me. Added to that, there wasn't a clear and simple way to begin the discussion of the central fact: during the 1880s, the will to meaning had been erased with great deliberation in the lives of Aboriginal children here in Canada.

To date, life on the reserve and on neighbouring reserves continues the story; the story remains every Canadian's living inheritance, present and future. Still, teachers labour under an extra load when it comes to teaching Aboriginal content. Their questions are difficult to answer: can I teach this well; what methods do I apply; and, what materials work best at this grade level?

These standard questions, second nature to every teacher, remain a starting point. Now I would have to confront a few more hard questions in order to foster my own professional development, questions like the apparently easy one of a five-year old: why is fire hot?

As a First Nations teacher, I was as hard pressed to teach such content with its fuller perspective as any teacher without proper guidance and the instructional materials that are suitable for each grade. I told myself that I might need, at the very least, a biologist, a philosopher, an artist, and maybe two school board members to assist me on this journey of inquiry. I believed an easy place to begin would be to teach my family's history. After pondering this, I formulated a few questions suggested by my research. Success in my inquiry, I knew, depended on the questions asked. A lot more depended on how I might set out to answer them. My final task would be to link the new content and perspective together in a new way to form the instructional approaches and methods that teachers use as a matter of course. I would then be ready to turn my attention to a review of the residential school curriculum to compare the possibilities for success. With this much done, I would turn to the study of Canadian-Aboriginal relations in education.

Such questions and answers would have to consider the student, the teacher, and the parents, too, I supposed. My struggle began with the first straightforward question.

Is it possible to teach hard facts without causing a "fight or flight" response in the learner?

I believe I would teach my family history first as a kind of myth, a story that takes place in time and place some distance removed. This ground work could provide my students with the means to understand, without sacrificing their compassion, actual historical events as they move through the grades. Then when the students got a little older, I might provide the names of children who died in residential schools in a single year in the 1800s, say 1891, thus: Henry Clarke, age twelve; John F. Linklater, age six; Isabella Constant, age eleven; Annie McKay, age thirteen. There would be more than enough names to cover each student in today's classroom, with names left over. I would then have each of my students select a name and trace it to a First Nations family name of today. Stories, thus revealed, might then be explored with empathy, as we do with our war heroes' stories today. I might also have students explore facts in math period. Older students could analyze residential school enrollment statistics to compare the numbers of children who enrolled to the numbers who died in a particular year. They might also graph the months each student was alive and learning. A study of levels achieved and the factors involved would be part of the teachers' knowledge base when discussions begin. The difficulty is, the information tables and lists of students are not available in textbooks and remain almost impossible for teachers to find.

Can the long and painful story of Aboriginal education policy be told using short-story techniques?

When teachers ask hard questions—how do I teach this and with what?—professors in faculties of education are expected to have at least part of the answer. In preparation, if I had enough education to be a professor, I might ask my teacher candidates to view the history of First Nations education in Saskatchewan during the residential school period in, perhaps, a short-story format. Let us say that the theme of the "short story" centres on the politics of domination. Here, as in all good short stories, the aim and purpose is to confine human freedoms. The setting could be simply a box; that is, life hemmed in by inhumane policies that paralyze people's hopes, thus putting a strangle-hold on constructive reaction.

The plot unfolds when the protagonist takes the people's children away. Anxiety for their children is his means of control. This tactic increases in effectiveness as news of unexplained deaths begin circulating among the grief-stricken parents and grandparents. Parental suffering bolsters the story's conflict as powerful obstacles violate the human wish to see one's captive child. The action of the story leaps forward as the protagonist begins removing the people's power of decision through procedure and policy that keeps the victims off balance, psychologically, and in a beggar's position, physically. A rise in conflict is realized when the protagonist shows that he alone decides what the captive children will learn. The climax comes when the protagonist demonstrates his capacity to deny the people in the box their will to meaning.

This would make for a good short story but for one problem. Namely, that, the long story of Aboriginal schooling in Canada is still being written. Parts of the facts remain in living memory and parts lie buried in the country's uncovered history. Some of that history is coming to light through the painstaking research of people like Isabel Andrews. Her seminal work, "The Crooked Lakes Reserves: a study of Indian policy in practice from the Qu'Appelle Treaty to 1900," was submitted to the Faculty of Graduate Studies and Research at the University of Regina in 1972. Isabel Andrews's research tells us that at the signing of the treaties in the 1800s, government used starvation as key instrumentation to force Indian people on to small parcels of land called reserves. Once on the reserves, the people were compelled to work for rations, meager rations of wormy flour and salted bacon. That twisted policy, undemocratic to its core, helped to guide the cruel treatment of the people. There was no work on reserves and scant means by which to create work. Even had there been work, people didn't have basic tools. There were no animals. No territory wherein hunters might regain self-sustaining labour. Hunger gripped the people. Many died.

In the education of "Indians" in Canada, the human heart also proved no guide. The basic principles of teaching and learning were distorted, stunted, and abused. The importance of a child feeling at home in his or her family and community, of feeling loved, was a principle denied in the structure of "Indian education." Home, family, cultural community—all the mainstays of a learner's emotional security and identity—were removed. Parental love had no bearing on decisions made. Instead, the government searched for "solutions" to its "Indian problem" as it dismantled the home life of five-year-olds.

Can the writing of plays by students accurately portray Canadian historical figures?
As a teacher today in search of an instructional method for today's students, I might consider assigning certain elements of historical content to the writing and presentation of a play, complete with assigned parts. The introduction of archetypal metaphors, such as powers in exchange for one's soul, are universal to the stories that come from around the world, and might assist student playwrights. The story of Indians on reserves in the 1800s has all the hallmarks of a dramatic

play and is adaptable to metaphors such as: the "in the beginning" creation stories; the agreement won between the people and invaders; people's removal to a promised land; people's confrontation with an opposing force; the presence of a nurturing woman, such as a queen; the seers, such as elders; the monster that threatens liberation, and so on. These metaphoric prototypes provide fertile ground for school children's imaginations (if one counts the success of J.K. Rowling's Harry Potter in our time).

In such a play, the hero, in the name of church and state, explains his barbarism away. He goes to great lengths to manage perception. He distorts all that his actions represent. Despite wielding powerful tools of civilization: the Bible, the Magna Carta, the Royal Proclamation of 1763, and the treaties, it is seen that the hero lacks a conscience. Unfortunately, for teachers and student alike, this is where the playwright's difficulty arises. Although the playwright's research poses a challenge, the final hurdle is that the historical content makes for poor drama; the balance of power is too one sided: man versus child, or well-fed man versus starving man. Inglorious conflict is not the stuff of high drama and, as such, not suitable to its purpose. It is seen that here is the loss of yet one more potential instructional method—like the ill-prepared classroom debate.

How can the reporter's art be used to make academic research accessible to students?

In Isabel Andrews's research, one reads that in 1879 the government commissioned Nicholas Flood Davin to review and then report on Indian industrial schools by touring the United States. He was a lawyer, editor of the *Regina Leader*, the local newspaper, and a member of parliament. The decision to place Indian children in boarding schools was based on his report. The report also influenced decisions on the role of parents and the academic program.

In our time, a headline in the local newspaper might read: Parents Have No Say in Education. News headlines, however, deal with the present while history attends to the past. Thus, to some young minds, history may seem boring; archival reports and textbooks, dull and lifeless. Perhaps even to adults historical texts can seem abstract and remote in time. Yet, before their eyes might be a document at once rare and priceless. One such document is Isabel Andrews's thesis: "The Crooked Lakes Reserves," prepared for the University of Saskatchewan, Regina Campus, in 1972.

When I read Isabel Andrews's thesis, I found it exceptionally interesting. But then, I was an adult and, besides, this was my family's story. However, the thesis is more than that. It also contains every Canadian's history. And that is where the importance of newspaper reporters comes in. Their reports present the captivating facts. The story springs to life. Such reporting also helps the reader reflect upon someone's unique life story. In this sense, reporters are like teachers whose main responsibility is to gather fuel that fires up the power of the mind.

The more I thought about this during the late 1970s and early 1980s, the more I saw how a historical thesis might be made interesting for students and parents, as well as teachers. How history is taught matters. A Chinese pedagogical principle says: Tell me, I forget; show me, I remember; have me do, and I understand.

A possibly engaging instructional approach might be for be the teacher to ask students to imagine that they are newspaper reporters. As their teacher, I would provide a page of historical notes taken from the thesis. The student's job would be to write stories suitable for today's newspaper and for today's readers based on the document.

Can the teacher design media reporting in a way that captures difficult truth?
In preparing students for this task, teachers might share a few of their own attempts, as models, first establishing their lack of training and practice in newspaper reporting. Instead, a local reporter will be invited into the classroom to critique their headlines and stories. Thus, the teacher's sample might be as follows:

Headline: Parents Have No Say in Children's Schooling

Report: Parents of the Cowesses Indian reserve say their request for a community school is being ignored. They claim government is misguided in placing "duty and dignity" before needs of children. In response, MP Nicholas Flood Davin says that a guarantee from government displays ignorance of "the Indian character." He believes that once such schools are initiated, chiefs might be given to understand that they have a right to a voice in the running of the school. No comment regarding treaty rights was made due to confidentiality.

Source: Andrews p. 179: "Guaranteeing schools as one of the considerations for [the Indian's] surrendering the title to land, was, in my opinion, trifling with a great duty and placing the Government in no dignified attitude. It should have been assumed that the Government would attend to its proper and pressing business in this important particular. Such a guarantee, moreover, betrays a want of knowledge of the Indian character. It might easily have been realized, (it is at least thinkable) that one of the results would be to make the Chiefs believe they had some right to a voice regarding the character and management of the schools, as well as regarding the initiatory step of their establishment." N.F. Davin, "Confidential Report on Industrial Schools for Indians and Half-breeds," Ottawa, March 14, 1879, Appendix, Archives of Saskatchewan, copy from the files of the Indian Affairs Branch, Department of Citizenship and Immigration, Ottawa, p. 11.

Another sample report based on Andrews's thesis might be:

Headline: Government Plan Erases First Nation's Identity Parents Claim

Report: Parents of Cowesses Indian reserve voiced strong objection, today, to a statement made by Mr. J.A. Macrae, Inspector of Protestant Schools for Indians in Manitoba and the Northwest. Macrae states that the primary aim of the school is to produce "a moral, industrious, white character." When asked what he considers might be his preferred level of education Macrae replied, "an uneducated white character"—if it stands for civilization.

Source: Andrews p. 183: "Until it is clearly felt that the primary aim is to produce a moral, industrious, white character—even unlettered—with a cultivated antipathy to that which stands against, and sympathy with that which stands for civilization." Sessional Papers, 1892, No. 14, p.98. [Statement of the Inspector of Protestant Schools for Indians in Manitoba and the Northwest, J.A. Macrae.]

For variety of instructional approach, it might be worth the class's time to summarize sections of general information found within the Andrews thesis and then demonstrate the report's veracity with a citation, as in the following:

Headline: RCMP Captures Three Runaways

Report: Two Constables of the NWMP arrested three runaway boarding-school boys on the evening of August 24th. It was reported by Agent McDonald that Father Hugonnard, the Round Lake school principal, arrived on the Cowesses Indian Reserve accompanied by police. Parents hiding the boys complained that harsh measures are being taken against family life. Parents fear imprisonment if convicted.

Source: Andrews p. 201, footnote 1: "The Governor in Council may make regulations, either general or affecting the Indians of any province or of any named band, to secure the compulsory attendance of children at school...Such regulations, in addition to any other provisions deemed expedient, may provide for the arrest and conveyance to school and detention there, of truant children and of children who are prevented by their parents or guardians from attending: and such regulation may provide for the punishment, upon summary conviction, by fine or imprisonment, or both, of parents and guardians, or persons having the charge of children, who fail, refuse or neglect to cause such children to attend school..." Canada Statutes, 57–58 Vict., Chapter 32, Section 11.

The implications of government-driven research and policy, as defined in Davin's set of recommendations, were harsh and cruel. Family life, among "Indians" suffered under immense oppression and privation. Davin likely became increasingly aware of this reality and its significance as time passed. Education, a universal, democratic instrument of truth and justice, had become a tool of injustice in the hands of church and state. Today, the work of teachers has become, by necessity, one of reclaiming the image of education.

As for Davin, on an October day in 1901, he took a room at the Clarendon Hotel in downtown Winnipeg and there committed suicide. The newspaper reports of this can be read by teachers wishing to learn more about the times and to evaluate the content and skills of reporting among reporters back then. Students and teachers might recognize that pity differs from compassion by an assumption of innocence.

What questions about residential schooling ought educators be prepared to answer?
Their first task may well be to define the roots of failure in Canada of Aboriginal children in the public school system. Teachers would do well to prepare themselves to provide information regarding the past record of their profession. A key question for the teacher becomes: what should I know about residential school pedagogy and practice when asked by parents and those running for office such as school trustees?

Teachers might prepare for this question by referring to the section called "Standard Course of Study for Indian Schools" (Andrews thesis, Appendix B) for an overview of the residential school curriculum.

Andrews tells us that the "authorized" curriculum consisted of five standards aimed at achieving a grade three or four level of reading. In the late 1800s, the Indian child's school day was divided between class-room instruction and manual labour, almost half and half. The girls did the sewing, mending, laundry, and knitting in support of the operation of the school. Child labour for school operations and the hiring out of girls as domestics were priority outcomes for the curriculum. The boys cleared brush, planted potatoes, ploughed fields, and cleaned the stables. Here, instruction was aimed at competency in the mechanical trades and farming. The children could not excel academically because the program disallowed progress beyond a grade-four level of reading, and there were no libraries accessible to them. Academic learning was not the primary intent of the school.

Should inquiring individuals remain unconvinced, teachers might point to additional information that confirms children thrive best in schools where there are positive relations between parent and teacher, teacher and child, and parent and child.

The participation of parents helps to build mutual regard between learners and the teachers. However, in the 1880s, policy and procedure defined relations between parent and school. A Canadian statute shows that the Governor in Council had been empowered to make regulations to secure compulsory attendance of Indian children. The regulations provided for the arrest and detention of truant children. The regulations speak of punishing parents or guardians by fine or imprisonment, or both:

> ...in such districts as the advance towards civilization has been such as to render the measure politic, I have either withheld assistance from the parents who refuse to send their children to the school or have arrived at the same end by diverting a proportion of the rations formerly allowed for the consumption of the children at home to the provision of a meal at the school-house, which provides a strong inducement to regular attendance.[1]

It can be seen that respect for the parent and empathy for the learner, who would feel the effects of this, was absent. The power to choose, to state a position, to negotiate choice, and then to enact the result is a cherished process in a democratic society. Instead, the Indian Act built a framework for legal enforcement of management procedures that worked against parental decision making. Andrews reports on the attitude taken regarding adults and children, for that matter:

> Little can be done with him. He can be taught to do a little at farming, and at stock-raising, and to dress in a more civilized manner, but that is all.[2]

Often children fled. Families tried to hide them. Diseased and unsafe, the residential schools were death traps. Doctors assigned to the schools sent reports to the authorities of the extremely bad conditions under which many of the children grew sick and died. Dr. R.G. Ferguson, First Superintendent of Fort San (1917–28) wrote that tuberculosis was their major cause of death in the schools. Yet, authorities did not seek to protect the children. At the Qu'Appelle Industrial School, increase in the death rate was rapid from 1892 to 1893—of the 357 enrolled, seventy students died. According to Dr. Ferguson, the government received reports of the children so closely packed in the dorms that they had to breathe infectious air shared by all:

> The obvious conditions facilitating the progress of the epidemic and the spread of infection at the time were the concentration of the Indians in fixed residences on the reserves, lack of sanitation, their contact with the surrounding white settlers, and the concentration of the children in boarding schools for education. Under these conditions tuberculosis infection spread quickly.[3]

The plans and practices for teaching and learning had not changed by the time my parents attended Round Lake Residential School. My mother told of the unremitting work. She said she was happy enough to learn how to sew and cook but that the work tired her out. She was lucky, she said, because she was a member of the girls' choir in the school that won competitions throughout the province. The joy that singing gave my mother was evident. Even so, she said, she was glad she didn't have to send my older brother, my younger sister, and me to the Round Lake school. As a boy my father learned all he could in the hope of becoming a farmer one day. Despite the lack of emphasis on academic learning, my parents loved to read and, as adults, read whatever they could. A library would have brought them great happiness; but, there were no libraries on the reserve, even in my day.

Today, the education system in Saskatchewan is organized with checks and balances that support shared decision making. The decision as to what is taught in the public school is the result of both influence and authority as shared by parents, teachers, trustees, administrators, and faculties of education. Teachers can rely on curriculum guides that are authorized and respectful. As a curriculum developer in my new job at the department of education beginning in 1983, I saw how the concept of relevance prompts lively debate that rises to fever pitch with the word "relevant" itself. Arguments, however, still affirm the relevance of community and culture to learning. Curriculum guides offer defined links between a learner's life experiences and the instructional approaches teachers may choose. With the passing of years, particularly during the 1970s and 1980s, concern for stereotyping in instructional materials grew. Outrage was expressed by Aboriginal parents, students, and educators and people began to take action to rectify the high dropout rate among Aboriginal high-school students. To the present date, Aboriginal people are better organized to develop and implement a bicultural education in their communities. They define relevant curriculum from a foundation of identity. The people of Red Earth in Saskatchewan, for example, define bicultural curriculum from this perspective.

Over time, I gained a better understanding of what silences history. My colleagues and I lacked the same knowledge background. Though we had come through the same educational system together, we were oblivious to the black holes of memory's destruction. I asked myself this question as a maturing teacher and, again, as an experienced curriculum developer nearing retirement: If teachers of today (approaching 2010) were to know the history of Aboriginal education, would they look at a picture of failing Aboriginal pupils and seek a reversal? I thought about the school principals and teachers I had worked with over the years; I knew the hours they put in after school, the searches they undertook on weekends to find interesting materials to teach with, the kindness and respect with which they treated children. My response to my own question was a resounding yes.

Yes, where departments of education lead in the setting of a new inclusive standard for teaching and learning. Yes, where trustees encourage and track their systems' progress based on that standard. Yes, where administrators support teacher development in areas of missing pedagogy. Yes, where faculties of education lead the development of knowledge and its instruction. Yes, where teachers' federations raise the bar for professional pride. Yes, where publishers and governments, independently and in partnership, publish a range of instructional materials consistent with the new standard for historical knowledge and contemporary reality. Yes, where the office of the treaty commissioner develops understanding of the foundational relations between Canada and the First Nations in all sectors of society. The perspectives and the voices of Aboriginal and non-Aboriginal community people are inestimable to the endeavour. This is true for all peoples whose lives are bound by stereotyping and a lack of knowledge in fellow Canadians.

Anything short of all children graduating to college, or to university, or to apprenticeships, or into the various arts, or to jobs and careers with a full understanding and appreciation for Canada's history, will mean that educators today, in their various roles, must be involved in the most costly pretence of the century: that the conditions for failure in which failed students find themselves are of their own design.

FOURTEEN.

INNOCENCE I CAN NO LONGER CLAIM

I CAME TO THE DECISION that I would leave teaching. After my sabbatical leave, I fulfilled the obligation to my school division to remain working within the system for another three years. I taught for one year after I moved to a school closer to home and was then seconded, for the remaining two, to the department of education. The change from classroom to the department meant I'd be joining forces with a new generation of teachers who, coming to the aid of their profession as curriculum developers, would renew the curriculum for the next generation's insight into our country's full story. This would be one important aspect of our work. Curriculum developers would also seek to forge a connection between a vast imported European history and that of the unexplored pre-existing civilizations in the Americas.

Many curriculum developers would scarcely start out thinking this was their task. However, critical thinkers generally were commenting on the need for a new synthesis of our time. There could be no escaping the responsibility.

Artists, ever on the forefront of visionary truths, had drawn attention to the need for integrity in both subject and its representation. They saw that American landscape paintings begged for American skies. The old master-wrought skies of Europe, though beautiful, evocative, and various in their rendering, nonetheless carried the light of a different time, a different continent. But the skies over the Americas shone with a distinctiveness that needed to be captured by American painters. New insights were being wrested in other fields of inquiry, too. As curriculum developers, our generation had to catch up to our poets, writers, and artists. Had we known the work ahead, and had we known that we would have to start out alone, many of us might have turned away, resigned to refusing the call.

Following the lure of defining new insights about Canada's past, a new team of curriculum developers, teachers, such as myself, would set aside our comfortable beliefs, the very beliefs that held us steadfast and made us good but unsuspecting thinkers. We might have fled, at least those of us who realized that a new curriculum must be hewn from the bedrock of people's beliefs, with the sludge of mistaken beliefs removed. But together we forged ahead. Change would mean teachers helping each other find their way in new territory. It wouldn't be long before subject-based teams set to work, and I would be in the middle of this momentous dialogue.

It had taken a discussion with Vania, a few years after my B.A. degree, to start me thinking about curriculum development. The visit with Mr. Wouters intensified my interest. Now it was the month of May and we were having tea at Vania's house. This was the time of year when busy teachers looked forward to summer holidays. Vania and I sat down to discuss the future and what this might mean to us. Things were changing in Vania's life. Instead of teaching, she was going to a brand new job. I had grown fond of Vania over the years and was glad our friendship had not grown into an over-reliance that stunted individual life-changing decisions in our professional development. We'd helped each other out at Christmas concerts, went to sporting events after school, and attended teachers' conventions together. For all that, neither of us was sad to know that we'd set out in different directions.

Actually, we were excited. Vania was going to work at the department of education as an early childhood consultant in curriculum development. She was ecstatic.

"It's such an opportunity. Imagine being able to share your thoughts on how to improve the curriculum with other teachers. It's a new Jerusalem, if I have anything to say."

I reminded her of my belief that the act of teaching remained at the heart and soul of what was called education. I believed in an inclusive curriculum complete with approved textbooks, but becoming a curriculum developer was still not all that appealing to me. The very idea of sitting in an office writing down what the next generation should think was a tremendous responsibility. Wasn't it the case, I asked, that reading a curriculum guide cover to cover was all the more reason to put it down, since such documents lived and breathed only with their actual teaching?

Vania laughed, "That's just my point. The curriculum is so outdated something has to be done. I aim to give it a try."

"Surely a good curriculum has more to do with its interpreters than with its date of issue. Teaching teachers what the new curriculum means, and how to put it into practice is critical. It's every bit as important as a new one," I said.

"That may be the case. It may be that there is no guarantee against its bastardization, but nothing lasts forever and I stand up for a new one. Rule Armenia!"

"In a way, it's always been outdated," I replied, tentatively.

"I wouldn't wonder you'd think so," Vania said, "especially when you recall what that one old professor of yours said—and don't tell me you never thought about that wolf in sheep's clothing all these years."

Vania was probing my memory to keep me on track. It all came back now with Vania and me sitting in the sun pretending we were talking about small matters. *If I were head of this institution, you wouldn't make it through the front door.* Those fear-provoking words instilled in me a sense of vulnerability that haunted my career, still stinging to this day. Vania wore that big sunny smile of hers.

"Well?"

"Well, nothing. That professor really didn't figure into my imagination as a teacher."

Yet, when I thought about the incident, I saw in retrospect that during my teaching life, and because of what people had been taught and not taught in school, I felt compelled to manage my identity accordingly.

"What about his effect on you as a possible curriculum writer?"

"He wouldn't figure, at all," I said. "Only teachers and kids do."

"There you are!"

There I was. I could no longer sit quietly in a box of psychological oppression. It was time to reclaim my identity, to speak my mind, and to confront the fear of others' loss of trust in me as a competent professional. I began to truly explore the idea of curriculum development then. At any rate, curiosity always got the better of me. Why wouldn't I try to help set out a few signposts for my fellow teachers? I vacillated between good judgement—teaching until I should become one of the great teachers—and sound judgement—helping to build a new vision for the profession. On one hand, it would be possible to stay and find ways, with fellow teachers in the school, to turn my knowledge into instruction suitable for children. In many an after-school meeting, I saw master teachers take complex knowledge and create from it learning objectives for all grade levels. But there was more to the problem than a single school.

Up until that Saturday when Vania and I said our goodbyes, like two young school girls setting out on a summer adventure, I still held firmly to the image of myself with chalk in hand. Then, a turn of events took us both by surprise.

The following week, Vania announced that she'd be moving, come summer, to British Columbia. Her husband had found a job as a product manager in the lumber business and had closed the deal on an acreage in a nearby valley.

"My curriculum consulting days are over even before they begin," Vania said. "Kevin's job pays enough so that I won't have to go to work at all. I can stay at home, have babies, and bake pies, if I want. Imagine an Armenian woman not working from sun up till sundown, inside and outside the home. Now that's the real Jerusalem."

I heard her happiness, but there were points I wished to make. Take the curriculum—she was going to leave that behind. We would not be able to continue our talks about a new curriculum. She might lose her interest in curriculum development altogether. In my mind's eye, I saw the department of education on College Avenue kitty-corner from our old teachers college building. It had been within Vania's grasp to make important changes. In fact, she had raised the idea! Now, here she was talking about moving away. We'd visit every summer, she said, and sit under big luscious hydrangeas and ornamental dragonflies stretching their wooden wings out in her garden, mosquitoes aside. I shared in the humour, but I could only think that our curriculum talks were over before they began. Vania answered by saying that, professionally speaking, I should focus on the fact that the best was yet to come.

Another chapter was opening up in my life, a chapter wherein I would, one day, leave my classroom for a consultant's office in search of that ever-elusive wisdom. And this was mainly because Vania, and children like Vincent, Tatiana, Ivan, not to mention all the others that might have had a say in it. The new beginning loomed even larger when I met Myra.

Myra

The day she entered the classroom in 1981, I knew things could never be the same; neither for her nor for me. Her records showed an all too familiar pattern. Myra and her family had moved to the city from the reserve and then transferred from school to school in search of friendly moorings and true financial security.

Her family came from a northern reserve in the province. The principal handed me her file but gave no further information. There was none to give. "We don't hear much here from those remote schools, you know—different jurisdiction, different system. You lose some." His dark, bushy eyebrows worked in tandem, as if he grasped the totality of an ill-defined problem.

It was nine o'clock when the memory of Vincent came flooding back: black shiny hair framing a tanned face flushed with the running games at recess, standing at his desk over one of his drawings. My thoughts of Vincent were interrupted when, out of the blue, the new student entered the room in a single stride. She sailed from the doorway to the empty desk at the back of the classroom as though unbroken action forestalled her turning back. She swept a quick glance over what must have been a recurring image of desks, blackboards, and lockers, different yet the same. Her assessment stopped where interest might have begun. She sat down and waited.

Myra was older and much taller than the other children. I knew what it felt like to be the tallest kid in the room and older than the little ones bending over their exercise books. I mentally reviewed Myra's file that I'd read that morning: Age: thirteen; Grade: five; Reading: below average; Math: good–excellent.

Good to excellent! That rating might have described Myra herself. She was simply beautiful, fine boned, with olive skin and short glossy hair. We would see. I reminded myself to do whatever I could to help develop her hinted-at excellence. I smiled at her, and we began the day.

Myra's situation presented a familiar problem. Children whose first language is not the language of instruction tend to get report cards that only hint at their talents. Mathematics, a universal language, was a subject in which many non-English speaking children might excel. However, a child's progress report stopped short of saying that the second language itself hindered progress and even hid real aptitude. As it was, non-English speaking children were marked in the same way as everyone else, even in math where problems to be solved are written in an unfamiliar English language. A child's highest mark hovering around computational skills told something of this.

Other than that, I had no idea where Myra stood. She showed no interest in putting down roots. Her approach to assignments was direct. She attended to these in fine clear handwriting, minding her own business. She restricted her involvement with her classmates. "I will leave this, too," was what she seemed to think. We'd win her over gradually, I decided, should she be able to stay with us long enough.

Myra, I discovered, seemed to enjoy anything to do with numbers. She perked up during math period; in fact, a light went on in her eyes any time measurement and calculation was involved. I formed a strategy for getting Myra into our circle, using math period as the lure. I devised group projects that required thoughtful calculations. Each time Myra encountered a classmate in her group struggling with a problem, she'd slide into the seat beside her without saying a word. I'd make myself scarce so that a spirit of helping one another took hold. In time, other children called on Myra for help. Then it was Myra who insisted that a classmate was struggling with a problem and needed her.

Myra had been with us two months, now, seven weeks more than she'd been at any other school. She came every day, growing a little taller and a little more self-conscious every day and wearing a jacket to cover her budding figure. Mother Nature, I'd think ruefully, forever forcing little girls to face all kinds of unwanted vulnerabilities.

A real trial began during the annual science fair. This was when children put science projects on display for parents and community. I thought it best to leave it up to the children to decide who would work with whom, what their projects would be, and who in the community they thought might give a hand. I helped them sort out their choices. If desired, a student could work alone. The rules were clear: the project could be as simple or as complex as they wished, as long as they knew their background material thoroughly and the project could be ready on time. I'd be coach and resource person.

Soon, the children began carting all manner of materials to school; cardboard boxes, strings, balloons, lumber, jars, and measuring tapes arrived by the bushel. My job during this construction phase was to make certain that exits and doorways remained clear in case a fire alarm sounded. It was a happy, exciting time for everyone, except for Myra. She'd grown reclusive, again, and pulled her leather jacket even closer around her shoulders, as if to shield herself. It seemed she viewed the action around her on a television screen and wanted no actual part in it. Here was a familiar pattern. Just as the children began to choose their partners, a singular mid-motion silence enveloped Myra. I sensed aloneness there, a dwindling presence that seemed to say: You won't want me. This doesn't interest me anyway.

I knew Myra too well to believe she'd stay long in her cocoon. Her curiosity always got the better of her. I decided not to pressure her with customary appeals. I'd wait. In the meantime, I shared my worries with her regarding the night of the science fair. Would everything go right, did she think? Would everyone be ready on time? She smiled and said yes, it would be okay. Suddenly, Myra's mind caught fire. I saw it in those onyx eyes. She had been sitting at her desk, her hands folded in her lap, thinking. Then she came to see me. She asked if it was possible to get wires, miniature lights, and a battery or two. I ran down the hall to find what she needed, smack into the principal, just as he emerged from the science room.

"Robbed blind," he muttered to himself. "Robbed blind, and we have an austerity budget to contend with."

"Pardon?" I tried to focus my racing mind on his words as he stood there, rocking on his heels, his suit and spectacles neat as a pin, as usual.

"Austerity and robbery will do us in with the board is what I'm saying. The cupboards in the science room are, alas, quite bare."

He paused, fixing his gaze on me. "Are you all right? You're as frantic as a teacher at a science fair." I ignored the humour.

"I need lights, miniature ones, a battery or two, and wires. That is all I ask. Myra wants them, needs them. I need them. I demand them!"

"Tsk! Tsk! A bad sign. Signs of desperation, signs of distraction, of dissembling. Myra, you say? Of course, anything you ask. What is she going to do with them, then?"

"At this point, Mr. Harold, I don't care."

"Right! One mashed light bulb coming up."

He quickly helped me fill a small shoe box with odds and ends of wires, bulbs, and batteries, plus a magnet for good measure, as he put it. I turned to dash back to my room and he called out, "I'll make an announcement over the intercom that if any teacher is going to have a nervous breakdown, to please do it in the hall."

Back in the classroom, Myra received the materials with feigned nonchalance. She held her smile in check. Then, with that direct singular motion that was hers alone, she got busy on her project. As I watched her from a distance, I thought how there are times a teacher has to recognize a child's encounter with his or her inner resources. The importance of absenting oneself from the internal dialogue of a child at the crossroads of self-recognition is as vital as leaving the prayerful to their private communion. Such moments require no teacher.

I secretly watched Myra with a kind of longing in my heart. I struggled knowing that she might fail and that I might be unable to prevent that. On the other hand I was unwilling to intrude. Myra spread out a maze of wires and bulbs on her desk top. She screwed the bulbs into their sockets and tested their connection with batteries and wires, which she connected quickly and with certainty. I watched the astonishing dexterity of her long fingers. Next she rummaged about in a box of odds and ends temporarily stashed behind the classroom's movable bookcase and drew out a large piece of cardboard. She poked holes into it with a pen and strung wires through.

As usual, there was only so much time to concentrate on one student. The others needed my attention. There was Jackie, for example, painstakingly painting a raccoon she had molded out of clay, her love of these creatures obvious in her dark shining eyes. There was Lizzie with Chris hovering over Anne's volcano arguing whether or not its form could withstand the blast intended for the night of the science fair.

It's the kind of day a teacher either loves or hates; a day when there is a great stepping over of this and that, with children lying on the floor surrounded by scissors, paper, rulers, string, crayons, and with the noise level higher than that of crews at work in a construction site. It's the right kind of noise though, I'd think. A working sharing hum is different from unproductive chatter.

Myra tapped my shoulder. Did I have a book of dates she could borrow? Dates, does she mean dates in history, or holidays?

"Any kind, I guess, but not too easy, ones people should know. Holidays is too easy. I guess those history ones."

We made our way toward the bookcase, stepping over and around children. I mentally reviewed Myra's manner of speaking as I picked my way across the floor. No matter what she said, it was as though she pegged English words to the rhythm and cadence of another language, Dene, a language I didn't know. Myra, likely wishing to speak English perfectly yet sensing something amiss, kept her words to a minimum.

She chose a set of encyclopedia and indicated that she needed no further help. It was plain enough. Myra had embarked upon a self-directed journey. It was up to me to mind my own business.

Besides, that very minute, the principal was making an announcement: Invitations for the science fair are ready now for parents. Can someone from each room come and pick up a batch to take home?

Time was running out. I scurried about surveying the class projects. It always seemed a miracle as each display neared completion. Children were capable of so many things. Their minds and hands were busy. A jarred tarantula, infinite in repose, seemed to guard the report about its life that lay beside it. The raccoon with masked eyes held out its hands, perfect to the last tiny black finger tip. Inclined planes and pulleys were ready for action. The volcano appeared positively smouldering. Myra's project was ready now, too.

All the while, Myra had kept to her task, rarely letting up on her concentration. Over the course of the last couple of days, she wrote down information read from the encyclopedia on small pieces of paper. On the morning of the science fair she began putting everything together. Keep to your own counsel, I reminded myself. The projects looked close to ready. I felt my very bones begin to relax. I surveyed the room from one end to the other.

Myra and the children were gathered around her project, squealing with delight. I went over. I saw then, in an instant, that she had constructed, of all things, an electrical game board, which she now demonstrated. Across the face of the board were rows of tiny light bulbs. Beneath each bulb, glued to the board, were slips of paper with questions printed on them in Myra's neat hand: What year did Columbus discover America? When did John Cabot arrive? Who was Canada's first prime minister?

These and other questions corresponded to the dates glued to the bottom edge of the game board in neat rows. The children demanded their turn at making correct connections. Each time a bulb lit up, they jumped up and down, laughing. Myra's project was a winner. I tried my hand at connecting fact to light, too, and fairly jumped for joy each time a bulb lit up. We were all excited.

The cardboard Myra used to back her project, though, worried me. It looked ready to collapse, and I was afraid that it might not be able to withstand much action when others began to try it out. There had to be a way to avert disaster.

"Myra," I asked. "Do you want me to bring a piece of plywood from home? We could get the janitor to drill holes in it, same as you did. He has all kinds of equipment downstairs and you can help him."

I noted that the back of the cardboard was a maze of wires criss-crossed together, and that it hadn't taken Myra any time at all to twist the ends. She thought for a moment and said, "No, it's okay."

"We'll leave it for tonight," I said, relenting. "It's such an excellent project, Myra. I think it should be a permanent one."

Myra nodded, satisfied. She plunged into tidying up the room with the others, helping to make everything perfect for the evening's visitors. Books were straightened on shelves, blackboards and brushes cleaned, desks placed in neat rows, window sills dusted, and lockers tidied.

A peace we had not known in days settled over the room. The children were glowing with pride. Everything was ready. The projects were set. With an hour before dismissal, there was time for a story.

They ask for the story of Marie Antoinette, a favourite of theirs; a story of drama, glamour and intrigue, complicity, nights of terror, triumph, and death. During the telling of the story, they sat riveted to a time and place of opulence for the few; a time of silken gowns, of lace and pearls in the Petit Trianon. Here was a time of greed, when starved citizens fell in the streets, weak and helpless, lying in gilded doorways; a time of cruel schemes, when conspirators turned children against their mothers; a time of cold imprisonment, when Marie Antoinette with no place to hide her sullied gown, had tucked her only personal possessions—a jagged piece of mirror and a borrowed comb—away in a broken niche in the prison wall on the day she must step down onto a manure cart brought round to the back door of the prison for her to ride in, on her final journey, down the Champs-Élysée, facing backward. And here, too, the guillotine, and the milling crowds in the Place de la Concorde.

The story swept us away in timelessness where all life seemed to embrace some vast unravelling mystery, a mystery that might one day be resolved. The power of the story held us once again. I saw ripples of sadness, of doubt, of anticipation, and of shock registering in the faces of the children, affirming that stories unify mind, spirit, and hearts.

Here, in our room, was beauty realized; a sense of purpose inherent in helping the young grow in their feeling for a common history. This was worth everything, I would think to myself, this feeling of connection to the world and its humanity. The past engenders good in those who appreciate their connectedness to it, I would say to myself, and this was one more reason to love life as a teacher.

The hour was up and the children filed out.

"Everyone to their station at seven o'clock sharp!" I called.

The children knew they were to arrive just before their parents to stand beside their displays, ready to explain their projects. Before dismissal, the children paired up, as partners. Everyone wanted to be Myra's partner. She didn't wish to pick a partner, she said, so we settled it for her. Bruce and Jackie would be her helpers. I squeezed her arm as she went past me out the door. She stopped as if to say something but then hurried off with the others.

The evening might have been a perfect success.

Parents, uncles, and aunts milled about the displays, asking the obligatory questions. I watched the door for Myra and her family. It was 7:30 and no sign of them. The raccoon was admired for its expressive eyes and dainty fingers. The tarantula held its pose even as the glass jar was lifted and peered into. The volcano exploded on time. It was already 7:45. Jackie and Bruce took turns minding the electric game board. It was a hit, all right.

"Everyone is getting Columbus right!" Bruce called out.

Myra didn't come to the science fair. Nor did her family. I wouldn't be able to share my pleasure in Myra's progress with them after all. Nor would I have the opportunity anytime soon, it was discovered. On the morning of the science fair, the family had decided to leave for Calgary where Myra's father was promised a job on an Alberta pipeline. When the principal came to inform us just before noon hour, the next day, I had yet to notice that Myra had already taken her belongings from her desk. She had known exactly what to take, and what to leave behind. The school's speller and math textbooks remained, as did a worn pencil and her partially used notebooks. She had taken her crayons, plastic ruler, and pencil case. It might have been anyone's desk now.

"They never seem to be able to stick it out," the principal said. "They don't come to our assemblies. It's no wonder these kids have no commitment..."

In the still of that Friday afternoon when the children went carting their projects home to treasure as they might, I sat at my desk, pondering my life as a teacher. It was a hard life, for certain, but a good life so long as I stayed within the confines of a kind of innocence. But I knew I could no longer claim that innocence.

I had come to terms with my progress as a teacher far earlier than I let myself believe. There was tactical evidence of this I could see. Myra left and that might have been the end of it, but my commitment to an improved curriculum and my sense of direction to its development was gathering momentum. I wondered what I might have given Myra. As I thought about her deftly twisting those wires together, all the while making connections between past and present, I felt a true determination and a powerful realization of unfinished business well up. Myra, and Vincent, too, stood waiting at the edge of truth. I sensed I must leave this cozy world of teaching and its out-dated knowledge in search of ways to secure a clearer connection to the past for these ones, too, I told myself; and for all the others. I could no longer be a keeper of half-truths, such as: "In 1492, Columbus sailed the ocean blue..." There were stories to find—and stories to tell.

FIFTEEN.

THIS WILL FORCE US TO THINK

I REMEMBER THAT LAST YEAR OF TEACHING at my very first school. In many ways, the four years I taught there laid the groundwork for my future learning, its lessons as fresh in my mind as if it were yesterday. That year ultimately helped inform my decision to leave the Regina public school system where I had taught all my teaching life. Though I can't say I was aware until later, the lessons I received from students at the beginning of my career stayed with me.

It was 1966. I wondered what new lessons this set of pupils might have in store for me. I vowed to stay alert to fleeting instances wherein my ignorance might be transformed by some new insight. I was, after all, a growing child myself, with an identity keenly constrained.

The 1960s forced me to think about my work as a totality, although I didn't see this right away. Only in retrospect could I appreciate fully how prior decades had brought a potential for the change that excited our generation. I came to see such change as more than the decade's own inventiveness. Instead, the 1960s generation had inherited a foundation of economic wealth from the prior generation, and with that came real luxuries for some, resources for many, and the time to think for all. Importantly, it offered time to reflect on what such progress meant in the deepest sense. The assassination of President Kennedy, the Vietnam War, the Middle East crises, the Cold War, and student protests, among other forces, helped us understand that our global village on planet Earth faced new realities: "And hard rain's gonna fall..." sang Bob Dylan.

Looking back, I would say with certainty that the world of grown-ups is very much like the world of children, no matter the historical time period. Society doesn't automatically give shelter to its innocents. Confusion enters children's dreams like it does those of adults who find themselves momentarily stopped by a glimmer of an odd reality beyond their conventional lives. A former pupil once said that children know reality better than most grown-ups. My journey meant that I had to leave behind the illusions I once held about the protected state of children's lives.

In this last year of teaching at my first school, I realized I had observed recurring patterns of behaviour in children that I couldn't explain. It took me a few years to realize that there really was a pattern. No sooner did grade-six boys have pencil and paper in hand than did they draw airplanes in combat. Inevitably, tracer bullets went racing from one end of a sheet of paper to the other, with warplanes diving and swooping earthward and heavenward, some wreathed in smoke, some with wings falling away, some bursting into flame. A boy could be so engrossed in the drama that he supplied his own sound effects: Rat-a-tat tat! Zing! I'm hit! I'm hit! I could be standing right beside him and he wouldn't notice.

It seemed boys were transfixed by warplanes and bullets. The boys were, after all, the grandsons of soldiers, and I wondered if their propensity toward war games presented something of Carl Jung's theory of the collective unconscious. I had only just finished reading Jung's book *Memories, Dreams, and Reflections,* written in 1965. Perhaps expo-

sure to war on television and in comic books compelled their imaginations? Still it seemed strange that girls who watched television, as
well, didn't draw scenes of violence. Give a twelve-year-old girl a blank
sheet of paper and she drew horses with flowing manes, arching necks,
and long tails that swept the ground. In Jungian terms, these images
appeared to be akin to those found on the walls of the catacombs. Yet
again, equine movies, like *National Velvet* with Elizabeth Taylor, could
be another reason. There was no telling. Nothing I read offered a satisfactory explanation. Over time, however, I found out that no matter
what they draw, children worry about conflict, war, and destruction.

I came face to face with this startling fact during the Middle East
crises with this year's class of grade-six pupils. In 1966 things were not
getting better in the Middle East. They had, in fact, worsened. What I
learned made me more aware of the fear children experience.

Political circumstances had been brewing for years. In 1948 Jewish
forces had secured control of western Jerusalem while the Arab districts
in eastern Jerusalem that included the Old City and religious sites were
annexed by Transjordan. During the 1967 Arab-Israeli conflict, East
Jerusalem was brought under Israeli control. Israel declared Jerusalem
its eternal capital. New hostilities seemed to spring up every day. An
all-out war seemed inevitable. The children brought newspaper clippings to school, sometimes twice daily, sharing what they had heard
on radio and seen on television. More and more bullets flashed across
the grade-six boys' exercise books; there in the margins of math and on
spellers, new warplanes droned over Red Cross trucks speeding across
deadly expanses. And on other sheets of drawing paper, horses pranced
with graceful intensity.

I knew some of the children in my class had relatives living in the
Middle East. Although years had passed and this generation had
grown up in Canada, their ties to the Middle East remained strong.
They worried about aunts, uncles, and cousins. Their questions were
increasingly difficult to answer. Why did people start wars? Why didn't
they get punished for starting them? Why didn't they send children

and old people to another country first or at least move the fighting? Their questions covered the territory of the human psyche. Grown-ups might draw comfort from scripture and any insights to be found there; "A little child shall lead them," for instance. But the very ground these children lived on was captive ground. Whither and whom could they lead?

As their teacher, I tried to respond as best I could, but my knowledge was meagre and the consequences of superficial reply might never be redressed. This was painful for me to think about. So, in trying to grow as a teacher, I decided to cast embellished reality aside, starting with my own. It was too easy to say that people had always gone to war and that there is little to prevent their going. People by the number gave children that answer and left it at that. It was easy, too, I could see, to take sides and depict one people as being more hostile and warlike than another. Historians of old were the keepers on that front. No, I would think, answers sought by children are not easy to find and hand down. In any case, as discussion of war surfaced in the classroom I began to see that it isn't the job of teachers to "hand down" pre-packaged answers. Instead, it was their job to raise the children's sights for the long search. I also began to see that sometimes in the circumstance of change, it is, indeed, a child who leads.

PAUL AND DANIEL

This year's grade-six pupils were exceptional. There was an added quality of friendly banter and academic seriousness that was even more apparent than last year's class. They ignored my wavering. They questioned persistently. They wanted answers. I was being taken to task. Something had to be done.

I proposed a plan of study. If they were up to it, I told them, we'd hold our own United Nations summit on the current Middle East crisis. We'd form teams to do the research and then debate the issues. That would mean getting the facts. And facts, I told them, repeating the caution of some old philosopher, are slippery things. Hard facts and information had to be found, scrutinized, and presented with clarity and objectivity. Since no single person could cull through the pertinent information alone, we agreed that, as a beginning, our task would be to study the crisis situation in the Middle East from predominant points of view. Those points of view were just that, I warned, and not those of some biased mind looking for easy answers. Did they think they were up to it? They clamoured for the opportunity to prove they were.

They found their predominant views easily enough in the newspapers of the day, and these young minds were quick to grasp the magnitude of the task. They certainly were up to it, they said. In fact, they'd get ready for the summit the second I gave the go ahead. Yes, they could collect information and judge the credibility of its sources. Yes, they could prepare their arguments and counter arguments. You bet they could!

I cautioned them that the geographical area in question, though a mere dot on the map, was packed with many races and religions as varied as Islam, Judaism, and a variety of denominations of Christianity. In my preliminary sketch of the area, I clarified that the Greek and Russian Orthodox, the Copts and the Armenians, as well as Catholics and Protestants, lived there. Thanks to Vania, I had learned something about this. I was careful to emphasize that a debate is extremely difficult to do well, especially with as many points of view as these to consider. Emotion, instead of clear ideas, might ruin good information, I said, and that was why most teachers believed only higher grades could handle this. For this grade-six class, that was all they needed—"Only higher grades?" they sniffed. The search was on.

A great sorting of information was carried out among stacks of encyclopedia, travel books, newspaper clippings, United Nations speeches, letters from home, atlases, and tape recordings. Research teams began refining some critical points, determining their importance and reordering them, again and again. Scissors and pots of glue figured into the structuring and restructuring. Debaters' heads bent over written materials and in discussion, all in preparation for the summit.

A few weeks later we were ready to begin the summit. I prevailed upon the principal of the school that for the next entire two days we were not be disturbed by the fire alarm, the intercom, impromptu visits, or anything else for that matter. We were entering a sensitive and prolonged debate, I told him, for which weeks of preparation hung in the balance. "Anything short of complete isolation," I said, "will put us all in a beastly false position."

"A beastly false position," he repeated, trying on the words as he stood in the hall, looking at me over his spectacles.

"Yes, a beastly false position."

I didn't know exactly what I meant by that but I had to let him know I was serious about my request. I turned to go, thanking the English writer whose name I couldn't for the moment recall, but whose quotation made our principal stop in his tracks and listen.

"Right," he called after me as I turned to go back down the hall to my classroom. "Quoth the Raven, Nevermore!"

At least he's heard, I fathomed, thanks to Poe. No one would bother us, now.

The memory of that grade-six summit would ignite my hope for the permanence of intelligence and empathy in human affairs in the future. Though the exact words faded and the arguments dimmed over the years, what happened that day and the next strengthened my resolve thereafter to become a real teacher, the teacher I was to feel I had never truly become. The children would grow up to be men and women of sound judgement, I knew. They would be leaders in society, leading with charity, good purpose, and integrity. The debate conducted by these young thinkers confirmed the ancient lesson that an examined past does help in the search for meaning and direction. I was deeply impressed, overwhelmed, in fact, to see the boys and girls—Grade Six, Room 12—put aside emotional bias in favour of weighing the facts.

Eleven-year-old Paul, the red pencil behind his ear partly hidden by a mop of black curls, was standing beside his teammates, with a series of glued-together pages streaming from his hand, all the way down to the floor. He spoke clearly and confidently, his free arm making arcs in the air, lending emphasis to his points. And here was his twin brother, Daniel, seated at the opposite table writing down notes in the margins of his sheaf of papers, dark eyes glowing with concentration. Daniel's rebuttal would be delivered in a clear decisive manner. A young statesman in the making, I wondered? I was thrilled and humbled, too. The two Jewish brothers had elected to sit on opposing teams, one taking the Arab view, the other, the Israeli.

"It will force us to think," Daniel said.

During the course of the debate, each presiding twin advanced his points earnestly, and each defended his own findings with carefully chosen facts. The boys encouraged their teammates to steer clear of contaminating comment; they patted this boy on the back for showing restraint and they nodded affirmation at that girl for bringing solid information to the debate.

It was also a time to worry that, as an elementary-school teacher, I might have taken too big a risk. Some members of the community might get upset. After all, war was close in recent memory for many and realities of the day brought ideas and instances of destruction to family members closer still. Our reasons for holding the debate, I knew, might have to be clarified to a parent or community leader who might misjudge the intent of our summit. Some might think us war mongering. Others might say the school glorified war. Still others might think teachers were tarnishing the minds of the young with dreams of arms and soldiering.

Worse, the children had to take sides. Each child had been compelled, by the very nature of the exercise, to present a point of view and hold to it, even if personal considerations implied otherwise. One young lady in the class, from an orthodox Jewish family, for example, was now arguing on the side of the Arabs.

At first, she had been reluctant to participate in the debate at all. Correct and self-righteous, Pearl had been loathe to enter into certain activities. She tended to be firm in her thinking. I was afraid her inflexibility might one day find her waxing superior in an imagined world, one that would be hers alone. So, when all was said and done, the end justified the means: she would be an Arab. Besides, the Arabs needed her as their team was a person short. There being no way out was the final push. Now here she was, in the middle of the debate, her gaze like a widening sky.

By now, in the middle of the debate, I was really sweating. It was true after all, I thought, turning things over in my mind, that there are those who seek to contain good by building fences, installing safes, erecting iron gates, stifling free speech, and, in fact, devising all kinds of barriers against all manner of evil. Ideas alive in human hearts, however, accept no boundary. On the contrary, fierce ideas cross trenches, foxholes, and moats with incredible ease through time and space. And sadly, guns and knives generally follow.

Ideas and their sources are what we felt we must contemplate, and that much we would say to our critics. To our parents. To the school board.

It never came to that. I needn't have worried. There were no reprisals. The children talked of many things after the summit. They agreed among themselves that no one wins a debate, least of all a war, no matter how well prepared. And having learned about truth-finding, they said, made them glad.

They had come to a serious view about the world and their role in it. They didn't need me to explain, or explain away, such complex matters. These boys and girls helped me understand as a teacher that children want to learn about real life in meaningful ways and that adults have to keep on learning to keep pace with their questions.

Real learning takes time. I was living proof.

In those post-summit days, as I thought about how one comes to gain true knowledge, I realized that throughout all my teaching years, little had pierced my fondest belief: a world of absolutes. In my own mind, and for so long, an imagined arena of justice prevailed in marvelous totality that we might all access, but exactly where that was was unknown to me. Plato and Aristotle had taught otherwise; their arguments, however, had cast steel bands around my sense of an extant and absolute world order. I had thought, too, when I left teachers college, that I knew a lot about teaching and that I would only need to brush up on what was missing, and even then only as the need arose. It was a case of "me and my Kingdom for a chalk."

My single-minded belief, when I mounted the steps of that fine red brick building on College Avenue, was that I might learn, over-night, all there was to know about teaching. This would remain my life-long embarrassment—which was just.

Had all my college colleagues come to a similar conclusion, I wondered? As young untried idealists, we entered teachers college with such hope. It was hard to say what their experiences were: we'd gone our separate ways so quickly. I had only fragments of infor-mation, gossip from here and there about my old classmates. To hear tell, Rusty Boulin turned out to be quite the married man and a family man at that. He had become an excellent teacher, much to his parents' dismay. Now, as a serious, community-minded person, he was committed to leading a church choir in his home-town. It was Eric Jones they worried about, they said. He was skit-tish and had great difficulty settling down. There was something of the superintendent in him yet, it was said, and his head had gone quite bald. I also learned that the two fundamentalist females, conservative anti-evolutionists, had become towers of strength in their community, but that their male counterpart had fled. His was a sordid comical story, they said, that involved messy scenes in preaching and philandering. His was a trio, all right, but not the Trinity for which he once seemed destined to seek.

If I had once harboured strong convictions, they had proven false. It had taken time to understand that goodness rarely takes care of itself. Children, like Daniel and Paul and all the others, helped me to see that being a teacher means being a helpmate. It means that, in the end, the teacher and his or her pupils are each other's teachers.

It was June, and the children and I were saying our last goodbyes. The children slipped notes and cards and little gifts onto my desk as they filed out. By the time I turned around to find the classroom empty of their belongings and personality once again, I was weeping inside and out. This would be my last year at this school. I wouldn't be seeing these little ones next year, or the next. It was time to get hold of my emotions all over again, and in a firm way at that.

The halls were silent now. I went to sit at my desk. It was time to go through the notes and drawings: I'm going to miss you. I'm glad you were my teacher. Here, a red heart with a tiny piercing arrow... there, a white horse with a flowing mane...there the bending flowers, a rainbow, and a shining sun.

Here was something new, though: a letter in a white business envelope with my name carefully written across it in blue ink. It had been written at home, possibly even the night before. I opened it and the young Paul Shapiro's handwriting leapt from the page. I settled back in my chair, struck with the thought of Paul's having taken the time to fill up a whole page, and then some:

I think that this is probably the most enjoyable year I have ever had and ever will have. I have learned and made and created things that

I know would not have occurred with others. For instance; I learned how to really appreciate the feeling of art and in this year I have advanced more than I have advanced in all my life. You have gone out of your way for us so that we could do interesting things. Also I have begun to realize that it is quite hard to discuss war. Other teachers think that kids should be treated like infants and therefore they think we cannot truly understand the meaning of war but you treat us like we were young adults and for the first time in my life I have been able to talk freely about war and other things knowing that the teacher understands. Probably others do not think we don't know about war, but there are many kids which I know who have read books like "Auschwitz" and who may have a clearer picture about war than most of the teachers in this school. One of the experiences I have enjoyed most, (and still am enjoying it) is the debate on the Middle East crisis. The people involved in this debate are truly going through a rare experience for such a low grade, because most of these kinds of debates are not held till grade nine or ten.

Another thing that you have created best of all is the free atmosphere in the room. We don't have to put up our hand for every detail as in the past and when something awful happens and somebody gets it, you just laugh it off with a joke afterwards. When it's a hot miserable day and nobody feels like working, you arrange something so that we can read or draw. In the past year I have really enjoyed the thought of school. You seem to make every subject seem more interesting by being a non-conformist.

Before I never really enjoyed Music but this year I really do. I have learned something this year that not many people will be gifted to learn.
Sincerely,
Paul

Gifted to learn. His simple words burst into my mind, quickening my conviction that one is ever both teacher and pupil. There was no mistaking it. If my professors had long ago set me and other young idealists on the road to examining the nature of truth and its revelation through time, children would take us farther.

Over the course of my teaching career, I had come to accept a scattering of proofs about children and classrooms. Children are more than a tumble of angels in need of a rounding up and a dusting off. They are neither free from troubles nor immune to them. One might say that the seeds of their lives are sown early and circumstances that shoulder them along are as difficult to ignore as those that assail adults every day. The names of my pupils recall a medley of feelings in me, still.

Teaching is like holding a lamp so that the learner comes to see the fragile and shifting balance between darkness and light in our lives. Teaching means coming to regard our common past as a kind of clearing, like a pool of light set deep within ancient woods to which each of us, man, woman, and child, is truly and magnificently bound. If I had somehow lost Inga, with the tiny message of longing pasted on her self-portrait, Paul's letter would help ease the pain of that over the years. At times, I could even imagine Inga from Holland having found someone to look at her and see her, both. Perhaps her teacher, somewhere in Belgium where her family had moved, was a teacher to whom she might write letters.

Paul's letter gave hope for little Rico who had stood outside himself the day he was strapped. Rico might have caught up with himself as the man he was promised to be. And if the world had somehow removed Vincent from our midst, Paul's letter bore the reminder that written histories, as well as yet unwritten ones, provide, at very least, a starting point when truth itself is the prize. For me, Paul's letter helped put into perspective remembrances of the long road that had told so little in its beginning and held so much toward its end.

Gifted to learn. I, too, might have written letters to those gone away:

Dear Myra,
If it is you they will talk about, if it is you as a young girl caught up in something undefined, something beyond your control, I would like to be able to say that your project at the science fair was something wondrous. And yes, everyone had guessed Columbus.

Letters sent out from me would not do, even if I knew their destination. I would go the way of my old teachers. This would mean closing the classroom door for others to open. It would mean dislodging my mind from its cherished moorings in ancient Mesopotamia if only to see the farther reach of God's hand in the Americas. It would mean taking all I had learned and then sharing this with fellow teachers who would soon be setting out the guiding principles for a new curriculum. And, yes, one day it would mean leaving the classroom. I accepted that two decades later when the call to work as a curriculum developer came.

Teachers in the making must learn to teach from the ground up, as necessary, and from Heaven down, as needed. Such things I told myself that final day as I walked, minus the chalk, down the long cool corridor into a summer afternoon.

AFTERWORD

FINALLY, AT THE END OF 1982 OR THEREABOUTS, it came to me that I would leave teaching, perhaps, forever. I was no closer to the big answers in my profession. Instead, more questions had sprung up around me. My new life plan meant that I would keep an eye out for a job opening in curriculum development. When an advertisement appeared I would apply.

I knew I'd miss the children. I had enjoyed their laughter, the dandelion bouquets on my desk, the Christmas carols, the shouts and cheers rolling across the school's softball fields. I'd miss the stories, the humour, and a child's way of saying and writing things down:

> "When I was real young I took all my grandma's pills by mistake, and they rushed me to the hospital and put me on an ironing board..."
> "I woke up in the night because I heard footprints in the hall..."
> "We called our calf Elmer, but then we found out he was a girl..."
> "I read in a book that cats were scared in ancient Egypt..."

But it was time to pack my suitcase and pay Goldie a visit. Her most recent note ended with her poem titled, "Come East, Old Woman":

> *The lady with the crumbling chalk doth make her last and final mark,*
> *There on the rock beside the sea, a glorious, furious, curious sea!*

My visit to her home in Toronto that August was just what I needed. Once there, I spent hours stretched out in her backyard on a lawn chair sorting through my thoughts and feelings and sipping lemonade from a long cool glass. When it came right down to it, Goldie's home was a needed refuge and her company, a balm. This would be the summer to figure out what I had learned and would do with the rest of my life.

Goldie told me that she'd read my "sheaf of papers" as I had suggested and came to a couple of conclusions: one, I had gone to considerable pain to answer her question as to why I left teaching, even if it were true that people didn't just walk away from the work they loved. And that it was lunacy to have sent all that paper, all at once.

"After a while I felt so much was coming at me. You might try chapters, you know."

That evening, we sat in her living room on soft white leather sofas set at angles on a calming sandstone-and-eggplant carpet lit by ivory lamps and cacti in bloom—an oasis of calm where the lighting had a soft yet immediate and luxurious clarity and where talk could find focus. "I no longer believe teaching is the worst profession," she smiled, slyly. "But those kids' stories would give anybody a start, coming on them cold. I wish you could find out what happened to each of them and let me know." I told her that it might take some digging but they were, none of them, exactly as I remembered them anymore. They'd be grown up, even if I couldn't bring myself to believe it. Whenever I met former pupils as young adults, it was like being thrust into a time machine that proved a kind of test. I told her that I felt this when I met Jay again. With his head held to one side and reading in my mind's eye, I wasn't prepared for the fact that he had taken time to grow older, and that he was not living up to his abilities. He loaded trucks in a warehouse for a living, was married, and loved reading. I asked him why he was stalled when he had such a brilliant mind. His reply was immediate.

"Brilliant? You must be mistaken! You must be thinking of someone else."

I stared at the dark circles under his eyes.

He said the whole time he was in school he thought he was dumb; because reading was so easy. He thought teachers let him do the only thing he was capable of doing—read.

Goldie, hearing this was incredulous. "What did you say to him?"

"I told him that most of anyone's time in school is devoted to learning how to read in the first place."

Goldie shook her head. "What about that Diana? The one who was to sing a carol but her parents didn't let her. Did she turn out?"

"Last I heard she was working in a bank. She's a single mother."

It was strange to think Diana would not be walking down the runways of fashion houses after all, as I once imagined she might, those long bones adding a final coup de grace to moments of aesthetic precision in the industry. No, Diana would remain the missing factor where the designer's art met the world's fascination with beautiful things. Now she was back, living with her parents. "I think she might still manage a company of her own, one day," I said.

"And that boy who got strapped. Did he stay out of trouble?"

"Rico? He worked evenings all that year. My talks with his mom got us nowhere on that score."

I told Goldie that Rico's family business grew to include a restaurant with trips back to the old country. Rico went along, apparently. He wore linen shirts and smart jackets. Thinking of Rico, I recalled the liveliness in his mother's face and hoped his own reflected the same expression of deliverance.

And then there was Ryan...red and blue welts on his arm, forever associated in my mind with cowboy boots of finely sewn leather. I was glad Goldie didn't ask about him. I didn't want to recall how, as professionals, the school did not involve itself in his situation. I was relieved as his teacher to hear that the business of the home wasn't my business. And I let myself off the hook.

Thank goodness Goldie was on to something else.

"The more I think about it, Pillar, the more I believe you could turn those stories into a book," she said. "I always thought teachers knew everything and that it was their fault entirely if a child had problems in school."

That was the first night. Goldie had a way of getting straight to the point of everything. She said I should sleep on it. In the morning, we would go shopping, first thing, as I wanted to see more Giorgio Armani jackets up close. She had two of her own and let me try them on. Both were of lightweight carved-dream construction that draped like orchid wings over the shoulders and down. Goldie said I could wear the taupe one with a pair of jeans and look super, but the shoes would have to go.

I couldn't sleep. Writing a book would be impossible. I would have a new job to go back to and so much to learn that it scared me. Curriculum research and writing at the department of education, in Regina, my proud city of hand-planted trees—what had I gotten myself into? And writing a book? The pages I had sent Goldie were just that, pages, with a few points set down in layman's terms about teaching. The last thought I had before finally falling asleep was that I would have to see if my reams of paper had succeeded in making a connection between the so-called Old World and New World. I fell asleep toward dawn losing myself in a dream about a Peruvian boy, weeping, his head on my shoulder, and my husband pulling me along in a wheeled contraption (perhaps something like the cart Marie Antoinette had been forced to ride in, so long ago) down a Peruvian city road that descended among a tumble of degraded buildings.

By degrees during our August visit, Goldie convinced me to at least think about writing the book. She began her mission in earnest over lunch, downtown, after our Armani art show. I was hungry now in a way that said good food would have to do. We sat in the sunlight of the restaurant savouring wine and pasta on white plates laid out on a white tablecloth with gleaming silverware. Goldie, who looked wonderful against the fronds of green, said point-blank, "Consider this question. Can the Canadian psyche bear the weight of all that inherited guilt just when they are beginning to have a sense of who they are? As I see it, your book would still make the point about teachers and kids without going so deeply into delicate issues."

I told her the thought had crossed my mind in the dead of night but that there was a Peruvian boy to consider, and my family, too. Not to mention the next generation.

The waiter came round to pour wine from the carafe as Goldie peered across the table at me, puzzled. I told her about my dream and how my conscience wouldn't allow for omission. She said she had to admit that that the story about the emperor's bejeweled teeth, in a jungle in South American prehistory, touched her sense of pride; the work of dentists never got the same coverage other designers did. We laughed as in our schoolgirl days.

"I mean it, Pillar, you need to write this stuff as a real book, Aboriginal issues and all, I dare say."

Sitting there with Goldie, I realized this would be no small commitment. Canadian society, during the 1960s and certainly in years prior, held the serious belief that "Indian people" were victims of their own lack of initiative. Textbooks, movies, comic books, and newspapers said so, explicitly. Not a lot had changed in public schools by the 1980s.

"By implication, I belong to the past, Goldie, to a legally defined time and space. Tell me how I can write about that and not offend readers."

"You know as well as I that once you take the plunge there can be no beating about the bush. Come on, Pillar!" Impatience crowded her voice.

"How do I say that a massive thicket of bigoted information and policy goes far deeper than racism based on colour; that all of it haunted my professional life? Think what this says about fellow educators, most of whom I care about and admire!"

She levelled that gaze at me. "It says everything about the terror of ignorance. You have an obligation."

"Truth is, Goldie, I wanted only to see myself simply as a teacher who loved learning. I made the decision to lead my life as a person separate from an imposed identity."

"Oh. So you hid a part of yourself under a bushel."

Her remark made me realize that my life-long fears coloured my perceptions of the world I lived in. My personal trauma and reaction at times had placed limits on colleagues who had cared enough to let me be. Many respected my right to contend with my own temperament. My first principal, Mr. Hervey Sykes, knew that as a young professional I wished to be considered an ordinary person with ordinary expectations levelled at me, not an extraordinary reminder of society's search for its identity. Like everyone, I wished, foremost, to be self-defined. But, yes, a bushel was handy, especially as colleagues turned to enter their classroom doors to teach Saskatchewan's history. I felt caught between what was being said and what was being heard.

By the time our salad and pasta were eaten and the wine removed for coffee, Goldie and I concluded that Truth is like teeth; they needn't be extracted for mere appearance's sake. I had to admire Goldie's candour. Her approach to work might be clinical and technical in depth and detail, but her spirit and intelligence were large. Her seemingly easy off-handed manner masked gentle humour and a tender heart.

On my return trip to the prairies, I thought about the question Goldie raised on our way to the airport. "Is it in New York where kids bring guns to school? What I mean is, your kids seem so harmless. Surely you're missing reality?"

I told her that I didn't think so. Yet, by the time I got to considering how one turns "reams" into a book, the reality of schools and children had grown visibly worse, even as I sat in my office pondering issues associated with the provincial curriculum. Drug and alcohol abuse, racism, bullying, family violence, incest, and suicide crowded out childhood altogether. I realized how easy it was for teachers to feel overwhelmed by the enormity of the task society sets for them.

Life is increasingly complex for parents. That means life is difficult for children. The world they live in is undergoing profound change. Experts tell us that cultural and linguistic barriers are breaking down and putting a strain on the social bonds that hold local communities together. We need only consider the degree to which technology has affected how we live. Without our daily conversations at the well with water bucket in hand, so to speak, as in times past, our experience of communal life can suffer to the extent that a common language may fail to sustain cultural identity.

A question that schools will be expected to answer, time and again, is what it means to be a Canadian. What is Canada's identity? In the 1960s and 1970s, it seemed the world would retain its powerful geographic loyalties. Today, a new wall of China could not reverse changes affecting whole countries. The Berlin Wall failed in its original purpose by the time the picks and axes came out. Teachers are always faced by children who know only the world they are born into. Children lack historical knowledge and hence a sense of direction.

In the decades of the 1960s and 1970s, I had the privilege to ask: why is knowledge organized this way? In the 1990s, I would join others in another question: where does this information best fit, and how, and why? Today information moves incredibly fast. It is the difference between stepping off a boat onto a plane. Knowledge development lags behind information by more than a couple of airport stops. Yet the school curriculum, the machinery of knowledge that keeps the educational system aloft, has always to respond to turbulence. Educators have to make continual improvements while maintaining communication on land, sea, and air.

Still, a curriculum without teachers is only documentation. But the hard question—how will we prepare the next generation?—still depends on the flight plan. I recall my colleagues in the classroom and at round tables hammering out theory and practice in earnest because that documentation represented an intended safe landing for everyone.

Almost two years after my visit to Goldie's that fateful August, I recall how happy and excited I was to join the round tables of eager faces when a position in curriculum development came open at the department of education in 1983. Aboriginal colleagues, consisting of six government neophytes seeking to accomplish great things, recognized that curriculum issues articulated by the Aboriginal community might not be fully addressed. Our job assignment was to incorporate Aboriginal content into pre-existing subject areas and their related concepts, pre-defined. For example, teachers, familiar with the concept of "interdependence," would teach the many interconnections that enliven farms, villages, and cities of Saskatchewan. The Aboriginal team extended this to include First Nation's reserves and Métis communities. But now, the teachers had no textbook or materials to assist them in knowing what to say about economic relations, social interaction, historical developments, and rural infrastructure. The round table seemed oddly square. Still, a foundation for Aboriginal knowledge in the provincial education system was established that was to begin a dialogue between the federal and provincial education system and the Aboriginal community that continues today.

In the big-picture sense, the challenge identified for any single cultural perspective, world-wide, today is subsumed in a general search for the unity and coherence of knowledge itself. Nothing short of a new synthesis is called for. Subjects grow in their complexity. What schools once called science has spawned many specializations such as neurobiology, ecology, physics, and biotechnology, to name but a few. A similar issue arises for English as a subject. English literature has expanded to the extent that an entire book by Harold Bloom, *The Western Canon: The Books and School of the Ages* (1994), is devoted to exploring the integrity of the Western literary canon. It appears teachers have to think about and teach knowledge in a new way. For example, in his book *Consilience: The Unity of Knowledge* (1998), the American biologist Edward O. Wilson argues that "neither science nor the arts can be complete without combining their separate strengths." He also points out that problems vexing humanity cannot be solved without integrating knowledge from the natural sciences with that of the social sciences and the humanities.

It would appear that, at this juncture in knowledge development, curriculum developers and teachers need to think beyond "a slurry of minor disciplines" (Wilson). In my limited understanding, this means, for instance, that when teaching custodial responsibility for a green planet, a viewfinder is required that integrates biology, ethics, the social sciences, and environmental policy as Wilson says. Some curriculum developers say that basic concepts within Indigenous languages, world-wide, might prove a very rich resource for coming to a new synthesis of the separate disciplines. First Nations languages carry concepts, undif-ferentiated into specialized analyses, that nonetheless portray a unified meaning.

In my experience in education, as a teacher, I saw the whole as a kind of fable: a floodgate of values is loosed upon the world and arbiters of fate tend holes in the dam as they eye the foundation. Meanwhile teachers and children are set upon a course, some in the leakiest of boats, heading out to a predestined headland where, upon their arrival, judgement is passed. The teachers teach and also navigate. In rough seas, they search the horizon for a lighthouse hoping that the keeper has the authority and the means to keep the light shining—for the entire journey.

Goldie was right. The little stories I told paled in comparison to the tales of torn lives among the world's youth today. The tragic experiences borne by children in residential schools share in common the worst experiences suffered by children in other ages, and in this age. The picture of chimney sweeps in pre-dawn London and the horrific terrors visited on children in the concentration camps and as refugees in times of war, live on in our memories in tandem with the stories brought to light by today's media of children suffering at the hands of society's perverted humans.

Still, as I ruminated, there was another burning question in my mind: did we as a profession not owe to our young children the power to think inquiringly, comprehensively? Did this not mean that as their teacher I had to do something about my own thinking?

Teachers need time for personal reflection and research inside our repositories of memory, be that archives, the university, or the oral histories of people. The privilege to study made all the difference in my life. An immersion in textbooks at school was not an answer. I had found numerous accounts of the Western hemisphere and its development; some tales were told at such a slant as to be an embarrassing inheritance for schools. The past was presented in such a way that the big picture got lost, or got skirted around. A certain glory had gone missing, the glory of a thousand years, for starters.

As for the art and science of teaching, there had been no single answer, no single force that automatically pulled the great thinkers and practitioners together in meaningful concert. Oscar Wilde, for all his comedic irony, wrote quite accurately: "Truth is rarely pure, and never simple." Indeed, truth is an exacting force; it is the vitality in all information that teachers study in order to find and impart true knowledge. Certainly, for the teacher, there is never a single object on the desk within reach that reveals and sustains the whole of knowledge. This much is known, however: to become a good teacher, one has to remain a good student. It is a fine way to stay in the company of all who are gifted to learn. Goldie would agree whole-heartedly with that. I would just have to convince her, though, that the stories of my children took place when innocence itself might still be protected. And in many ways, I felt that my story would tell of a time to which none of us might easily return.

APPENDIX: A NOTE ON ISABEL ANDREWS

Isabel Andrews's research provides a fearless and searing exploration of government policy and its impact on First Nations education in Saskatchewan. I have incorporated direct quotations from her work that has given rise to the questions I explore and discuss in this book. These quotations spark two decisive questions: do all children deserve to know their country's full history? What is the foundation for failure of First Nations and Métis children in public education?

Andrews, Isabelle Ann. "The Crooked Lakes Reserves: a study of Indian policy in practice from the Qu'Appelle Treaty to 1900." A thesis submitted to the Faculty of Graduate Studies and Research in partial fulfillment of the requirements for the Degree of Master of Arts in History, Division of Social Sciences. University of Saskatchewan, Regina Campus, 1972.

Andrews, p. 176: "Little can be done with him. He can be taught to do a little at farming, and at stock-raising, and to dress in a more civilized manner, but that is all." N.F. Davin, "Confidential Report on Industrial Schools for Indians and Half-breeds," Ottawa, March 14, 1879, Appendix, Archives of Saskatchewan, copy from the files of the Indian Affairs Branch, Department of Citizenship and Immigration, Ottawa, p. 2.

Andrews, p. 179: "Guaranteeing schools as one of the considerations for [the Indian's] surrendering title to land, was, in my opinion, trifling with a great duty and placing the Government in no dignified attitude. It should have been assumed that the Government would attend to its proper and pressing business in this important particular. Such a guarantee, moreover, betrays a want of knowledge of the Indian character. It might easily have been realized, (it is at least thinkable) that one of the results would be to make the Chiefs believe they have some right to voice regarding the character and management of the schools, as well as regarding the initiatory step of their establishment." N.F. Davin, "Confidential Report on Industrial Schools for Indians and Half-breeds," Ottawa, March 14, 1879, Appendix, Archives of Saskatchewan, copy from the files of the Indian Affairs Branch, Department of Citizenship and Immigration, Ottawa, p. 11.

Andrews, p. 183: "Until it is clearly felt that the primary aim is to produce a moral, industrious, white character—even unlettered—with a cultivated antipathy to that which stands against, and sympathy with that which stands for civilization." Sessional Papers, 1892, No. 14, p. 98. [Statement of the Inspector of Protestant Schools for Indians in Manitoba and the Northwest, J.A. Macrae.]

Andrews, p. 199: "... in such districts as the advance towards civilization has been such as to render the measure politic, I have either withheld assistance from the parents who refuse to send their children to the school or have arrived at the same end by diverting a proportion of the rations formerly allowed for the consumption of the children at home to the provision of a meal at the school-house, which provides a strong inducement to regular attendance." Sessional Papers, 1890, No. 12, p. 170. [Statement of the Indian Commissioner of the day, Hayter Reed.]

Andrews, p. 201, footnote 1: "The Governor in Council may make regulations, either general or affecting the Indians of any province or of any named band, to secure the compulsory attendance of children at school... Such regulations, in addition to any other provisions deemed expedient, may provide for the arrest and conveyance to school and detention there, of truant children and of children who are prevented by their parents or guardians from attending: and such regulation may provide for the punishment, upon summary conviction, by fine or imprisonment, or both, of parents and guardians, or persons having the charge of children, who fail, refuse or neglect to cause such children to attend school..." Canada Statutes, 57–58 Vict., Chapter 32, Section 11.

Andrews, p. 211: "The obvious conditions facilitating the progress of the epidemic and the spread of infection at the time were the concentration of the Indians in fixed residences on the reserves, lack of sanitation, their contact with the surrounding white settlers, and the concentration of the children in boarding schools for education. Under these conditions tuberculosis infection spread quickly." R.G. Ferguson, "Studies in Tuberculosis," p. 6. [Dr. R.G. Ferguson, First Superintendent of Fort San, 1917–28, Director of Medical Services and General Superintendent, Saskatchewan Anti-Tuberculosis League, 1928–48, in his 1928 published study of disease among Indians of the Qu'Appelle Valley area.]

See also the section "Standard Course of Study for Indian Schools" (Appendix B of Andrews's thesis) for an overview of the residential school curriculum.

NOTES

1. Statement of the Indian Commissioner of the day, Hayter Reed in Sessional Papers, 1890, No. 12, p. 170.

2. N.F. Davin, "Confidential Report on Industrial Schools for Indians and Half-breeds," Ottawa, March 14, 1879, Appendix, Archives of Saskatchewan, copy from the files of the Indian Affairs Branch, Department of Citizenship and Immigration, Ottawa, p. 2.

3. R.G. Ferguson, "Studies in Tuberculosis," p. 6. Dr. R.G. Ferguson, First Superintendent of Fort San, 1917–28, Director of Medical Services and General Superintendent, Saskatchewan Anti-Tuberculosis League, 1928–48 in his 1928 published study of disease among Indians of the Qu'Appelle Valley area.